Printed and bound in Canada at Friesens. The text of this book is printed on 100% post-consumer recycled paper with earth-friendly vegetable-based inks.

Cover and text design: Duncan Campbell, University of Regina Press
Proofreader: Katie Doke Sawatzky
Indexer: Judith Brand

Library and Archives Canada Cataloguing in Publication

Salloum, Habeeb, 1924-
[Arab cooking on a Saskatchewan homestead]
Arab cooking on a Prairie homestead : recipes and recollections from a Syrian pioneer / Habeeb Salloum ; with a foreword by Sarah Carter.—New edition.

Previous edition published under title: Arab cooking on a Saskatchewan homestead.
Includes bibliographical references and index.
Issued in print and electronic formats.
ISBN 978-0-88977-518-3 (softcover).—ISBN 978-0-88977-519-0 (PDF).—
ISBN 978-0-88977-520-6 (HTML)

1. Cooking, Syrian. 2. Syrians—Saskatchewan—History. 3. Syrians—
Prairie Provinces—History. 4. Cookbooks. I. Carter, Sarah, 1954-, writer of
foreword II. Title. III. Title: Arab cooking on a Saskatchewan homestead.

TX725.M628S24 2017   641.595691   C2017-905021-4   C2017-905022-2

10   9   8   7   6   5   4   3   2   1

University of Regina Press, University of Regina
Regina, Saskatchewan, Canada, s4s 0A2
TEL: (306) 585-4758 FAX: (306) 585-4699
WEB: www.uofrpress.ca

We acknowledge the support of the Canada Council for the Arts for our publishing program. We acknowledge the financial support of the Government of Canada. / Nous reconnaissons l'appui financier du gouvernement du Canada. This publication was made possible with support from Creative Saskatchewan's Creative Industries Production Grant Program.

New Edition

ARAB COOKING
ON A PRAIRIE HOMESTEAD

Recipes and Recollections From a Syrian Pioneer

HABEEB SALLOUM

with a foreword by Sarah Carter

 University of Regina Press

CONTENTS

FOREWORD

Sarah Carter

Arab Cooking on a Prairie Homestead has long been one of my favourite books, not only because of the delectable recipes, but because it is a unique work of prairie history. It weaves recipes into a beautiful memoir about growing up on a Saskatchewan farm. Written by the son of homesteaders from Syria, it brings to light the experiences of Arab settlers whose contribution to the history of Canada is not well known. As Habeeb Salloum writes, "today people stare in disbelief when they hear that Arabs homesteaded in western Canada." They were the first to grow lentils and chickpeas, the pulse crops that are today central to the economy of the prairies. Acquiring seeds from relatives, Salloum's parents drew on the knowledge of their ancestors who had cultivated pulses in semi-arid conditions for centuries. The Salloum family survived Saskatchewan's dustbowl of the 1930s because of these ancient pulse crops. While other farmers abandoned their farms and headed north, the Salloums persisted.

Arab settlers have a long history in Canada, and they included Muslims and Christians. Paul Anka is likely the most famous Canadian of Arab ancestry, but there were many others. They worked as travelling salespeople, and they ran restaurants, bakeries, and shops. There were Arabs in the fur trade. Annie Midlige, born in 1864 near Beirut, traded furs and established stores across a vast stretch of territory in Quebec. She had a 400-acre farm near Baskatong, where she also owned a hotel. Syrian and other Arab traders were active in the Canadian North, such as Esmeil Muhammed "Sam" Jamba, born in Syria (Lebanon today) in 1890. They settled throughout the West, but there was a significant cluster of Arabs in southern Saskatchewan on arid marginal land bypassed by earlier homesteaders. While some of the children of these settlers stayed on the farm, others served in the Canadian forces (as did Habeeb and his brother), and they were engineers, lawyers, accountants, and politicians. Two of the most famous Saskatchewanians of Syrian ancestry were musicians: internationally renowned concert pianist George Haddad (born in Eastend in 1918) and "Canada's King of the Fiddle," Ameen "King" Ganam (born in Swift Current in 1914).

But it was not easy. Salloum's book documents the intolerance and prejudice Arab settlers encountered. He describes Saskatchewan as a "land where we tasted bitterness." He was called a "Black Syrian" and a "foreigner" by schoolmates. He left the parched prairies of blowing dust and piercing sand in 1940 at age sixteen, and returned only for visits, never to live. At that time, Salloum wanted to shed his Arab origins and assimilate, and he writes that because this was the desire of the children of other Arab settlers, few tried to write about their own history. Salloum even initially tried to replace Arab cuisine with food such as bologna and sardine sandwiches, but he soon longed for his mother's recipes.

Salloum shares his mother's dishes, the smells and tastes of his Saskatchewan boyhood, and adds other recipes from his travels. His attitude honours and echoes that of his mother, whose culinary work was always adaptable, inventive, and creative. Her Arab pastries were baked with saskatoon berries, for example, and she had numerous uses for dandelions. (There is a chapter on "the joys of saskatoons," and one on dandelions.) The Salloum children and their mother scoured the prairies for wild greens that she substituted for the herbs and spices of Syria, and they picked huge quantities of saskatoons at the Coulee of Saint Claire near the town of Cadillac, joining another Arab family in the annual expedition. When writing about saskatoons, and in other sections of the book, Salloum acknowledges that his family and other settlers were occupying the land and drawing on the resources of the Indigenous people of the Plains, but as a boy he had no knowledge of the people and their history.

This book showcases the contributions of Arab settlers to the fabric of Canada. Recipes are the key to reclaiming this history. Salloum concludes his book with this statement:

"The saga of the Arab immigrants is truly the story of Canada." I share the hope that this history will not be forgotten and the belief that the saga of Arab immigrants is truly the story of Canada. This is a particularly important message now, as Canada hosts a new generation of Arab settlers. Salloum's book helps us remember what being Canadian means, that we have always been a pluralist nation. It reminds us, too, that there have always been pernicious efforts to place limits on exactly who is deserving of full citizenship. We must continue to challenge and resist this prejudice and intolerance. And what better way than to sit down together and share food with our neighbours, old and new alike. �֎

Sarah Carter, Henry Marshall Tory Chair in the Department of History & Classics, University of Alberta, Edmonton, Alberta

PREFACE TO THE NEW EDITION

Tragically, since the publication of the first edition of this book in 2005, a terrible war has broken out in Syria and a heartbreaking refugee crisis has ensued, affecting the entire world, including us Canadians here at home. There now is a humanitarian crisis that has left five million Syrian refugees fleeing their country. Much fear has been generated about the Arab world and about immigrants and refugees in general. I hope this new edition of my cookbook can contribute, in some small way, to increasing awareness and understanding of this part of the world, and lessen the fear and animosity towards newcomers.

On a much more personal note, other changes that have occurred since the publication of the book's first edition include the loss of my wife, Freda; my three brothers— Eddie, Fred and Albert; and my sister Phyllis. They are greatly missed. But there have been gains too: I now have six great-grandchildren; I have increased the authorship of my books to ten; and I have received numerous awards for my cookbooks and my other writing.

With respect to this book's first edition, I have received hundreds of emails about it over the years, with people offering praise for the book and its contribution to Canadian history. Indeed, I had received so many requests for the book since it had gone out of print, I was at a loss until this new edition was suggested. I want readers to know that, despite the years that have passed, the dishes found in this cookbook—dishes prepared by my mother in the early pioneering days of my life—were settled deep within me and continue to reflect a part of my heritage and part of an immigration story, a piece in the ethnic mosaic of Canada that should forever be recorded for posterity.

Since the time Prime Minister Pierre Elliot Trudeau introduced official policies of multiculturalism in the 1970s, Canada has been a much more progressive country than during the time of my childhood. It is a more diverse society, with a growing awareness and tolerance for others. The 'Black Syrian' epithet that I was taunted with in my youth is today frowned upon by our society. Prime Minister Justin Trudeau appears to be continuing his father's legacy, encouraging Canadians to welcome the Syrian refugees who now desperately need a new home.

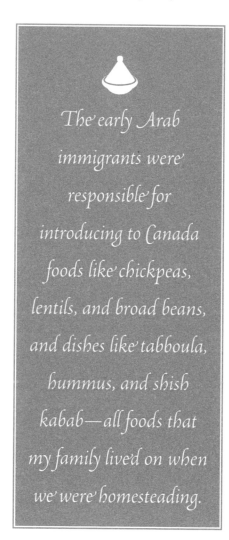

The early Arab immigrants were responsible for introducing to Canada foods like chickpeas, lentils, and broad beans, and dishes like tabboula, hummus, and shish kabab—all foods that my family lived on when we were homesteading.

Yet, despite this multicultural fabric, old prejudices have not completely died out. For those who still harbour bigotry against foreigners, immigrants, and refugees, a book like *Arab Cooking on a Prairie Homestead* provides a guide towards achieving a more tolerant society because it demonstrates first-hand how Arab immigrants have always played a part in building this nation. Indeed, along with tried and true recipes, the reader will find here an intimate, first-hand account of the Syrian immigrant story on the prairies and will discover that, like my own family, the other earliest immigrants left important marks for others to follow. My parents and their offspring would become part of the first wave of immigrant pioneers

calling Canada home. And despite hardships such as the drought and the Depression of the 1930s, our Syrian family, like others of my parents' generation, built a clear pathway for today's new arrivals.

In truth, there will always be immigrants and those seeking refuge in Canada for their new home. For the first immigrants in the early twentieth century, it was a world of neither internet nor email, no Skype and no Facetime, and thus immigration at that time literally meant leaving behind everything and everyone that the family had known for their entire lives. The conditions my family and others faced in the early twentieth century, especially concerning adapting to the new environment, will never again take place. When today's Syrian immigrants arrive, it is with some level of comfort that someone or some organization is there to assist them. The internet keeps them in touch with everyone and everything and with events taking place in the 'old country'—unlike during the time of my parents when news from the land of their birth depended on someone new arriving or on the odd Arabic newspaper that was sent to our home.

The early Arab immigrants were responsible for introducing to Canada foods like chickpeas, lentils, and broad beans, and dishes like tabboula, hummus, and shish kabab—all foods that my family lived on when we were homesteading. However, in order for us to obtain the ingredients for the Syrian foods my mother cooked we had to grow them ourselves, while newcomers can find the same at almost any corner store. In fact, those early foods are common now on the shelves of food stores. Hence, newcomers today need not go far to find what they are accustomed to eating.

Moreover, these Middle Eastern ingredients are fairly inexpensive, and in a world that is facing environmental threats, climate change, and future droughts, these foods will be heaven-sent. Chickpeas, lentils, and broad beans, which are adaptable to dry climates, along with burghul and *kishk*, two wheat by-products, formed the basis of our family's dishes for our nourishment during the years of drought and the Great Depression. It wasn't until years later that I would understand that the foods we ate then have become today's sought-after foods—healthy and nourishing ones. Today, chickpeas and lentils have become some of Saskatchewan's top export crops. The time when as children we ate these foods hidden away in the back of the schoolyard is gone forever. Everyone now knows about these pulses and their benefits.

Today, I am pushing ninety-four years of age, and as I look back through my years of both struggles and good times, I do believe that I have achieved most of what I intended to achieve. My health is good, and I credit it to having been raised on the foods my mother prepared for her family—which are the very foods found still today inside these pages. What my mother cooked—nutritious, vitamin-rich, tasty Arab dishes—contributed to a lifetime of wellness for me.

We are celebrating this year Canada's 150th anniversary. Ultimately, it is my hope that in these pages readers will discover ways to create good food and good relations, too, with their neighbours—whether they be long-time citizens or newcomers to Canada. To sit at the table together and to learn about each other through our food traditions can only lead to a better, more just world where there is tolerance, health, respect, and good food for all. ✵

Habeeb Salloum, Toronto, 2017

To understand a people,

acquaint yourself

with their proverbs.

In an effort to follow the advice in this Arab
saying, I have included amongst the recipes a
number of Arab proverbs, so that my readers
might come a little closer to understanding the
Arab people. There are also some excerpts from
my earlier writings included throughout.

PREFACE TO THE FIRST EDITION

Unknown to most Canadians, Arab immigrants settled in most parts of Canada in the late nineteenth and early twentieth centuries. From the shores of the Arctic to the 49th parallel and from the Atlantic to the Pacific Oceans, they made their homes and became fragments in the Canadian mosaic. My family was among them, and the story of our immigration, pioneering struggle, Canadianization, then urbanization will perhaps provide some insight into the integration of many Arab immigrants into the fabric of urban Canada.

Foremost in our family's saga is the story of how we fed ourselves during the Depression years, when the land in our area of southwestern Saskatchewan turned into a desert waste. How my parents used their ingenuity, inherited from thousands of years of civilization, to help our family survive, how we lived off our huge garden, watered by hand with pails of water from our well, and how the dishes Mother improvised and cooked kept us healthy—this is the core of my story.

Our saga is no different from many other tales in that part of Canada. It is my hope that the story of our family will give future generations, who will no doubt have forgotten the Great Depression, an inkling of what life was like for an immigrant family during those harsh years.

Much has been written about the innumerable ethnic minorities that make up the Canadian mosaic, but one must search almost in vain to find the Arab element in the picture. Perhaps, the most important reason that so little has been written is that these immigrants brought with them from their homeland the idea that their culture was inferior to Western culture.

These feelings of inferiority were to stay with most of the Arab immigrants until they fully integrated into Canadian society. Hence, very few tried to write their history or even retain the language of their forefathers or any segment of their culture. Today, people stare in disbelief when they hear that Arabs homesteaded in western Canada.

I believe that the history of our family and how they survived the Depression years is representative of how many of these virtually unknown Syrian pioneers lived, ate, worked, and, in the process, contributed to the Canadian mosaic and the establishment of our country. It is a fascinating story of a people who in less than a century have disappeared almost without a trace. Besides their Anglicized Arabic names, one of the only legacies of the descendants of these Arab immigrants is a collection of family recipes, foods prepared and eaten for centuries by their foremothers and forefathers.

A number of the foods that these Arab pioneers brought from their homeland—burghul, *hummus, taboula, tahini,* and Arabic bread (*pita*)—have found their way into health food stores and vegetarian kitchens throughout the world. These foods, which we ate virtually every day as children, carry with them my fondest memories of the land from where my parents came. Nourishing and tasty, they helped us, as they did the other Syrian pioneers, to survive our early homestead years. Today, as I look back at that era near the beginning of the twentieth century, what I remember most are the many gourmet dishes my mother prepared from our own basic garden produce, enhanced by ingredients we gathered from the wild.

I have included not only almost all the main dishes my mother cooked during my youthful years, but also others from the Middle East and North Africa. During my many trips to the Arab world, I have picked up countless Arab dishes which I today often cook. Hence, I have enlarged my mother's gourmet kitchen, especially with my taste for spicy foods. In my view, these dishes, although unknown to my mother, reflect more accurately the cuisine of the Arab world which, according to some food historians, consists of some 40,000 dishes.

As to condiments, during our early homesteading days, my mother had to improvise for herbs and spices. Since my father made only a few trips to town, mostly during summer, and since we had very little money, my mother usually did not have the herbs and spices she needed. Yet, she made do. During the summer months, she sun-dried numerous herbs which we grew in our garden or found in the wild, and these enhanced our daily dishes. (For those who are not enamoured with herbs and spices, the amounts called for in the recipes can be reduced, increased or eliminated altogether).

By adding some of my own creations to Mother's delights, I hope that I have given the Arab cuisine a more universal appeal. I am sure that if my mother were still alive today, she would approve of my additions. All her life she created and acquired new recipes. Hence, I feel that I am only continuing her great work in the culinary world.

Habeeb Salloum, Toronto, 2005

ACKNOWLEDGEMENTS

I wish to thank my daughters, Leila Salloum Elias and Muna Salloum, for proofreading the completed manuscript and for the many consultations we had together. Their suggestions for certain changes helped immensely in the final phases of completing this newly revised manuscript.

I wish to express my genuine appreciation to Sarah Carter for her detailed review and comments about my book and for understanding the nature of the process of immigration and settlement in western Canada, especially for the Syrian community.

I also wish to thank Bruce Walsh, director of the University of Regina Press, for recognizing the importance of my book as a contribution to the history of Canada. Thanks also to editors Karen Clark and Donna Grant, and Duncan Campbell, designer, and all of those at the University of Regina Press for their efforts to retain the multicultural aspect of Canadian history. ❈

In June 1979, at a family reunion in Kelowna, British Columbia, I recited a long poem of which these lines were a part, telling the story of our branch of the family. I believe that from these few words one can draw a picture of our family's history in Canada after they left Syria—the land of their ancestors. The story which follows serves as an expansion and elaboration of these verses.

From the east of this country I am now coming,
Not from the East where winds of centuries blow.
In that land where prophets once were speaking,
Our proud tree was planted and began to grow,
Then a few of our forefathers came seeking,
This land where the honey was said to flow.
For a few, their pampered sons now are tasting,
The sweet honey that they, their fathers owe.
While many others for it still are searching,
'Tis the ambitions of fathers that still glow.

As a youth in Saskatchewan I remember thinking,
Why did my parents come and bring us in tow,
From the far Syrian desert with sands blowing,
To the Saskatchewan desert of wind and snow?
Did my father love the desert way of living,
Or did fate on him the desert hardships throw?
For instead of honey, he found when farming,
The bitterness of poverty as in India or Mexico.
His harsh life was one long path of struggling,
To build a future by making grain in desert grow,
But how many times did he with his offsprings,
See the hot wind burn the grain row after row.

CHAPTER 1

THE LEGACY OF THE FATHERS: OUR FAMILY'S HOMESTEADING DAYS

In the fall of the year 1923, the warm rays of the sun reflected on the walls of the mud and stone houses of the (Qarʿawn) Karoun, a town in the Biqaʿ Valley, located in the then French Mandate of Syria and Lebanon. The dry air was invigorating as my father, Jiryas Yaʿqūb Sallūm (George Jacob Salloum), who, in the same fashion as his fellow townsmen, was part peasant-farmer, part trader, hurried back and forth putting his affairs in order before departing for North America.

He was excited but at the same time sad, for he was leaving his young wife, Shams, my older brother Adīb (Eddie), and myself, not yet born. The world he was leaving was not a tranquil place. The Ottoman and then the French occupation of Syria and the unsettled conditions this brought in its wake had prompted many of the townspeople to leave for the Americas. My father, even though he made a good living, wanted to enhance his status and decided that he, too, would join the exodus and try his luck in the beckoning so-called "New World."

In the early twentieth century, to the minds of most peasants, not only in Syria but in much of Europe, any location in the Americas was viewed as a place of opportunity. The United States, Brazil, Mexico, and Canada were the main destinations and it mattered not in which country these seekers of a new life disembarked. They had visions that every land in the "New World" had streets paved with gold.

Where a previous fellow townsman or relative had settled, they usually followed. In *The Arab Americans:*

Threshing crew, 1926: my father is the one standing.

Nationalism and Traditional Preservation, Arab-American Abdo Elkholy writes that, due to the linguistic barriers, ninety percent of the early Arab immigrants went directly to relatives or friends. In just such a fashion, my father landed in Canada, a land that, according to the 1921 census, had barely 3,000 immigrants of Syrian origin.

From the far-off land of Syria, how did he end up in Saskatchewan? I have been asked this question countless times by Arab-Canadians and others. I am sure it was not a well-thought-out plan, but an unusual circumstance of fate that brought him to this wind-filled land. A relative of his, Dāwūd Sallūm (David Salloum), who had immigrated sometime in 1913 and who was a farmer in Hazenmore, a town in southern Saskatchewan, had written and asked if someone from the village wanted to come and work for him as a farmhand. Already a peasant farmer in his home village of the Karoun, but having always dreamt of emigrating to North America, my father quickly wrote and accepted the offer.

After a two-month voyage through the Mediterranean, then across France, where he was delayed for a month, he crossed the Atlantic, landed in Quebec City, then took a train to Hazenmore. He made this voyage speaking only the Syrian colloquial Arabic with no knowledge of any other language. I remember as a child listening to amusing tales of his adventures in France. One story he always related, and which I remember vividly, was of how each time he asked for a drink of water in a restaurant or hotel he was served wine, never being able to make the waiters understand that all he wanted was water. He left the country believing that everyone in France drank nothing but wine. Tales such as this were repeated many times and enthralled me in the same way that a child would sit and listen, captivated, to the stories in *Alice in Wonderland*.

In those years, unlike my father, most Syrian immigrants had settled in the eastern Canadian provinces of Quebec or Ontario. They made their living, in the majority of cases, through peddling or shopkeeping. Only a few went into farming. These early Arab immigrants were prepared to do almost anything to make a decent living. However, rarely did they cross the country to live in Canada's prairie provinces.

To immigrants unfamiliar with the English language and accustomed to a close-knit village life, country living in southwestern Saskatchewan was indeed lonely. Living on the prairies appealed only to those who had a little knowledge of Canada, to the adventurous, and later, to their relatives.

My father's work as a farm labourer lasted only a few months. The glittering gold of America, the dream of almost all the immigrants of that era, was not to be found working sixteen hours a day on a farm for a few dollars a month. In addition, having been an independent peasant farmer, he was not accustomed to being ordered around by another person; thus he could not adapt to having his relative telling him what to do.

He left the farm with no regrets, and moved to the town of Gouvernor to live near another relative, Moses Salloum (Mūsa Sallūm), who was related to both my parents. Moses owned a general store, a mark of prosperity in that era, and agreed to outfit my father with a horse and buggy. This enabled him to become a peddler selling clothing and trinkets to the farmers in the surrounding countryside. Many Syrian emigrants before him had worked and prospered in this business, and he hoped to follow in their footsteps.

Like the other Syrian immigrants, my father was unaware that many Canadians looked down upon his new profession and ethnic origin. In that era, in the eyes of many Canadians, few qualities attributed

Passport photo, 1924: My brother Adīb and me as a baby sitting on my mother's knee.

to Arabs were positive and most were negative. In one of the early studies of immigration to Canada, J.S. Woodsworth, in his book *Strangers Within Our Gates*, cites a Dr. Allan McLaughlin, author of a series of articles between 1903 and 1905 on "Immigration" in *Popular Science Monthly*, whose interpretation and subsequent definition of the Syrians provided the general attitude towards this ethnic group. McLaughlin stated:

> The mental processes of these people have an oriental subtlety. Centuries of subjection, where existence was only possible through intrigue, deceit and servility, have left their mark,

and through force of habit, they lie most naturally and by preference, and only tell the truth when it will serve their purposes best. Their wits are sharpened by generations of commercial dealing and their business acumen is marvellous. With all due admiration for the mental qualities and trading skill of these parasites from the Near East, it cannot be said that they are anything in the vocations they follow but detrimental and burdensome.

During this period when my father was becoming established in his new trade, my mother, my brother (not yet three years old), and myself (less than a year old) followed our father's footsteps across the Mediterranean to France and then crossed the Atlantic. After a month of travelling, my mother, with her two small children, landed in Quebec City, then took a train to Gouvernor. The tales of how she travelled halfway around the world with no knowledge of French or English and the tribulations she encountered were, like my father's stories, to hold us spellbound during many cold Saskatchewan winter nights.

A few years after my mother arrived, my father decided that he had had enough of peddling and its servile ways. Even though he was making a fair income, he hated the trade. He could not become accustomed to begging people to buy his few pieces of clothing and household trinkets.

During the time my father was peddling out of Gouvernor, my eldest sister Ramza (Rose) was born. Our family was growing and the one-room shack was becoming overcrowded. This gave my father the incentive to leave the work he loathed and set him searching to find a farm. He yearned for a piece of land he could call his own. For him, hard work was a fulfilling way of life, not a bogey to be feared.

Our family's early social and economic hardships were mirrored by other Arab immigrants. The isolated rural areas proved to be the experimental laboratory in which their survival in the new land was to be tested. However, the hardy nature of the Arab immigrants and their readiness to work were, in many cases, not appreciated by old-time Canadians. McLaughlin typified this attitude when he wrote:

In their habits of life, their business methods, and their inability to perform labour or become producers, they do not compare favourably even with the Chinese, and the most consoling feature of their coming has been that they form a comparatively small part of our total immigration.

In the same vein, J.S. Woodsworth in 1909 added that the Syrians "are manifestly not fitted for life in Western Canada."

My father's wish to be a farmer was soon fulfilled. He was granted by the federal government a quarter section of land as a homestead eighteen miles north of the town of Val Marie. In the meantime, he had not been idle. He had saved a few hundred dollars from peddling, and with this he bought another quarter section of land, a team of horses, a wagon, and a plough. Unlike many other Arab immigrants of the time, my father did not intend to save money, then return to the old country to buy a house or a piece of land. He had decided that Canada was to be his future and permanent home.

I have often wondered how my parents felt when they reached their empty land. In the old country they had been used to seeing relatives and friends; now they were alone with not even a neighbour's house in sight. As they looked across the barren land, how they must have longed for their home in the Karoun or even their little shack in Gouvernor, which at that moment must have seemed like a palace. Surely they must have known that homesteading on the unbroken prairie was no easy task.

Nevertheless, in that summer of 1927, my parents were young and ambitious. To begin from noth-

> To begin from nothing must have been an unnerving experience; but there was no turning back. They were pioneers in a land they had chosen and were determined to settle, ready to conquer whatever came their way.

ing must have been an unnerving experience, but there was no turning back. They were pioneers in a land they had chosen and were determined to settle, ready to conquer whatever came their way.

Their first task was to build a habitable structure before the cold winter winds blew across the land. The previous owner of their quarter section had partially constructed a small framed building. However, he had left before even the outer walls had been completed. This unfinished shell served as a shelter for our family during the hot July and August days, but my father knew he had to do something before the icy winter blasts compelled both man and animal to seek a warm refuge.

Without money, he could not buy the materials he needed, but his background came to his aid. In Syria, people had built their homes from the soil and rock of the countryside, and my father was well-acquainted with their building methods. He had helped many of his relatives and friends erect their homes, and now he put this knowledge to work.

Near the frail structure where we lived, a part of the land was pure clay. With my mother's help, my father mixed clay with straw and water, creating a building mixture known as adobe—a word derived from the Arabic al-ṭūb. They filled it into the inner walls and ceiling of the frame structure, and when the adobe hardened, the building became a habitable home, comfortable in the extremes of both summer and winter. In later years, the adobe was painted and proved both pleasant to see and highly durable. I remember returning to visit the abandoned homestead fifteen years after the home was built to find the walls were still like new.

At the same time as the house was being finished, my father started to plough the land to ready the soil for the next year's crop— our first harvest, which my father thought would set us on the road to prosperity. However, preparing the soil was no easy task. Not only did it need to be ploughed, but thousands of rocks had to be hand-picked from the fields.

Every morning my father would wake my brother and me at 4 a.m. and take us to the fields to help remove the many rocks. As tiny tots, we could pick only the very small stones, while my father laboured with the large boulders. We picked stones morning after morning. The task was unending, so that, even as a child, I came to loathe the sight of piled rocks.

Around 7 a.m., we would return to enjoy a hearty breakfast which my mother always prepared. After the meal my father would go to plough the fields while my brother and I helped with the chores around the house. These were pleasant tasks, however, compared to the picking of stones.

The virgin land being plowed by my father hosted many wild animals and birds which were found on the south Saskatchewan plains. Almost every day when my father returned from the fields, he would bring a few prairie chickens or rabbits for our daily meals. There was no problem keeping the extra meat. In summer, we put the meat in a pail, then lowered it into the well to just above the water line; in the winter, an outside shed served as an excellent refrigerator.

Even though meat was important, it was only one item in our diet. During the spring and summer months, my mother would scour the nearby fields for the roots and edible greens known to her in the old country. In addition, every year she had a thriving vegetable garden which, with my brother's and my help, was watered by hand. From this excellent garden she kept us fed for the whole year. What we did not eat during the summer, she dried or cooked in jars for winter use. Hence, even though money was very scarce, we always ate well.

The excellent crop in 1928 made my parents forget the hardships of their first homesteading year. They planned for a rosy future, but fate did not look kindly on their many dreams. Thereafter, the bountiful years were few and far between.

In 1929, there was a small crop but nothing to compare with the previous year. The stock market crashed, bringing on the Depression, and, as if to magnify the catastrophe, Mother Nature refused to send the life-giving rains. It would be some years before the grain would again grow.

In no time, the land in that part of southern Saskatchewan became a desert waste. For the next three years, nothing grew, and the soil blew back and forth like the deserts of Arabia. How many times my father and mother must have cursed the day they came to this land where they had thought the streets were paved with gold.

During these years our neighbours, the nearest being three miles away, began to abandon their parched farms, but my father, with an expanding family, could not afford to move away. Besides, the harsh life which was forcing many of the people to leave did not affect us in the same way as it did our neighbours.

Like many Arab immigrants, we were able to survive better than many members of various ethnic groups due to the experience of agrarian, subsistence-level living that had been practiced by my parents in their homeland. In the Biqaʿ Valley, my parents had grown chickpeas and lentils—crops that had, through the centuries, adapted to the desert climate. These we now seeded, and every year our garden of chickpeas and lentils thrived, aided by hand-drawn water from our well. For meat, besides the wild partridges and rabbits, we raised chickens and a few sheep and cows that lived off the little grass and bushes which grew in the valleys.

Although we had enough to eat, clothing was another matter. My mother made our shirts, overalls, and other garments from canvas or flour bags and any used, discarded clothing she could find. Like most Arab immigrants, my parents' desire to survive and try to prosper in a foreign land gave them the impetus to improvise.

For us children there was not much excitement growing up during

Our family on the homestead, 1930. From left to right: Rose, Habeeb, Helen, Mother Shams, Mary, Fred, and Eddie (standing behind Fred).

these years. Going into the town of Val Marie was an event my older brother and I looked forward to with great anticipation. In the period we lived on the homestead, I remember journeying only twice with my father to Val Marie, which appeared to me to be a huge metropolis—a fairyland centre which filled my dreams.

The eighteen-mile trip to Val Marie by horse and buggy or sleigh was usually, especially in winter, a two-day ride. With no money for a hotel, we slept overnight with our horses in the livery barn, spreading out bales of hay for our beds. Years later, I returned to that town which by then had only forty-eight residents. No one I talked to knew that there had once been a livery barn in their town. In the intervening years, I had realized that my childhood thoughts had been far from reality, but I did not know how far. All there was left from that metropolis of my dreams was a number of businesses and a few homes. "'Tis better to live in a world of fantasy," I thought to myself as I surveyed the scene.

During the homesteading years, our prolific family increased by four: a brother, Fu'ād (Fred), and three sisters, Hilla (Helen), Mariyam (Mary), and Furzlīya (Phyllis). With the closest doctor twenty-two miles away in Ponteix, the children were delivered by a neighbour's wife, who had some training as a nurse, assisted by my father.

Births were not the only occasions when a doctor was needed but could not be reached. I remember vividly many a cold winter night with my mother crying in pain, having no medical help to relieve her torment. There is no doubt that these undiagnosed pains—caused, as she found out later, from gallstones—affected her in the coming years. But the pains of childbirth and gallstones were only the visible, physical suffering.

Deep inside she had other torments. During the long winter evenings she would relate to us nostalgic stories about life in Syria. Her eyes would shine as she talked about the orchards and vineyards heavy with grapes that, at that time, I had neither tasted nor seen. She talked

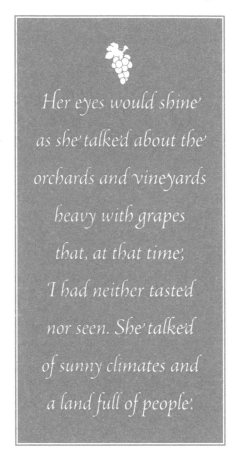

Her eyes would shine as she talked about the orchards and vineyards heavy with grapes that, at that time, I had neither tasted nor seen. She talked of sunny climates and a land full of people.

of sunny climates and a land full of people. She would reminisce about the village of Karoun, where she had many relatives and friends, comparing it to the homestead, where we had a visitor perhaps once or twice a year. Even as a child, I deeply felt that her life was lonely.

I was nearly eight years old and my brother ten when the first school was built three miles away from our home. We attended it for a year, but by the next summer the majority of the farmers had moved away and the school was closed. The process of the Canadianization of the older children began in this early period of our lives. Attending school and associating with our schoolmates made us feel we were different and, at times, inferior.

"Black Syrian! Out of my way, Black Syrian!" were the epithets with which we were taunted every day. In later years I came upon a book entitled *Which Way to Mecca, Jack?*, written by William Peter Blatty (also author of *The Exorcist*), a second-generation Arab-American. I found that I totally identified with him when he asked his mother, "Mama, why can't I talk American like the other kids?" Indeed, he could well have been speaking about my youth when he described himself as a "foreigner in the land of my birth" or when he reminisced about his boyhood fantasies, stating:

> As for my own dreams, the only one I really harbored in those days was the dream of waking up some morning and finding myself an Irishman. How I envied the Irish boys their snub noses, their pale skins, and their incredible reflexes! I had daydreams in which my name was Miles O'Malley or Fairfax McLaughlin, and I had blond hair and was the champion boxer of Ireland. . . . Meanwhile, I would have given a million dollars for just one crummy freckle.

Feeling inferior, we aped everything our classmates said or did. This was especially true when it came to our attitudes toward First Nations peoples. Even when we were by ourselves, we wanted to be just like them, which, in our minds at that time, meant looking down on others, and so who better to pick on than the Indigenous peoples?

"Let's go and dig the Indian grave." My excited brother, shovel in hand, tugged me forward. I needed no urging. Eagerly I followed. To us children, the reputed Indian tomb on a hill overlooking our homestead was a site of mystery and romance.

Why this aura of intrigue had ensnared us children is to me today unfathomable. Yet, as a young boy, I was fascinated by the tale of an Indian grave under a tree, standing like a sentinel atop that knoll. All alone, encircled by the barren prairies, the lonely weather-beaten shrub signified to me something different—a symbol of Indian lore and buried riches.

Somehow, we children had come to believe that an Indian chief was interred under the only tree visible for miles around. Of course, we never did find the buried Indian, but the folk tale of a chief entombed at the summit of our homestead mound lived on in my youthful memories.

The tree eventually died, but the grave never did give up its secret. However, we had other irons in the fire. My older brother and I often found circles of stones where, we were told, the Plains Indians pitched their tents. Scattered around them we found a few vestiges of the people who once owned our land—a number of arrow heads and some stone hammers.

Growing up in the same manner as all our neighbours' children, we never dreamed that the land we lived on had been taken away from its millennia-old inhabitants, then given free to others brought in from the four corners of the

Earth. Our digging of what we thought was an Indian grave and our endless search for arrow heads were to us games in the world of fantasy. In our minds, the people who left these remains were not humans like ourselves. They were like the fictitious characters in the tales from the *Arabian Nights* stories that our mother often related during the cold winter evenings.

We must have picked up this outlook from our few playmates—no doubt, influenced by their parents' thinking. As poor Syrian immigrants with deep feelings of inferiority, we mimicked those we thought were real Canadians. The history of the conquest of the West with its broken treaties and betrayals was never known or discussed in our family circle. Yet, we had inherited the bounty of these unfulfilled promises. No one acknowledged the fact that, like almost all the western pioneers, we were living on stolen land.

Yet, for hundreds of years before the arrival of Europeans, on the vast expanse of the windswept and treeless prairies—a land which some say God could have given to Cain—the Indigenous Nations lived. They abided in a relatively secure world with their own laws, languages, and religions. The cultures in which they were immersed satisfied all their earthly and afterlife needs.

Like most of the western hemisphere's Indigenous Nations, the Plains Cree and Assiniboine peoples were exceptionally friendly and hospitable to the first white men who entered their lands—that is, until the strangers brought their gifts of guns, rum, smallpox, and syphilis. Equally damaging to the Indigenous Nations of the western plains was that the newcomers virtually exterminated the buffalo on which they depended. The herds of buffalo, from fifty to one hundred thousand each, that once darkened the prairies had disappeared.

In summer, they had eaten the buffalo meat fresh and made pemmican with the remainder for the harsh winter months. Hides, sinews, bones, and hair—everything was used in their daily life. After the bison were gone, ordeals of starvation became common and this, added to the diseases introduced by the Europeans, almost wiped out the original inhabitants of the western plains.

Weakened by lack of nourishment and almost continual sickness, the old and young often died in the cold winter months. Those who remained were put onto reservations. Their children were often taken away and sent to residential schools.

Those who left the reservations to try to better their lives were not, like my parents, given land or livestock or trained for jobs in the newly established towns. They often lingered on the fringes of society.

The settlers who had been given the lands of the Indigenous Nations either prospered or moved away and melted into mainstream Canadian society. But many of the Indigenous peoples, ensnared by the white man's laws and racist colonial policies, were never able to climb out of the abyss in which they had been forcibly placed. Still, to this day, many Canadians continue to reject the rightful upholding of the treaties that were signed and reject Indigenous self-determination and reconciliation. Sadly, it is apparent that a great many have not advanced in their thinking from the time when we immigrant children searched for days around the circles of stone for traces of a people who had been so dehumanized and mistreated. This is one of the tragedies of Canada's history.

CHAPTER 2

THE CANADIANIZATION OF OUR FAMILY

The improvisations of my parents, which included growing foods such as chickpeas and lentils from our desert homeland, helped us survive during those barren homesteading years, but my father knew he had to find another place if his family was to have a decent future. The turning point came when he met a fellow Arab immigrant in Gouvernor. Albert Hattum, who hailed from a neighbouring village in the Biqaʿ Valley, having immigrated to Canada sometime in 1909, was a farmer who had settled north of Gouvernor. They discussed their lives in this new world, and when my father informed him that he was looking for new land, Hattum told him there was a farm for rent a few miles away. Some weeks later my father rented this farm, and in early March of 1933, our friend came with a team of horses and a wagon to help us move.

A blizzard was blowing as we loaded our possessions in four wagons, getting them ready for the next morning when we planned to make the thirty-mile trip to the new place. My father, our friend, my older brother, and I each drove a wagon on that cold, blustery day. I still remember the biting winds cutting through the blanket wrapped around me as our friend, Hattum, from the wagon behind spurred me on with encouraging words: "Son, you are a man now. Take courage! The trip will end soon." I can still hear his voice as he shouted to my father across two wagons' length. "That son you have will be a great man one day. Look at him now driving the horses in this cold without complaint."

It was dark that March evening when we reached our new farm situated between the towns of Gouvernor

Minot School—our farm school.

and Neville. I felt elated, for we had driven through a countryside which was inhabited, unlike the deserted lands around the homestead we had left. On our new farm, there was a house with a barn and ploughed fields. In the coming days, like a general, my father organized us so that each was responsible for his or her own task. His instructions were carried out without hesitation. The house was in rundown condition, but habitable. That spring and summer we cleaned, repaired, painted, and reconstructed many parts of our new home.

To me, this new farm was heaven compared to the old homestead. Now we had neighbours who lived close by, and hardly a day passed when we did not see someone who would come over for a visit or just to chat. For me, even more satisfying, there was a school only three miles away. I was happy. School was to me then as social media, video games, and television are to the children of today. My mother also appeared happier as she went about her many tasks. Now she had friends among the neighbours, and on rare occasions some of our relatives would come to visit our modest home.

However, all was not bliss. Like the days on the homestead, the winds blew the soil from the parched land. Only in 1935 did we get a fair crop, the first since 1928. Until I left home in 1940, this was the only bountiful crop I can remember. In 1937, the land was so dry that even thistles failed to grow.

During sunny days the wind blew the soil so thick that midday became midnight. In those years, the town of Gouvernor gradually disappeared as the surrounding land became desert and the farmers moved away. Some years ago I visited the site where the town once stood to find that there was not one building left. In my mind, it was a strange irony. The desert seemed to have followed us from Syria. We were fated not to escape the blowing sands.

The year we moved to the new land, my youngest brother, Albert, was born. Although we were now a little better off, the hospital and doctor were still beyond our reach. In later years, my mother gave birth to two girls who died soon thereafter. Birth control was apparently unknown to my parents, especially to my mother, who wanted relief. Her cries from the pains of child-bearing and its side effects still ring in my ears.

Between 1933 and 1940, we children became prepared for adult life. In this period we attended Minot, a little prairie school which moulded our lives. With its few facilities this tiny place of learning did a better job of preparing the young for the outside world than most gadget-filled schools of today.

What I remember most vividly about this small house of knowledge is its miniature library, which to me, in my tender years, was the gold mine of the school. I cannot recall how many times I read, then re-read, every book. During the cold Saskatchewan evenings, their stories were my constant companions. From these few books, I became familiar with the outer world, and was prompted to dream of leaving the parched prairie land for the rich cities of western or eastern Canada. If the library was my companion, the young women teachers, who taught ten grades and still had time to give us advice, were my guides. With hardly any wages to sustain them, they put their hearts and minds into helping the children of the farmers to become adults, ready for the future.

During those school years, I was burdened with a feeling of imperfection. Like most other immigrant children I tried desperately to become part of the Anglo-Saxon world. I tried to imitate the ways of my Canadian classmates and sought their approval. Blatty aptly described this method of wanting to belong when speaking of his own Americanization:

> Now that I was away from home I was able to concentrate on filling in the elements of a new identity, stealing this habit and that grace, this way of dressing and that way of acting from the hordes of refined, wealthy young gentlemen of fine old New England homes who came to the Georgetown campus to study....

I plunged on with my college career, growing more and more urbane, more and more embarrassed by reminders of my alien upbringing.

As the Abrahams have written in *Arabs in the New World*, sharp differences developed between our parents and ourselves. The gulf between their values and attitudes and ours widened. For instance, when we had Arab and Canadian visitors to the house, my parents would speak to their Arab friends in Arabic in front of the Canadian guests. This would make me feel ashamed, and I would think to myself, "Why are we different?"

At the same time as I and my brothers and sisters were trying to shed our Arab origins and assimilate, we dreamt of the cities of Canada—these unreachable far-away fairyland places. It was apparent that we did not inherit a love for the land from our father.

During these farming years, our lives were enriched by visits to our neighbours, mostly those with an Arab background, and by rare trips to town. What I most enjoyed were the winter traplines and poetry, which often were combined, giving me a feeling of elation and fulfillment, such as on one particular day as I rode my horse across the rolling, white prairie landscape.

The cold Saskatchewan winter wind stung my cheeks like a razor-sharp knife as I urged my old mare on. Through a blowing snowstorm, I was making my weekly round along a five-mile-long trapline. Yet, I felt content. What I earned from the skins of rabbits and weasels was the only spending money I would ever see during my early teens.

To forget the searing cold, I recited out loud into the empty expanse of space the poems of Robert Service, who through the years was my favourite bard. The world around me became a land of fantasy, and I lived with Service on the frozen landscape of the Yukon. I felt that, like me, he understood the cold Canadian winters and the struggle to survive. With not a soul for miles around, I could hear my voice echoing through the piercing wind as I recited Service's "The Law of the Yukon":

This is the law of the Yukon,
    and ever she makes it plain:
'Send not your foolish and
    feeble; send me your
    strong and your sane;
Strong for the red rage of battle;
    sane for I harry them sore;
…
This is the Law of the
    Yukon, that only the
    Strong shall thrive;
That surely the Weak shall per-
    ish, and only the Fit survive.
Dissolute, damned and
    despairful, crippled and
    palsied and slain,
This is the Will of the Yukon—
    Lo! how she makes it plain!'

Near the end of the trapline, the storm became a gentle breeze. On every side, the landscape was like a large ocean covered with endless waves of snow. The atmosphere had become crystal clear, but the bitter cold had intensified. It was truly a living scene from the Arctic frozen terrain.

With two long-dead weasels tied to the saddle behind me, I made my way back through the deep snow. Of course, at that time, the suffering of these animals in the jaws of my traps and their subsequent cruel death did not bring a pang of regret. Like most of my fellow teen trappers, I was thinking only of the few cents the weasel skins would bring.

As my old mare plodded along, the winter scene around me, tailor-made for an artist's brush—that is, if the artist was sitting in the warm indoors and surveying the snow-covered landscape—did not entice me. My thoughts were still with Service and his poems. Wiping the icicles formed from the steam of my breath along the edges of the parka hood, I thought of the words in "The Cremation of Sam McGee:"

Talk of your cold! through the
    parka's fold it stabbed like a
    driven nail. If our eyes we'd
    close, then the lashes froze till
    sometimes we couldn't see;

Sam McGee's voice seemed to speak directly to me:

'It's the cursèd cold, and it's got
    right hold till I'm chilled
    clean through to the bone.

That night as I slept near the coal and wood stove that, during the long winter months, barely kept our home warm, I fell asleep, repeating again and again:

There are strange things done
    in the midnight sun
By the men who moil for gold;
The Arctic trails have
    their secret tales
That would make your
    blood run cold;

I wasn't always lucky when I made my weekly round of the trapline. Usually, if I found even one weasel, my spirits would reach dizzying heights. Most of the time, the traps were empty or closed shut by some sly coyote—an intelligent animal who often outwits the most experienced of hunters.

Nevertheless, during that winter, I had done well. From my weasel hides and the rabbits which I had shot—whose hides I sold for between five and ten cents each—I had saved five dollars for that day in spring when I would accompany my father to town.

Early in April that year, along with my father and older brother, we headed by horse and buggy to Neville for our spring shopping—to buy the essential foods and seeds needed for our usual large garden. However, my mind was elsewhere. The five dollars in my pocket made me feel like a millionaire. I was excited, thinking that soon I would be gorging myself on chocolate bars.

My thoughts were deep in this dream world of sweets when we drove from a dirt country road onto the dirt main street of town, lined on both sides with mostly business establishments. Neville, at that time a village of some 200 souls, was to me a glittering city, full of exciting things to see and do.

Among its establishments were two gas stations with their garages and machinery dealerships, four towering grain elevators, a railway station, two general stores filled with goodies, a lumberyard/hardware store, a post office, a busy restaurant, a hand-drawn fire-fighting engine, and the Neville Hotel which housed a beer parlour. It was a night spot that, as a child, I often heard our visitors discuss—at times not too kindly, especially when they talked about the barroom fights.

Today, most of this is gone. Neville is a fast-fading prairie village. Many years later, during a visit to western Canada, I travelled to my boyhood town. The fantasy metropolis of yesteryear had become almost a ghost town. Its population had dwindled to less than 50 and the main street, although now paved, was edged by empty spaces. Here and there, a few homes and businesses barely clung to life, and its inhabitants, in the main, were past their prime.

The railway station was no more; of the two gas stations, only one remained—a sad replica of its former self; the hotel had disappeared, and what businesses were still in operation appeared to be less than thriving. A relative accompanying me and who once lived in the area surveyed the town and summed up the scene: "It's a town waiting to disappear."

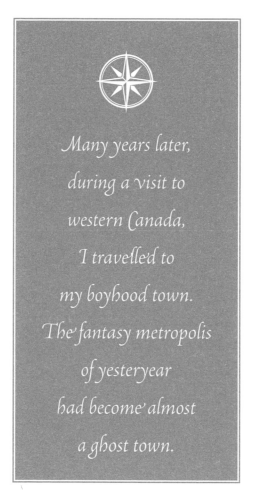

Many years later, during a visit to western Canada, I travelled to my boyhood town. The fantasy metropolis of yesteryear had become almost a ghost town.

Standing on the corner beside the remaining poorly stocked general store, my mind went back to that day when I left my father and brother and hurried down the wooden sidewalk to Towler General Store. That day, my emotions heightened as I neared my goal. The thought of feasting on not one but a dozen chocolate bars sent shivers through my body.

With great anticipation, I selected the bars, smiling all the time at the storekeeper. Sliding a hand first in one pocket, then the other, to draw out the money, I found them both empty. I was devastated. Bursting into tears, I rushed out, retracing my footsteps a half dozen times. Alas! My hard-earned money was gone. My dreams had come to naught.

How my few dollars had disappeared in the short space between where we had stopped and the store haunted me for days. It was a mystery that I was never able to unravel—to me, one of the greatest misfortunes of my youth. In later years, I experienced many pitfalls, but the loss of my chocolate bar money left with me the most unforgettable mark.

I was near sixteen when the Second World War began. I applied at the Moose Jaw Technical Institute to take a machinist course

offered to young men who desired to work in the war factories, was accepted, and in a few weeks found myself in the city of Moose Jaw. During the day I attended classes, but when the school day ended, I walked the town's streets, enthralled by the sights and sounds of the largest city I had ever seen. To a farm boy who had never left his parents' farm, it was a world of splendour and excitement.

Still, there was the loneliness of a strange city. However, my forlorn days were alleviated by Service's poems. To every incident and in every nook, I would see a connection with Service's verses, whether it be seeing a painting in a church and thinking of his poem, "My Madonna," to encountering for the first time Moose Jaw's ladies of the night and then being haunted by his words from "The Harpy:" "Mine eyes with wine I make them shine, that man may seek and take."

Subsequently, since those early days in Moose Jaw, I have roamed the four corners of the world, from the snows of northern Canada to the deserts of Africa and the jungles of South America and the Far East. Yet, I have never forgotten the poetry of Robert Service. His mesmerizing ballads still captivate me as a man in his nineties. At times, I still fantasize that perhaps these

lines from "The Men Who Don't Fit In" were written especially for me:

There's a race of men
  that don't fit in,
A race that can't stay still;
So they break the hearts
  of kith and kin,
And they roam the world at will.
They range the field and
  they rove the flood,
And they climb the
  mountain's crest;
Theirs is the curse of
  the gypsy blood,
And they don't know how to rest.

The Second World War broke into our narrow prairie world and drastically changed our lives. Unlike the previous years when there was not a job to be had, now the Armed Forces and armament factories were crying out for men. After a few months in the machinist course in Moose Jaw, I left to work in an armament factory in Regina. In 1943, I joined the Air Force and my eldest brother volunteered for the Navy. We served both in and outside of Canada and were discharged in 1945.

In those war years, most of the adult children in the family began planning to move away and seek a better life. We wanted to part with the harsh ways of farming and the cultural heritage of our parents, which were now significantly different from that which characterized Canadian society. Although, like almost all immigrants, our parents tried hard to teach us their customs and ancestral language, we rebelled. We felt that by making our homes in urban centres, no one would know our origins and we would become true Canadians. We were no different from Blatty, who wrote:

> Among my playmates on the Tower East Side and in Brooklyn had been many children born to Greek, Italian, Armenian, Polish, Spanish or Irish immigrants, and we were all, all of us, embarrassed and ashamed of the peculiar behaviour of our parents.

Like most Syrian immigrants of that period, we wanted to become white—what we saw then as being "undeniably Canadian." Abu Laban, a Canadian-Arab author, quotes from the 1935 report by Joseph Helal for the Canadian Syrian National Society in which, after much effort, the Syrians established with the Canadian immigration authorities that they were white in origin: "The Society succeeded in establishing, to the fullest satisfaction of the authorities, the fact that Syrians do not come under any racial category

other than that of the white race." In the towns and cities which we were to make our home, unlike the farm where everyone knew us, we were convinced that we would lose our foreign background.

Not one of us children ever thought of following in our father's footsteps and working the land. The cities of Canada were our El Dorados. Even my father could not stem the coming tide. He was forced, to some extent, to accommodate the children. The beginning of the urbanization of our family was at hand.

While we were serving in the Armed Forces, my parents moved to Neville, where they opened a restaurant. My sisters and my younger brothers, unlike myself and my older brother, now had a chance to finish their schooling if they so desired. Although my father opened a restaurant, he could not give up the farm. I recall, in later years, when I raised the subject of farming and indicated how happy I was that he had left the farm to open a restaurant, he became very angry and insisted that "farming is the best life for any man." The heartaches and sorrows of the homestead had clearly slipped from his memory.

My two younger brothers did the farming while my mother, helped by my father and sisters, operated the restaurant. Although

In uniform during the war years.

Our family in 1962, after all of us children had left the farm and made our lives in various urban centres. Back row, left to right: Eddie (Adīb), Rose (Ramza), Habeeb, Phyllis (Furzliya), Fred (Fu'ād), and Albert. Front row, left to right: Mary (Mariyam), our mother, Shams, our father, George (Jiryas), and Helen (Hilli).

their profits from the restaurant were modest, compared to the farming years their standard of living had risen manyfold.

When the war began, the Depression ended and, strange as it may seem, so did the drought. The rains came, and, while the crops were in some years not as good as in others, the wheat grew every year. With the money he made from both the restaurant and the farm, my father at last decided he had had enough of work. He moved to Swift Current, bought three houses and lived in semi-retirement, but he kept the farm and sold it only in his last years. He also kept the restaurant, but it was operated by my eldest sister and youngest brother to whom he sold it a few years later.

One after another, the members of our family left the land

behind. The movement to the urban centres was irreversible. A family which for hundreds of years, generation after generation, had lived from the soil, now, in a few decades, became fully urbanized.

Eventually my four sisters all married. Rose remained in Swift Current; Mary moved to Manitoba; Helen went to Kelowna, British Columbia; and Phyllis lived in Saltcoats, Saskatchewan. She and her husband were the last members of the family to become urbanized. Eddie and Fred became residents of Vancouver, while Albert, like myself, moved to Toronto.

The process of urbanization occurred quickly due to a number of factors. The most important of these factors were the opportunities urban living offered when compared with the hard, seemingly unrewarding life of the prairies. In the old country, people rarely moved away from their birthplace or trade, mainly because of traditions and the lack of economic evolution. Here, in the Americas, these shackles of the past were non-existent. Unlike our parents, for whom linguistic and other cultural barriers hindered their full assimilation, we believed that in urban society our Canadianization would be complete. In the cosmopolitan centres, we would not be pointed out as different. Radios, schools, library books, catalogues, and advertisements which came to our Spartan rural home enticed us with the glamour of the rich world, and in the ensuing years the dreams became a reality. Every member of the family ended up in an urban centre and never considered returning to the land.

Our family was like most other first- and second-generation Arab immigrants. We started out with very limited educational and monetary resources and an equally limited grasp of the English language. However, as the years progressed, the children's education and especially their mastery of the English language made them yearn to cut their ties with their ethnic background.

Like the first-generation Arab-American immigrants, we believed that Arabic was a sign of backwardness and English was the glamorous future. In fact, we came to understand that to be a real Canadian the Arab immigrant would have to learn how to speak English without an accent. We would have identified with Salom Rizk, whose 1943 autobiography is entitled *Syrian Yankee*. After winning a school contest, he had this hope: "Maybe I would be an American yet, a real American speaking English like other Americans."

According to Elkholy, in 1969 twenty percent of second-generation Arabs and seventy-one percent of third-generation Arabs in the United States neither understood nor spoke Arabic. The Jabbras in their book, *Voyageurs to a Rocky Shore*, note that the use of Arabic virtually disappears amongst the third generation and all that remains are a few mispronounced words for items of food.

Driven by economic ambition, Arab immigrants began early to imitate their neighbours and seek their approval. They wanted desperately to be accepted into Canadian society. Their assimilation was aided by their small numbers relative to most other ethnic groups, and by their limited education acquired from missionary schools in the Middle East. These places of learning did not emphasize pride in their origin and history. Most of the Syrian immigrants to North America were more sectarian than nationalistic and thus ready to cut their old country bonds.

Added to this is the fact that almost all the early arrivals at the turn of the twentieth century were Christians. Elkholy puts the figure at ninety percent. Many of these immigrants came with a feeling that they belonged to the Christian West. They tried, in the majority of cases, to assimilate to the point of becoming invisible. Even when rejected, they could not believe they were not accepted as true brother Christians. I remember rushing home crying as a child, asking my father what to do, after being taunted as a "Black Syrian." I can still hear my father's angry voice instructing me: "Go back! Tell them Christ was a Syrian!"

Carrying their servility to a ridiculous extent, some of the Christian immigrants I knew even taught their children that they were descendants of the Crusaders. Some parents did not wish to have their children learn Arabic. Others tried to Frenchify or Anglicize their family names, claiming they were returning them to their true European origin. A vast number, like our family, gave their offspring both Arabic and Western names or simply gave them Anglo-Saxon Christian names. With this yearning to be considered Western, it is no wonder they were so easily assimilated.

The Muslims, although on a somewhat smaller scale, followed the path of their Christian brethren. A good number of them fell over each other in trying to disappear. According to Barclay in his studies of the second generation among the Muslim Arab community in Lac La Biche, Alberta, in their attempts to gain acceptance in a Christian world, Muslims emphasized the common features of Islam and Christianity and minimized the differences. The assimilation of the Muslim Arab immigrants led some to be lost to their religion altogether.

The religious disparity between Christians and Muslims was significant, however, in preserving traditional values. Elkholy writes that these values were more vivid among Arab-Muslims and their children than among Arab-Christians, whose American-born children were especially susceptible to the sweeping processes of assimilation. Unlike the Christian parents who seemed to want to shed their Arab past, the Muslim parents, so it seemed to me, emphasized pride in their Arab-Muslim heritage, hence holding off the process of complete assimilation.

In the urban centres of western Canada, where they were few in numbers, the Arab immigrants found they could assimilate quickly. Thus, in the overwhelming number of cases, they made their homes in the towns and cities. Even the ones who settled, like our family, on the land, had in one generation moved into towns. In these urban centres, they found an atmosphere conducive to being accepted.

As a whole, more than any other ethnic group, the early Arab immigrants, because of their lack of nationalism and because of their religious divisions, plunged headlong into assimilation. As they grew more and more urban, they seemed embarrassed by reminders of their alien upbringing and thus rejected the ways of their ancestors. The only aspect of their traditional culture a few of them retained was some interest in Arab food, music, and dance. However, even these relics from the past were forgotten by the vast majority as they Canadianized themselves out of existence.

In the Swift Current area, where many of the Arab pioneers settled, over eighty percent married outside their community, while their children had little or no connection with the Arab world. Educated in Canadian culture and institutions, they have no memories of a "foreign homeland." Like almost all the other first-generation Syrian immigrants to Canada, my father and mother, even if they reminisced about farming, eventually made the town their permanent home.

Retired and living comfortably in Swift Current, they forgot the misery of the farming years and always praised Saskatchewan, the part of Canada that was their adopted land. Unlike myself and some of my brothers who remember this province as a land where we tasted bitterness, my parents, in their later years, thought of it as paradise.

If one lives in paradise, one does not want to leave it, and my parents never left. My mother died in 1965. The gallstones that had caused her so much torment during the farming years eventually ended her life. My father, who had weathered hundreds of sandstorms, died in 1968 from emphysema, a disease caused by the sand that through the years had gathered in his lungs. Both are now buried in one grave in Swift Current, a city in the prairie land they loved.

As for myself, urban life gave me the chance to pursue my education, and, in the process, I lost my feelings of inferiority and began to search for my roots. In the succeeding years, as I read about the Arabs and their civilization, my knowledge and horizons expanded. The more I learned about the Arab contributions to humankind, the more I wanted to tell the world about this rich and intellectual civilization. First I became proud of my Syrian ancestry, then, as I became more enlightened, of my Arab heritage.

The city and its educational institutions gave me the dignity that my homesteading years had erased. I have no doubt that if I had not left the farm, like the majority of the early Arab homesteading immigrants I would have disappeared into Anglo-Saxon society, too ashamed to expose my origin.

CHAPTER 3

WHO WERE THE ARAB PIONEERS?

There is little doubt that our family's experience in Canada was mirrored by other immigrant families from a multitude of lands. Many of the newcomers from European countries have written the history of their pioneering days and their integration into Canadian society. However, rare is the Arab immigrant who has recorded for posterity his experience or that of his family. The struggle of the Arab pioneers who came from the Middle East at the beginning of the twentieth century is a silent saga waiting to be told. This chapter will tell a small part of that story by giving a short overview of the history of the Arab-Syrian immigrants (by the mid-1940s, generally referred to as "Lebanese" after the creation of Syria and Lebanon as two separate countries) who came to southwest Saskatchewan, and more specifically, to the Swift Current area.

In the early 1900s, most who travelled to this relatively unknown area of Canada at that time were searching for a better life. Leaving their Syrian villages behind, the majority landed in New York at Ellis Island—the American port of entry where millions of immigrants poured into the United States. From there many worked their way westward.

Toiling as labourers or peddlers, they moved onward always thinking that over the horizon they would find their El Dorado. When a number of these newcomers reached North Dakota and Montana, they heard that the Canadian government was handing out virgin prairie land in southwestern Saskatchewan within a 100-mile radius of Swift Current. The adventurous and ambitious men went on to investigate. Here, at last, their search was rewarded—in what then appeared to be virtually uninhabited land, they found the space and freedom to create the future of their dreams.

At the beginning of the 1900s, Saskatchewan had just become a province. Consequently, the government sought out immigrants to populate its empty territory. It was an ideal situation for these Arabs of peasant origin. On this land of endless space they found they could build the life for which they yearned. Acre after acre, more than they had ever known, could be owned by one man—something almost inconceivable to a people who came from an overpopulated land. In this newly opened area one person could possess more acreage than all of the farms owned by perhaps a dozen villagers in their homeland.

Almost all of these immigrants originated from the Biqaʻ Valley in the Ottoman province of Syria—a rich, fertile area which the French were later to detach and hand over to Lebanon, a country they had created from parts of what was then known as Greater Syria. This had been done to give birth to a Christian nation that would always remain under their influence and be divided from the Arab hinterland.

To a large measure, the French Mandate Government succeeded in its plan. Even the Canadian Arab immigrants were eventually affected. The vast majority of the early

pioneers in their first years called themselves, and were known as, Syrians. After the Second World War when new immigrants came to Canada in large numbers from what had become Lebanon, they influenced the thinking of a good number of the descendants of the first migrants. In the ensuing years, these Canadian-born Arabs began to propagate their origin as Lebanese.

ʻAin Arab, al-Biri, and Karoun, which today still send their sons and daughters in large numbers to the Americas, were the villages where most of southern Saskatchewan's early Arab pioneers had their roots. These towns were only a few miles apart—the furthest being less than a day's walk from the other. Hence, some knew each other long before they landed in America. No sooner had the first settlers begun their new lives than others from the same villages followed. Rarely did a Syrian immigrant from another town settle among them. Like their ancestors, the Bedouins of the Arabian desert, whose lives revolved around tribal loyalties, the early immigrants preserved, to some extent, their village connections. In the succeeding years, this familiarity was often an asset, as the immigrants tended to associate and help each other out in times of crisis. With homesteads scattered and many miles apart, this relationship was useful, especially in the limited social world of these early Syrian pioneers.

The homesteads given to the new immigrants were the bases upon which they commenced their new lives. Each person was granted a quarter section (160 acres) of virgin land, never before touched by a plough. The only stipulation was that it be lived on and cultivated. This had been what the newcomers wanted—land they could work and call their own. With great energy they set about cultivating their parcels of land. By hand, oxen, or horse, they began to build their lives in this new place. Day and evening they worked, at first by themselves, then later—when they returned to the "old country," married, and came back to Canada—with their wives and children.

As long as there was daylight, they picked rocks, ploughed the previously untouched soil, and planted their life-subsisting gardens. At the same time they built their humble abodes and dug their wells. Holidays and recreation were virtually unknown to them. However, their many hours of toil would not be in vain. In the years to follow, their descendants became some of the most prosperous farmers in southern Saskatchewan.

Hardship was no stranger to these early Arab pioneers. Like their ancestors who had lived in the Ottoman province of Syria, they had to struggle for a bare existence. Thus, on their homesteads, the hardship of establishing themselves in a new environment was not an insurmountable task. Rather, they relished the uphill road before them.

Following the methods used by their fathers, they set about organizing their farms. Some, like our family, bought extra land on which there was already a structure, usually a primitively built shack. Others built their homes with sod, adobe, or any lumber they could afford or find. At the same time as they readied their homes, they began to cultivate the land and prepare large garden plots—the products of which were to be the mainstay of their lives.

In the same fashion as our family, these early settlers thrived mostly on dishes of broad beans, chickpeas and lentils. In addition, they consumed great quantities of burghul

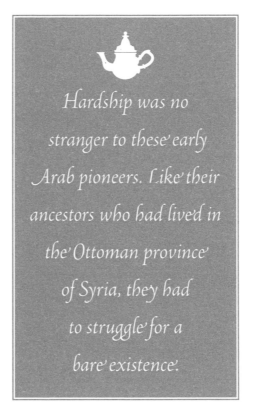

Hardship was no stranger to these early Arab pioneers. Like their ancestors who had lived in the Ottoman province of Syria, they had to struggle for a bare existence.

(called by the early Arab immigrants *smeed*)—a cooked, cracked wheat made by Middle Eastern farmers since the dawn of civilization. There was no problem in producing this cereal, for the hard Saskatchewan wheat was ideally suited for the production of this staple. Like our family, Arab homesteaders typically owned at least a few cows. These were, of course, very important to their diets. From the milk they made yogurt—a then unknown food to the other homesteaders in that era. With yogurt and burghul they produced a food called *kishk*—the oldest cheese known to man. For meat, an old cow or steer was butchered once a year and a part preserved frozen during the winter in an outside shed. The remainder was used to prepare *qawarma* for the summer—a way of preserving cooked meat in fat, long practiced in the eastern Arab world.

During the Depression years of the 1930s, when some neighbours found it difficult to feed their families, the farmers of Arab origin had very little problem. Today, many of the foods on which these early Arab immigrants thrived are found in Middle Eastern markets of the large Canadian cities. A number of them like burghul, chickpeas, lentils, and yogurt, have become well-known foods in North America.

However, this was not due to the influence of the Arab pioneers. They preferred to keep their dishes hidden away in their kitchens, well concealed should an unexpected neighbour arrive. Even though they ate tasty, nourishing foods and were generally healthier than the other settlers, they believed their foods were inferior to those eaten by the farmers of European background. Imbued with this unfortunate attitude, they felt that consuming Arabic food was something to be ashamed of, especially in the midst of their non-Arab neighbours. The days of multiculturalism were yet to be implemented. During those homesteading years, not one of these former Syrian peasants would have been able to imagine a time when their food and ways of life would be considered equal to that of Canadians of European ancestry. This feeling of inferiority was even transmitted to most of their descendants. Thus, rarely did they pass on to other Canadians of non-Arab descent their foods or any other aspect of their culture.

The vast majority of Arab immigrants to other parts of North America were Christians, but those who settled in southern Saskatchewan were almost evenly divided between Christians and Muslims. Having the same culture, they differed very little in their ways of life. On the other hand, when it came to assimilation, it was another story.

The Christians, on the whole, were more likely to have received a more formal education than their Muslim brethren, as a result of the Christian missionary schools in Syria. They firmly believed that they were a part of the Christian West and tried to assimilate as quickly as possible—not an easy task in those early days of prejudice. Pride in one's national origin did not exist for the Arab-Christian pioneers who saw themselves as the descendants of the first Christians of the world.

However, the social climate at the beginning of the 1900s was not conducive to assimilation. The Christian immigrants found it almost impossible to become thoroughly "Canadian" or, more accurately, were not accepted as equals by the society of that era. Hence, their children, having been left with no connection whatsoever to the land of origin of their fathers, had no choice but to reject their past. Even more than the immigrants from the British Isles, they wanted to become true Canadians. For them there were no roots of which they could be proud. The only connection some retained was an adherence to the religious sects of their parents.

To a much greater extent, the Muslim pioneers took pride in their Arab heritage. Though many were illiterate or semi-literate, they nevertheless knew their Muslim religion and bits and pieces of Arab/Islamic history through oral tradition. They passed on to their children what they knew of their Arab heritage and therefore imbued in them a feeling of pride in their ancestry and land of origin. The descendants of the first Arab-Muslim immigrants to Canada have tended to preserve and maintain a number of the

virtues of the Arabs. Civility, generosity, and hospitality are still to be found, to some extent, among the first- and second-generation descendants of the first Muslim pioneers.

There is little doubt that these pioneers have contributed to the Canadian mosaic. For example, a number of neighbours from other ethnic backgrounds who have associated for years with these Canadians of Arab ancestry have taken on some of their Arab virtues. Today, should one visit the homes of these third- or fourth-generation Muslim descendants, they will always be invited for a meal—the tradition of their fathers.

As the years passed by, the first- and second-generation descendants of the first Arab-Christians, in the majority of cases, moved to towns or left for other parts of Canada. On the other hand, many of the Muslims down to the third and fourth generations retained their love for the land and today are prosperous farmers in the country that their fathers had helped to develop.

As for their heritage, with the passing decades, both Christians and Muslims seem to have become almost totally assimilated. The only attachment a few retain with the "Old Country" is memories of Arab food. The vast majority are now intermarried and, I would guess,

are not familiar with their origins. Perhaps, more than any other ethnic group, they have melted into the Canadian mainstream. For them, the push towards multiculturalism of the past few decades in Canada has had little meaning. They have come to see themselves simply as being as Canadian as the descendants of the United Empire Loyalists see themselves. ✖

CHAPTER 4

BURGHUL:
THE CORNERSTONE OF OUR DIET
IN THE DEPRESSION YEARS

Arab food, retained by many of the descendants of these pioneers—including my own family—is today spreading throughout the Americas. I believe that my telling of our family's culinary history of the Arab dishes we ate on the Canadian prairies during our farming years—hidden away from our neighbours—will give the reader an insight into why this is the case.

Perhaps the most important of the foods that helped our family survive the Depression years was burghul—an ancient food. When our Saskatchewan neighbours found it difficult to find enough food to eat daily, my own family at least ate well. Much of our bounty of dishes was due to this nourishing and healthy cereal, for thousands of years one of the mainstays of Middle Eastern peasant food.

I remember returning home to help in the harvest after the Depression years had faded away. The rains had come and this year there was plentiful wheat, but no market for the grain. The wheat was being stored in elevators and they were full. My father appeared upset: "If Canadians only ate burghul, we could easily sell our wheat!" My father was angry as I helped him shovel yet another load of grain onto a pile open to the elements. Our granaries were full and that autumn the elevators in town, overflowing with grain, had stopped purchasing wheat. The drought, grasshoppers and other ailments of the Depression years had cut grain production almost to zero and this was one of the few bountiful years that we farmers in south Saskatchewan were to enjoy. But the Wheat Board, awash with grain, had quotas, and we could only sell a limited quantity.

My father's words had a ring of truth, even though at that time I did not consider them relevant. Burghul was not a word with which we children were enamoured. I always loathed the July days when it was burghul-making time.

As youngsters, we had to partake in all the phases involved in the production of our yearly supply of around two hundred pounds of bur-ghul, commonly known as cracked wheat. First, we had to scour the bare prairie for the odd pieces of wood discarded by farmers and then build an outdoor fireplace over which we were to cook the burghul. After washing the wheat we placed it in an oil drum cut in half, and cov-ered it with water. The hardest part of all was to carry buckets of this water from a nearby well. How I cursed burghul. "Why could we not be like our neighbours' children who have never heard of that accursed food," I often thought to myself.

After the wheat was cooked, but not overdone, we spread it out on white sheets of cloth under the hot sun. In about two days when the kernels turned bone-dry, we dunked them again into water, then put them through a grain chopper. My mother would then winnow the crushed-cooked-wheat to remove the loose bran and again spread the burghul on the sheets until all the moisture was gone.

Making burghul in southern Saskatchewan.

Today, this method of making burghul is only a memory. In all the large cities of North America, this first-rate wheat product is produced by machines and elec-trically controlled ovens. Very few of the descendants of the early Syrian immigrants or even the new arrivals now make their own burghul. It is available in a good number of supermarkets, health food stores and Mediterranean food shops in most urban centres.

Called by some "the noblest food achieved by wheat," burghul, also known as bulgar, bulgur and bulgourl, was first eaten in the Middle East about seven thousand years ago. The Armenians, Syrians and other immigrants from that part of the world introduced it to North America at the beginning of the twentieth century. However, only in the last few decades has it become known to the general public of the large urban centres in the western world.

It has become a much sought-after food by vegetarian and other health-conscious people in North America. Research has proven that this cereal is unequalled in food value. The cooking of the wheat preserves most of its nutrients, even when some of the bran is removed after the cooked grain is crushed. The calcium, carbohydrates, iron, phosphorous, potassium, vitamin B and protein content are almost all retained. Furthermore, these nutrients are not lost when burghul is stored. It will last for years without loss of food value or any other type of deterioration.

Unsurpassed as a nourishing food, burghul has more food energy than cornmeal; more iron than rice; less fat than uncooked wheat; six times more calcium than cornmeal and three times more than rice; and more vitamins than barley, cornmeal or rice. An inexpensive, natural, wholesome and succulent versatile product of wheat—a great replacement for rice—it can be used in all types of dishes and in every course and every meal of the day.

Today, burghul can be purchased in bulk or packaged and comes in three sizes: coarse, medium, and fine. The coarse is used in pottage dishes; the medium as an ingredient in salads; and the fine as a main component in vegetarian and meat patties, in tabboula, as a breakfast cereal, and in a number of desserts. With all these multi-purpose uses, there is no doubt that the Canadian wheat surplus would soon disappear should burghul become a feature on the daily menu.

The following few easy-to-make dishes are but a sample of the many others found in the culinary world of this healthy eatable. Many of the spices that I have included in the recipes were not available during our farming years. However, my mother always found substitutes. Burghul blends well with almost all spices and herbs and on the prairies there was a variety of wild herbs. The dishes she prepared never fell short when it came to taste.

BURGHUL AND YOGURT APPETIZER / KISHKEH

SERVES 4 TO 6

Modern medicine has confirmed what the ancient civilizations in the Middle East always knew about burghul and yogurt—they are healthy foods. This simple dish combining the two, which is a favourite food of both the rich and poor in Damascus, is not only healthful but also tasty. My mother often prepared this appetizer on our homestead, especially during the hot summer days.

½ cup	medium burghul	125 ml
¾ cup	plain yogurt	175 ml
1 tsp	dried mint, finely crushed	5 ml
4 tbsps	finely chopped cucumbers	60 ml
½ tsp	salt	2 ml
¼ tsp	black pepper	1 ml
2 tbsps	finely chopped fresh cilantro	30 ml

1. Soak burghul for 10 minutes in warm water, then drain by pressing water out through a fine strainer.

2. Combine all ingredients, except cilantro, then spread on a serving platter. Chill, then decorate with cilantro and serve.

Health is a crown on the heads of the healthy that only the ill can see.

BURGHUL PILAF / BURGHUL MUFALFAL

SERVES 4

Called "a poor man's food" in the Middle East, this dish, which graced our table hundreds of times, is simple to prepare, healthful, and wholesome.

4 tbsps	butter	60 ml
2	medium onions, finely chopped	2
1 cup	coarse burghul	250 ml
2¼ cups	water	560 ml
½ tsp	salt	2 ml
¼ tsp	black pepper	1 ml

1. Melt butter in a frying pan, then sauté onions over medium heat for 10 minutes. Add burghul, then stir-fry for further 3 minutes. Stir in remaining ingredients, then bring to boil. Cover and cook over low heat for about 20 minutes or until all the water has been absorbed. Shut off heat, stir, then re-cover and allow to cook in own steam for about 30 minutes. Serve hot as a side or main dish.

The nut cannot be enjoyed except by the one who breaks it.

BURGHUL AND PARSLEY SALAD / TABBOULA

We enjoyed this delightful dish only in the summer months when our garden flourished. In those days there were no supermarkets where vegetables could be found year-round. I would never have imagined that the tabboula of our homestead days would someday grace the tables of people throughout North America.

¼ cup	medium burghul	60 ml
2	medium bunches of parsley	2
2	medium tomatoes	2
1 cup	finely chopped green onions	250 ml
½ cup	finely chopped fresh mint	125 ml
4 tbsps	olive oil	60 ml
4 tbsps	lemon juice	60 ml
1 tsp	salt	5 ml
½ tsp	black pepper	2 ml

1. Soak burghul for 10 minutes in cold water, then drain by pressing water out through a fine strainer. Wash, stem, and finely chop parsley. Dice tomatoes into ¼-inch (6 mm) cubes.

2. Place burghul and all vegetable ingredients in a bowl, then thoroughly combine and set aside.

3. Combine remaining ingredients, then pour over burghul and vegetables. Toss, then serve on a bed of lettuce leaves.

BURGHUL WITH TOMATOES
/ BURGHUL BIL BANADOORA

SERVES 4 TO 6

To survive, our family had to rely on the traditions of the peasant farmers in Syria. My father had come from the Biqa, an area in Syria where they grew a variety of wheat that was particularly suitable for making burghul. This was and still is one of my family's favourite dishes. Wholesome and tasty, this dish is as old as time among the peasants of Syria.

½ cup	butter	125 ml
2	medium onions, finely chopped	2
¼ cup	pine nuts	60 ml
4	medium tomatoes, finely chopped	4
2 cups	water	500 ml
1 tsp	salt	5 ml
½ tsp	black pepper	2 ml
½ tsp	ground coriander seeds	2 ml
¼ tsp	cinnamon	1 ml
¼ tsp	allspice	1 ml
1 cup	coarse burghul	250 ml

1. In a saucepan, melt 3 tbsps (45 ml) of the butter, then sauté onions over medium-low heat for 8 minutes. Stir in pine nuts, then sauté for a further few minutes. Add tomatoes, then cover and allow to stew for 10 minutes. Add water, salt, pepper, coriander, cinnamon, allspice, and burghul, then bring to boil. Cover and cook over medium-low heat for about 20 minutes or until all the water has been absorbed, stirring a few times. Shut off heat, stir, then re-cover and allow to cook in own steam for about 30 minutes. Stir in remaining butter, then serve hot.

CHICKEN WITH BURGHUL STUFFING / DAJAAJ MIHSHEE BI-BURGHUL

SERVES ABOUT 6

In the homes of the affluent in the countries of the Middle East, chickens and turkeys are usually stuffed with rice, but the peasants and poorer people of the cities, because of cost, substitute burghul for rice. With no money to buy rice in the Depression years, Mother substituted burghul.

4 to 5 lbs	roasting chicken	2 to 3 kg
1 cup	coarse burghul	250 ml
½ cup	pine nuts	125 ml
½ cup	butter	125 ml
½ cup	finely chopped onions	125 ml
1 cup	chicken stock	250 ml
1 cup	chopped parsley	250 ml
2 tsps	salt	10 ml
½ tsp	black pepper	2 ml
½ tsp	allspice	2 ml
1 tsp	ground coriander	5 ml
1 tsp	cinnamon	5 ml

1. Wash and dry chicken, then set aside. Soak burghul in water for 5 minutes, then drain thoroughly. Sauté pine nuts in butter over low heat until golden, then remove with slotted spoon and set aside. Reserve butter in pan.

2. To make stuffing, sauté onions over medium heat in reserved butter until limp. Add burghul, then stir-fry for a few minutes. Add remaining ingredients, except cinnamon, then cook over medium heat until stock is absorbed. Remove from heat and allow to cool, then stir in pine nuts.

3. Stuff chicken and sew up, then place in a roaster. Brush with additional butter and cinnamon. Roast covered in a 350°F (180°C) preheated oven for 2 hours. Remove cover and bake until chicken turns golden brown.

BURGHUL

Medieval Arab writers illustrated in their compilations of recipes the importance of wheat as a staple of good nutrition. To the Arabs, pleasure was defined by drink, clothes, sex, scent, sound, and food. Al-Baghdadi, a thirteenth-century epicurean, considered eating as the finest of all pleasures and therefore wrote a book on cooking. We do not know if al-Baghdadi knew about chicken with burghul stuffing, but, if he had, he would have considered it among the top culinary delights.

BURGHUL CABBAGE ROLLS/
MIHSHEE MALFOOF BI-BURGHUL

SERVES 8

*With cabbage from our garden and the always-in-storage burghul,
this savoury dish, costing virtually nothing to prepare, was often
served at home, especially during the summer months.*

1	medium cabbage	1
2½ cups	cooked chickpeas	625 ml
1 cup	coarse burghul	250 ml
2	medium onions, finely chopped	2
4 tbsps	tomato paste	60 ml
2 tbsps	finely chopped fresh cilantro	30 ml
2 tbsps	butter	30 ml
2 tbsps	finely chopped mint	30 ml
½ tsp	allspice	2 ml
½ tsp	cumin	2 ml
⅛ tsp	cayenne	½ ml
	salt and pepper to taste	
8	cloves garlic	8
2 cups	tomato juice	500 ml

1. Place cabbage in a pot of boiling water; then cook for a few minutes to soften leaves. Remove from water and loosen leaves with a knife from the bottom, then trim down thick ribs. (If leaves are still not soft, boil again for a few minutes.) When all leaves are cut free, cut large outer leaves in half, then set aside.

2. Place all remaining ingredients, except garlic and tomato juice, in a bowl and thoroughly combine to make a stuffing.

*Squeeze the past like a
sponge, smell the present
like a rose, and send
a kiss to the future.*

3. Place some stuffing, according to size of leaf, on the wide end and roll, tucking in the ends in the process. Continue until all leaves are finished, then set aside.

4. Cover bottom of saucepan with pieces of ribs and extra leaves, then add rolls, arranging them tightly side by side in alternating layers. Between each layer, sprinkle a little extra salt and distribute the garlic cloves evenly among the layers. Then place an inverted plate on top of last layer. Add tomato juice and enough water to cover plate. Bring to boil, then cover and cook over medium heat for 50 minutes or until burghul is well cooked. Serve hot or cold.

BURGHUL-MEAT TARTARE / KUBBA NAYYA

SERVES *6 TO 8*

Kubba Nayya was one of the tasty kubba dishes that I feasted upon in my adolescent years. Anyone who has a taste for French or Australian tartare will enjoy this dish, which can be served as a main entrée or as an appetizer.

1 cup	fine burghul	250 ml
1½ lbs	fresh lean beef or lamb	680 g
2	medium onions, finely chopped	2
2 tsps	salt	10 ml
1 tsp	crushed dried mint leaves	5 ml
¾ tsp	black pepper	3 ml
1 tsp	cumin	5 ml
1 tsp	allspice	5 ml
½ tsp	cinnamon	2 ml
⅛ tsp	cayenne	½ ml
a few sprigs	fresh mint	a few sprigs
2 tbsps	olive oil	30 ml

1. Soak burghul for 15 minutes in warm water, then drain by pressing water out through a fine strainer.

2. Place meat in a food processor and process until well-ground, then add burghul and remaining ingredients, except sprigs of mint and olive oil, and process into thick paste. Spread on a platter, then decorate with mint sprigs. Sprinkle with olive oil just before serving.

   NOTE: *The way that I enjoyed eating this dish as a youth was to scoop the kubba with round, pliable loaves of Arab bread (pita), freshly cooked by my mother. We would tear pieces of this bread, then fold in a form of a tiny shovel, to scoop up the Kubba Nayya.*

KUBBA STUFFING

Instead of being served raw, kubba can be stuffed and cooked in various ways. This stuffing can be used for the next six recipes of kubbas.

3 tbsps	butter	45 ml
½ lb	ground lamb or beef	227 g
¼ cup	pine nuts or chopped walnuts	60 ml
1	medium onion, finely chopped	1
1 tsp	salt	5 ml
¼ tsp	nutmeg	1 ml
¼ tsp	allspice	1 ml
¼ tsp	cinnamon	1 ml
¼ tsp	black pepper	1 ml

1. In a frying pan, melt butter, then sauté meat over medium heat until it begins to brown. Stir in remaining ingredients, then sauté further until onion is limp. Set aside for use as stuffing.

The key to the stomach is one mouthful.

Kubba

Kubba is one of the best known dishes in the eastern Arab world, and the Arabs of the Middle East consider kubba of whatever kind as the epitome of all food. There are many types of kubba, but the kubbas made with meat are the most popular.

When I was growing up in southern Saskatchewan, I remember the countless times my mother made us the various types of kubbas and how each time we found that we enjoyed our kubba dishes even more than the time before.

(continued on next page...)

MEAT KUBBA—STUFFED AND FRIED / KUBBAT ARAAS

SERVES 6 TO 8

The word kubba comes from the Arabic verb meaning "to form into a ball."

one *Kubba Nayya* recipe (page 36)
one *Kubba* Stuffing recipe (page 37)
oil for frying

1. Place in the palm of one hand a ball of *Kubba Nayya* about the size of a golf ball. Using your forefinger, press a hole and begin expanding the hole by rotating and pressing against palm of hand until you have a shell of ¼-inch (6 mm) thickness. Place a heaping tablespoon (about 15 ml) of stuffing into the hollow shell. Close end of shell, then form into an egg-like shape. (Use cold water on hands to help shape and close shells.)

2. Deep fry in oil over medium-high heat, turning until golden brown. Serve hot.

KUBBA PIE / KUBBA BIL SANEEYA

SERVES 6 TO 8

For a busy person, this type of cooked kubba is the easiest to make. Only a few moments are needed to make the kubba ready for cooking.

	one *Kubba Nayya* recipe (page 36)	
	one *Kubba* Stuffing recipe (page 37)	
¼ cup	oil or butter	60 ml

1. Divide *Kubba Nayya* into two portions. Spread one portion on the bottom of a greased 9- × 13-inch (23 × 28 cm) baking pan. Spread stuffing evenly over top, then evenly flatten remaining portion of the *Kubba Nayya* over the stuffing. Cut into 2-inch (5 cm) diamond or square shapes, then dot with butter or spread ¼ cup (60 ml) oil over the top.

2. Bake uncovered for 50 minutes in a 350°F (180°C) preheated oven, then broil until top becomes golden brown. Remove and serve.

(...continued)

Not only to us, but to the immigrants from the Greater Syria area who are spread throughout the world, kubba evokes memories of that never-to-be-forgotten dish eaten in their land of origin. Some traditions and ways of life may eventually be forgotten, but never the delicious and various types of kubba.

Kubba has spread like wildfire throughout the South and Central American lands. It was brought to these countries by the immigrants from the Greater Syria area, beginning in the late 1800s. Today, kubba has become a national dish in many of these countries. In Brazil, for example, it is called kibbe and can be found in many of the restaurants of the urban centres. In Mexico and the Dominican Republic, it is known as kipe and is part of the national cuisine of both countries. However, in all of the Latin American countries, kubba is much more spiced than in the land of its origin.

BURGHUL AND POTATO PIE / KUBBAT BATAATA

SERVES 6 TO 8

Kubba made with potatoes is a great vegetarian dish, or when stuffed with the kubba stuffing, it will make a delightful main course. During our farm days, we often relished this mouth-watering dish during the potato season.

1 cup	fine burghul	250 ml
3 cups	mashed potatoes	750 ml
1	medium onion, finely chopped	1
4	cloves garlic, crushed	4
3 tbsps	flour	45 ml
2 tsps	salt	10 ml
1 tsp	black pepper	5 ml
1 tsp	dried basil	5 ml
1 tsp	cumin	5 ml
½ tsp	cinnamon	2 ml
½ tsp	allspice	2 ml
⅛ tsp	cayenne	½ ml
	one *Kubba* Stuffing recipe (page 37)	
4 tbsps	olive oil	60 ml

1. Soak burghul for 10 minutes in warm water, then drain by pressing out water through a strainer.

2. Thoroughly combine all ingredients, except stuffing and oil, then divide into two even portions. Spread one portion evenly in a 9- × 13-inch (23 × 28 cm) well-greased pan, then spread *Kubba* stuffing evenly over top. Spread second portion of burghul/potato mixture evenly over top and smooth. Cut into 2-inch (5 cm) squares, then sprinkle with the oil.

3. Bake in a 400°F (200°C) preheated oven for 50 minutes or until the edges of *Kubba* turn golden brown. Broil for a few minutes until top is golden. Serve hot or cold.

LEMON KUBBA / KUBBAT LAYMOON HAAMID

SERVES ABOUT 8

Another type of kubba that I cannot forget is kubba cooked with lemon juice. During the cold winter days of my youth in southern Saskatchewan, I remember how I waited in anticipation for my mother to make this delicious dish.

½	*Kubba Nayya* recipe (page 36)	½
½	*Kubba* Stuffing recipe (page 37)	½
½ lb	lamb or beef, cut into ½-inch (1.25 cm) cubes	227 g
2 tsps	salt	10 ml
1 tsp	nutmeg	5 ml
1 tsp	allspice	5 ml
½ tsp	black pepper	2 ml
8 cups	water	2 L
1	large onion, finely chopped	1
19 oz	canned chickpeas, drained	540 ml
4	cloves garlic, crushed	4
1 cup	lemon juice	250 ml

1. Form *Kubba Nayya* into balls and stuff with *Kubba* Stuffing (see method for Meat *Kubba* on page 38), then set aside.

2. Place remaining ingredients, except lemon juice, in a saucepan and bring to boil, then cover and cook over medium heat for about 45 minutes. Gently slip in the *kubba* spheres, then cook for another 30 minutes. Add lemon juice, then cook for another 10 minutes or until *kubba* is well cooked, adding more water if necessary. Serve hot.

CHICKPEA AND BURGHUL PATTIES / KUBBAT HUMMUS

MAKES ABOUT 50 PATTIES

The vegetarians of our affluent society are always searching for a new dish to add variety to the limited vegetable dishes. One day they will discover Chickpea and Burghul Patties, which were often made by my mother in the summer when meat was scarce. When they do, I am sure they will place this dish near the top of vegetarian culinary delights.

1 cup	medium burghul	250 ml
19 oz	canned chickpeas, drained	540 ml
2	medium onions, chopped	2
4	cloves garlic, crushed	4
¼ cup	finely chopped fresh cilantro	60 ml
1 tsp	baking powder	5 ml
1 tsp	baking soda	5 ml
2 tsps	salt	10 ml
½ tsp	black pepper	2 ml
½ tsp	cumin	2 ml
½ tsp	allspice	2 ml
⅛ tsp	cayenne	½ ml
1 cup	flour	250 ml
	oil for frying	

1. Soak burghul for 10 minutes in boiling water, then drain by squeezing out the water in a strainer.

2. Place all ingredients, except flour and oil, in a food processor, then process until a soft paste is formed. Place in a mixing bowl, then add flour and mix thoroughly. Form into balls about the size of golf balls. (If batter is too sticky, add more flour; if too dry, add a little water.) Flatten into patties, about ¼ inch (6 mm) thick.

3. Pour oil in a saucepan to ½ inch (1 cm) deep, then heat to medium-high. Fry patties until golden brown, turning them over once. Remove and place on paper towels to drain.

4. Serve either hot or cold. (They reheat well on foil plates in the oven.)

    NOTE: *To make Kubbat 'Adas (lentil kubba), one 19-ounce (540 ml) can of brown or green lentils may be substituted for the can of chickpeas.*

Examine what is said,
        not him who speaks.

PUMPKIN KUBBA / KUBBAT LAQTEEN

SERVES 6

Another vegetarian dish which would delight a person who has left the world of meat is Pumpkin Kubba. In the fall when Halloween is over and the North American farmers are left with thousands of pumpkins, how happy they would feel if they knew everyone was waiting to make Pumpkin Kubba.

1 cup	fine burghul	250 ml
2 cups	baked, mashed pumpkin	500 ml
2 tsps	salt	10 ml
½ tsp	black pepper	2 ml
½ tsp	ground coriander seeds	2 ml
½ tsp	allspice	2 ml
½ tsp	cumin	2 ml
⅛ tsp	cayenne	½ ml
1	medium onion, finely chopped	1
4	cloves garlic, crushed	4
1 cup	flour	250 ml
½ cup	water	125 ml
	oil for frying	

1. Soak burghul for 10 minutes in boiling water, then drain by squeezing out the water in a strainer.

2. Place all ingredients, except oil, in a food processor and process into dough that should stick together when squeezed, adding more flour or water if necessary.

3. Form into balls about the size of golf balls. Flatten balls into patties, then set aside.

4. Heat oil in a saucepan to a depth of 1 inch (2.5 cm), then fry patties at medium-high heat until golden brown, turning them over once. Drain on paper towels, then keep warm until ready to serve.

NOTE: *Another way of making this dish is to place the mixture in a 9-inch (23 cm) square baking pan greased with oil, then pat down and, with a wet knife, cut into 1½-inch to 2-inch (4 to 5 cm) squares. Spread a little oil over the top and bake in a 350°F (180°C) preheated oven until golden brown, about 45–50 minutes. Broil a few minutes until top is golden. Serve warm.*

BURGHUL DESSERT

SERVES ABOUT 6

After making burghul, Mother would take the finest that we had and sieve the burghul in order to produce a fine semolina-type product she called swee'. This she used to make a delicious pudding which we enjoyed when we finished our burghul production—a treat after our hard work. At other times, she used ordinary fine burghul to make this dessert; the result, in my view, is not much different.

1 cup	fine burghul	250 ml
½ tsp	salt	2 ml
4½ cups	water	1125 ml
1 tsp	cinnamon	5 ml
¼ tsp	ground cloves	1 ml
½ cup	honey	125 ml

1. Place burghul, salt, and water in a saucepan, then bring to boil. Cover and cook over medium-low heat for 30 minutes or until burghul is well cooked, adding more water if necessary. Stir in remaining ingredients, then serve hot.

If you cannot be a lighthouse, at least be a candle.

CHAPTER 5

YOGURT KEPT US HEALTHY ON THE FARM

"Not again," I thought to myself as I angrily opened my lunch bag. Mother had this day, as she had for a whole week, made us children ʿarous bi labna (a yogurt paste spread generously on paper-thin Arab bread, then rolled into a long cylinder shape). How I envied my schoolmates munching on neat sandwiches made with white bread. As I moved away to eat my lunch in a semi-hidden corner, I childishly resolved that when I grew up there would be no more ʿarous bi labna for me.

Little did I know in those homesteading days, and in fact long thereafter, that the yogurt which I once detested is one of the healthiest foods known to humankind. My parents had brought with them from Syria a love for this delectable and nutritious dairy product, consumed in the Middle East since the dawn of civilization. Perhaps they did not know its many benefits, but they, as I do now, relished its taste. We ate it almost every day for breakfast and for snacks and I am now sure that this healthy food was one of the reasons we children were rarely sick during our childhood years.

The ancient yogis of India mixed yogurt with honey and called it the "food of the gods." Cleopatra bathed in this milk product to give herself a clear and tender complexion, and Genghis Khan fed it to his soldiers to give them courage. One of the earliest prepared foods, yogurt can claim few equals in the folklore of the culinary arts.

Yet, even though yogurt has been a cherished eatable in the Middle Eastern and Central Asian lands for millennia, in the West, before the turn of the twentieth century, it was barely known. Only recently has yogurt gained universal popularity and become a staple in the diet of many North Americans. Today, in the same fashion as in other parts of the world, especially in Asia and Eastern Europe, its image as a life-extender has taken hold. Some label it "the miracle milk product"; others call it "a mystery food"; while the romantics call it "the elixir of life."

A milk curdled by the actions of bacterial cultures with the consistency of custard, yogurt was discovered about five thousand years ago on the Mesopotamian plains. Later, the Turks, who carried it into eastern and central Europe, gave it the name we still use—yogurt. From the early days of its introduction in that part of the world, especially in Bulgaria, it caught on like wildfire.

Yogurt has long been considered "a health food *par excellence*," and today modern nutritionists have established that its reputation as an almost medicinal food is justified. It has been found that yogurt contains a digestive enzyme that prolongs life. Humans naturally produce this enzyme in their childhood, but it becomes deficient as they reach adulthood. It has also been proved that besides all the healthful elements found in milk, yogurt contains a teeming load of bacteria— about 100 million per gram. These multiply in the intestines and, by getting rid of the accumulated germs, relieve stomach ulcers and dysentery and promote excellent digestion.

Much more easily digested than milk, yogurt is ideal for the aged, pregnant women, children, and the sick. In addition, it is believed that regular eaters of this fermented milk tend to have clear skin and find no problem in enjoying a good night's sleep.

All types of milk, ranging from reindeer to cow, can be used in the making of yogurt. However, the fat and nutrient values vary depending on whether it is prepared from cream, whole, partly skimmed, or skimmed milk, and whether it has additives like fruits or syrups included. On average, 100 grams of regular plain yogurt contain 77 calories, 7.1 g carbohydrates, 5.3 g protein, 3 g fat, 229 mg potassium, 181 mg calcium, 142 mg phosphorus, 75.5 mg sodium, and vitamins B_1, B_2, and B_{12}.

For those wishing to cut down on the amount of fat, cholesterol, and calories in their diets, this near-perfect food when made from skimmed milk is a godsend. In preparing meals, brands labelled low-fat and low-cholesterol can be substituted for mayonnaise, sour cream, or similar products. This will constitute a tremendous improvement in their diets—at times, working wonders.

Besides its nutritional value, yogurt is a marvellously versatile and adaptable food. It adds richness, flavour, and an appetizing aroma to myriad dishes. The possibilities of cooking with this tangy, cultured milk are infinite. It blends well with cheese, eggs, grains, meats, fruits, and vegetables and makes an excellent marinade. Delicious when flavoured with syrups, nuts, herbs, and spices, it enhances and is enhanced by other foods. The gastronomic repertoire of this so-called "milk of eternal life," which I had once shunned, is endless. ✺

TUNISIAN FOOD

The red-hot embers kept us barely warm as we huddled around a Tunisian earthenware *Qanoun* (tiny stove) on that cold January day. However, we were not thinking of the cold. The aroma flowing from the kitchen had aroused our hunger as we waited for the maid to prepare lunch.

Soon the young lady came in with two steaming, mouth-watering dishes of *leblabi*, a spiced chickpea soup, accompanied by *tajine*, a Tunisian shepherd's pie that is filled with meat, eggs, and cheese. To add flavour to the meal, she set before each person a small dish of *harissa*, a fiery sauce of red-hot peppers, garlic, and salt. When we praised our host for the tasty food, he smiled: "Wait until my wife returns from her vacation. After you dine on her food, you will never forget the culinary delights of the Tunisian cuisine."

True to his word, when his charming wife came back a few days later, we were invited to an authentic Tunisian feast. Plates of *mechouia* (grilled vegetable salad), *briks* (fried pastry stuffed with meat, cheese, and eggs), *shakshouka* (a fried vegetable dish), *doulma* (stuffed zucchini), *kamounia* (a liver and meat dish flavoured with cumin), *mechoui* (seasoned barbecued lamb), and *couscous* (the king of Tunisian cuisine) were laid out and decorated in an appetizing fashion. It was apparent she had cooked for us a royal feast. We could hardly wait to begin enjoying these Tunisian delicacies so diligently prepared by our hostess.

In the usual Arab fashion, our host urged us on as we savoured dish after dish, each more tasty than the last. While we dined, soft strains of Andalusian Arab music playing in the background put us at ease. The soothing melodies and the subtle spicy taste of the colourful food created a happy and relaxing atmosphere at our friend's hospitable table. ❖
—*Habeeb Salloum, "Do Nations Express Themselves in Their Foods?"* Contemporary Review, 278.1621 (2001): 107-11.

YOGURT

Yogurt can be made from all kinds and types of milk. If made from skim milk, it is lower in fat and calories but somewhat weak in flavour.

8 cups	milk	2 L
4 tbsps	plain yogurt	60 ml

1. Place milk in a pot and bring to boil, then lower heat to medium-low and simmer uncovered for 3 minutes. Remove from heat and transfer to a bowl. Allow to cool to lukewarm temperature. (You will know the milk is cool enough if your finger in the milk can stand the count of ten.)

2. Thoroughly stir in yogurt and cover, then wrap with a heavy towel and allow to stand for 8 hours.

3. Refrigerate overnight before serving or use in preparation of food.

NOTE: *Always set aside part of the yogurt for the next batch.*

He who is scalded by the soup blows on the yogurt.

SOLIDIFIED YOGURT DIP / LABNA

Even third- and fourth-generation immigrants from the Greater Syria area never seem to lose their love for labna. *My grandchildren, when asked what they enjoy most in Arab food, without hesitation respond "labna." They can eat it morning, noon, and night! For me, it is better than the hundreds of expensive cheeses found on the shelves of fine-food supermarkets.*

Delicious when served as a snack food with crackers or Arab bread (pita).

4 cups	plain yogurt	1 litre
1 tsp	sumac *	5 ml
½ tsp	crushed dried mint	2 ml
¼ tsp	salt	1 ml
⅛ tsp	black pepper	½ ml
1 tbsp	olive oil	15 ml

1. Place yogurt in a cheesecloth bag, then tie with a string. Suspend over a receptacle and allow to drain for 48 hours.

2. Combine remaining ingredients, except oil, in a bowl, then set aside.

3. Spread strained yogurt on a platter, then spread spice mixture evenly over yogurt. Sprinkle with oil just before serving.

* Sumac can be purchased from Middle Eastern grocery stores.

Example is better than precept.

YOGURT AND EGGPLANT APPETIZER

SERVES ABOUT 8

Yogurt and eggplants complement each other. Dishes made from these two ingredients are always tasty and are excellent as side dishes or as entrées. The yogurt takes away the bitterness of the eggplant, and the eggplant gives the yogurt a smooth subtle taste.

1 lb	eggplant	454 g
1 cup	plain yogurt	250 ml
2	cloves garlic, crushed	2
½ tsp	crushed dried mint	2 ml
½ tsp	salt	2 ml
¼ tsp	black pepper	1 ml
2 tbsps	chopped fresh cilantro or parsley	30 ml
1 tbsp	olive oil	15 ml

1. Pierce eggplant with fork all around. Bake eggplant in a 350°F (180°C) preheated oven for about an hour or until thoroughly baked—peel should be crispy. Remove and allow to cool.

2. Peel cooled eggplant and place in a food processor, then add remaining ingredients, except cilantro or parsley and oil, and process into paste. Spread on a platter, then decorate with cilantro or parsley and sprinkle with oil just before serving.

YOGURT GAZPACHO

SERVES ABOUT 8

Excellent on hot summer days.

1	cucumber, about 8 inches (20 cm) long	1
4 cups	plain yogurt	1 L
2 cups	water	500 ml
2	cloves garlic, crushed	2
½ cup	pulverized almonds	125 ml
4 tbsps	finely chopped green onions	60 ml
2 tbsps	finely chopped cilantro	30 ml
2	hard-boiled eggs, peeled and chopped	2
1 tsp	salt	5 ml
1 tsp	black pepper	5 ml
⅛ tsp	cayenne	½ ml
	croutons	

1. Peel cucumber and chop into small pieces.

2. Thoroughly combine yogurt and water in a serving bowl, then stir in cucumber and remaining ingredients, except croutons. Chill, then serve in individual bowls, with each diner adding croutons to taste.

God sends almonds to those without teeth.

YOGURT-RICE SOUP /
SHAWRABAT RUZ MAʿ LABAN

SERVES ABOUT 10

Serve piping hot on cold winter days.

2 tbsps	olive oil	30 ml
½ lb	beef, cut into ½-inch (1 cm) cubes	227 g
1	large onion, chopped	1
4	cloves garlic, crushed	4
4 tbsps	finely chopped fresh cilantro	60 ml
6 cups	water	1.5 L
½ cup	rice, rinsed	125 ml
1 tsp	salt	5 ml
1 tsp	black pepper	5 ml
2 cups	plain yogurt	500 ml
1 tsp	cornstarch	5 ml
2	eggs, beaten	2
1 tsp	crushed dry mint	5 ml

1. Heat oil in a saucepan, then sauté meat over medium heat for 10 minutes. Add onion, garlic, and cilantro, then stir-fry for a few more minutes. Stir in remaining ingredients, except yogurt, cornstarch, eggs, and mint. Bring to boil and cover. Cook for 40 minutes over medium heat.

2. Combine yogurt with cornstarch. Stir yogurt mixture into saucepan, then turn heat to low.

3. Simmer for 10 minutes, stirring clockwise most of the time, then stir in eggs and mint. Serve immediately.

YOGURT-ZUCCHINI SALAD

SERVES ABOUT 6

This salad goes well with barbecued meats, especially in hot weather.

2	zucchini, about 6 inches (15 cm) long	2
3 cups	plain yogurt	750 ml
2	cloves garlic, crushed	2
1 tsp	salt	5 ml
4 tbsps	finely chopped fresh cilantro	60 ml
½ tsp	black pepper	2 ml
2 tbsps	chopped fresh mint	30 ml

1. Peel zucchini, quarter lengthwise, and slice thinly.

2. Combine all ingredients, except mint, in a salad bowl, then chill. Sprinkle with mint, then serve.

Believe what you see
and lay aside what you hear.

YOGURT-POTATO SALAD / SALATAT LABAN WA BATAATA

SERVES ABOUT 6

A cup of yogurt is borrowed from a neighbour or a friend in the Middle East as often as a cup of sugar is borrowed by a next-door neighbour in the West.

1 lb	potatoes (about 4 medium)	454 g
2 tbsps	olive oil	30 ml
1	large onion, finely chopped	1
4	cloves garlic, crushed	4
2 tbsps	finely chopped fresh cilantro	30 ml
½	small hot pepper, seeded and finely chopped	½
1 tsp	salt	5 ml
½ tsp	black pepper	2 ml
1 cup	plain yogurt	250 ml

1. Peel potatoes and dice into ½-inch (1 cm) cubes.

2. Heat oil in a saucepan, then sauté onion over medium heat for 8 minutes. Stir in garlic, cilantro, and hot pepper, then sauté for further few minutes. Add potatoes and remaining ingredients, except yogurt, then barely cover with water and bring to boil. Cover, then cook over low heat for 30 minutes or until potatoes are done, adding more water if necessary. Stir in yogurt, then serve.

Every day I taught him the bowman's art and when his arm got stronger, he shot an arrow right through my heart.

DUMPLINGS IN YOGURT / SHEESH BARAK

SERVES 6 TO 8

Dumplings

1 lb	frozen bread dough, thawed	454 g
1 lb	ground beef or lamb	454 g
2 tbsps	butter	30 ml
4 tbsps	pine nuts or slivered almonds	60 ml
½ tsp	salt	2 ml
½ tsp	black pepper	2 ml
½ tsp	ground coriander seeds	2 ml
¼ tsp	cinnamon	1 ml
2	medium onions, finely chopped	2
2	cloves garlic, crushed	2

Yogurt Sauce (Labaniyya)

2	eggs, beaten	2
3 cups	plain yogurt	750 ml
3 cups	cold water	750 ml
2 tbsps	butter	30 ml
2	cloves garlic, crushed	2
1 tsp	salt	5 ml
2 tbsps	dried mint	30 ml

Give your dough to a baker,
even though he may eat half of it.

1. Make dumplings by forming dough into ¾-inch (2 cm) balls, then cover with a tea towel and allow to rest for 1 hour.

2. In the meantime, make a filling by stir-frying meat in butter over medium heat until light brown, then add the remaining dumpling ingredients and stir-fry for an additional 5 minutes. Set aside and let cool.

3. Roll out dough balls to make circles ⅛-inch (3 mm) thick. Place ½ teaspoon (2 ml) filling on each circle, then fold dough over filling and pinch edges to seal. Fold in half again to shape dumpling like a thimble and pinch to close. Place dumplings on a greased tray, then broil in oven, checking until lightly browned, turning them over once.

4. To make sauce, place eggs and yogurt in a saucepan, then stir until well blended. Add cold water; then stir well. Cook over medium-low heat and gently stir in one direction until mixture comes to a gentle boil, then reduce heat to low.

5. In the meantime, place butter in a small saucepan and melt; add the garlic, salt, and mint. Sauté over medium heat until garlic turns golden brown, then stir garlic mixture into yogurt sauce. Place dumplings in sauce, then cover and cook for 15 minutes over medium-low heat and serve piping hot.

NOTE: *The yogurt sauce can also be used to cook Meat Kubba (Kubbat Araas) (page 38), or Stuffed Zucchini (page 264).*

During the cold Saskatchewan winter, a steaming hot bowl of Sheesh Barak was heaven-sent. Its mouth-watering aroma and divine taste ensnared me, and I have been trapped in its web ever since.

In this recipe, precautions must be taken in order that the yogurt does not curdle or separate. This is done by gently stirring in one direction over medium-low heat until it comes to a gentle boil.

BEEF, RICE, AND YOGURT CASSEROLE

SERVES ABOUT 8

For maximum taste, this dish should be served hot from the casserole.

2 tsps	olive oil	10 ml
1 lb	beef, cut into ½-inch (1 cm) cubes	454 g
2	medium onions, finely chopped	2
4	cloves garlic, crushed	4
1 cup	rice	250 ml
6 cups	water	1.5 L
2 cups	plain yogurt	500 ml
1 tsp	crushed dried mint	5 ml
1 tsp	salt	5 ml
1 tsp	baking soda	5 ml
½ tsp	black pepper	2 ml
1	egg, beaten	1

1. Heat oil in a frying pan, then sauté beef over medium heat for 10 minutes. Stir in onions and garlic, then sauté for a further 5 minutes. Set aside and allow to cool.

2. In the meantime, place rice and water in a saucepan, then bring to boil. Cover and cook over medium heat for 8 minutes, then drain and allow to cool.

3. Place rice in a bowl, then stir in the sautéed beef, onion, and garlic, as well as the remaining ingredients. Transfer to a casserole, then cover and bake in a 350°F (180°C) preheated oven for 1 hour or until meat is tender. Serve immediately.

BANANA YOGURT DESSERT

SERVES ABOUT 6

2	medium bananas	2
2 cups	plain yogurt	500 ml
2 tbsps	melted honey	30 ml

1. Cut bananas in half lengthwise, and slice. Thoroughly combine yogurt and honey in a bowl. Fold in banana slices, then chill before serving.

YOGURT-DATE PUDDING

SERVES ABOUT 10

10 slices	whole wheat bread, cut into small pieces	10 slices
1 cup	chopped dates	250 ml
2 cups	plain yogurt	500 ml
½ cup	melted honey	125 ml
4 tbsps	pulverized almonds	60 ml
2 tbsps	butter	30 ml
½ tsp	nutmeg	2 ml
½ tsp	almond extract	2 ml
3	eggs, beaten	3

1. Thoroughly combine bread and dates in a mixing bowl, then set aside.

2. In another bowl, combine remaining ingredients, then pour over bread and dates. Thoroughly combine, then place in a casserole and bake in a 300°F (150°C) preheated oven for 40 minutes. Serve hot from the casserole.

NOTE: *Raisins can be substituted for the dates.*

YOGURT DRINK

In the hot lands of North Africa, the favourite beverage to quench one's thirst is similar to this yogurt drink.

4 cups	plain yogurt	1 L
2 cups	water	500 ml
4 tbsps	melted honey	60 ml
½ tsp	almond extract	2 ml

1. Place all ingredients in a blender, then blend for 1 minute. Chill before serving.

YOGURT AND PINEAPPLE DRINK

2 cups	plain yogurt	500 ml
4 cups	pineapple juice	1 L

1. Place both ingredients in a blender, then blend for 1 minute. Chill before serving.

When you are dead, your sister's tears will dry as time goes on, your widow's tears will cease in another's arms, but your mother will mourn you until she dies.

CHAPTER 6

KISHK: THE OLDEST AND HEALTHIEST CHEESE

From burghul and yogurt, we annually made a powdered cheese called *kishk*. There is no doubt that more than any other food, it kept our large family nourished and healthy, especially during the Great Depression of the 1930s. With this near-perfect food we made a variety of savoury dishes that not only stifled our hunger, but satisfied our taste buds. However, to produce this oldest cheese known to man was no easy task.

First we had to make the burghul during the hot summer month of July—a formidable venture, especially with no modern machinery (details of the process are on page 27). While preparing the burghul, we also made a large amount of yogurt, which was then placed in cloth bags to drain out the water and turn the yogurt into a cheese consistency. The solidified yogurt or *labna* (recipe on page 50) was mixed with coarse burghul, formed into walnut-sized balls and dried in the sun. When bone-dry, it was ground using a hand-operated meat grinder and put through a sieve—the final step in the production of our *kishk*. The whole process took from three to five days, if the weather was hot and sunny.

According to a number of food historians, this nourishing powdered product is considered one of the oldest cheeses known to man. Perhaps only the bone-dry yogurt, made by the Bedouin of the desert, goes back to earlier times. It is believed that *kishk* was discovered in the Greater Syria area of the Middle East when humans first mastered the concept of making their own food.

For thousands of years *kishk* was one of the main peasant foods which nourished farmers in that part of the world. During the nineteenth century, American missionaries travelling through the Syrian mountains noted that the peasants were poor, yet appeared as healthy as the farmers of America. After a number of years of research, their good health was attributed to the consumption of *kishk*.

This ancient food, produced from two of the main staples of humankind—wheat and milk—contains most of the nourishment needed by humans. With only *kishk*, perhaps fortified by a few fruits or vegetables, one could be a healthy specimen.

Since it has long been considered a peasant food, *kishk* is today rejected by almost all the "modern" Arabs who live in cities. As they trip over one another trying to tailor their menus to Western processed foods, they have forgotten this wholesome staff of life which kept their ancestors healthy. Only some of the farmers in the villages of Syria and Lebanon, and the sons and daughters of Arab peasant immigrants in the Americas, appreciate the taste and food value of *kishk*.

In the large cities of the eastern and western United States and the metropolises of Canada, *kishk* is available in most Middle Eastern markets. On the other hand, if this near-perfect food cannot be found, it can be made by following the recipe on the next page. ✄

MAZZA

I was introduced to mazza during my first trip to Lebanon in the early 1960s when, on the second day after our arrival, we were invited by a friend for a meal in the town of Zahlah—noted for its fine restaurants serving the best in Arab foods. After we sat down to eat, the waiters brought out dish after dish of mazza. Not being familiar with how a meal was served in that food-loving town, I partook of every tasty appetizer, even though warned by my friend that the main course was yet to come.

After I could barely push down another morsel, indeed, the main course did come— barbecued meat galore. The aroma was divine, but alas, I was so sated that I hardly took a bite. It was my first lesson of how one should only nibble in order to enjoy *mazza*. Unlike my friend's invitation and accompanying warning, the Arab code of hospitality forbids warning guests not to partake too much of the appetizers— in fact, a host or hostess will urge their visitors to eat on.

However, even experienced visitors will have trouble confining themselves to a reasonable number of appetizers. The *mazza* dishes seem to have their own way of ensnaring, especially guests who love fine food. ✄

—*Habeeb Salloum, "Tidbits to Delight Diners," The Toronto Star, March 24, 2004, D1 & D4.*

KISHK

MAKES ABOUT 4 POUNDS OF KISHK

Even though our early years of hardship are only a memory and I have travelled and enjoyed the foods of many countries, I still yearn for the wholesome kishk meals of my youth. I firmly believe that should kishk dishes become internationally known, they will, without doubt, grace the eating tables of the world.

3 lbs	coarse burghul	1.4 kg
2 quarts	plain yogurt	2 L
1½ tbsps	salt	25 ml
4 lbs	solidified yogurt (*Labna*)	1.8 kg

1. Rinse and drain burghul, then allow to stand for ½ hour.

2. Mix yogurt with burghul, then let stand for 6 hours. Add salt and half of the *labna*, then combine well and cover.

3. Allow to ferment in a warm place for 9 days. Every day add a little of remaining solidified yogurt and stir. (Make sure the solidified yogurt is divided evenly for the 9 days.)

4. Roll into walnut-size balls, then spread on a white sheet of cloth in sun to dry. (For fast drying, balls can be dried in oven over very low heat, but the taste will not be the same.)

5. After drying to consistency of half-wet, put through a grinder twice, then return to dry in sun, spreading out thinly on a white sheet of cloth. Rub between palms of the hands occasionally to break up the small balls, then stir *kishk* by hand. When *kishk* is bone-dry, divide into fine and coarse by rubbing through a sieve.

The recipe for Solidified Yogurt or Labna is on page 50. Labna can also be purchased in Middle Eastern markets.

Kishk need not be refrigerated. However, it should be covered and stored in a cool dry place.

Making kishk.

KISHK SOUP

SERVES ABOUT 6

Kishk soup can be cooked without meat or with a little meat. By itself, it is very appetizing. On the other hand, meat makes it a heartier dish.

2 tbsps	butter	30 ml
¼ lb	tender beef or lamb, cut into small pieces	113 g
1	medium onion, finely chopped	1
2	cloves garlic, crushed	2
¾ cup	fine *kishk*, dissolved in ½ cup (125 ml) of water	175 ml
¾ tsp	salt	3 ml
½ tsp	black pepper	2 ml
5 cups	boiling water	1.25 L

1. Melt butter in a saucepan, then sauté meat and onions over medium heat until meat begins to brown. Stir in garlic, then stir-fry for a few minutes. Add *kishk* and stir-fry for a moment, then add remainder of ingredients and bring to a boil over medium heat. Cover, then turn heat to low and simmer for 10 minutes. Serve hot with toast.

NOTE: *Makes an excellent breakfast dish, especially on cold winter mornings.*

Seek counsel of him who makes you weep, and not of him who makes you laugh.

KISHK DIP

SERVES 6 TO 8

Life is strange. We are always looking for that which is beyond our reach. In my youth, when Mother prepared the numerous kishk dishes, I longed for unattainable foods such as bologna and sardines whose costs were beyond our pocketbook. Later in life, when the harsh years of poverty were but a memory, I pined for the many kishk dishes I had once scorned.

1 cup	*kishk*	250 ml
	cold water	
¼ cup	olive oil	60 ml
¾ cup	finely chopped onions	175 ml
½ cup	finely chopped tomatoes	125 ml
	a few sprigs of parsley	

I.   Place the *kishk* in a small bowl, then gradually add cold water and stir until the *kishk* reaches the consistency of thick cream. Transfer to a flat serving platter, then sprinkle with olive oil. Spread onions and tomatoes evenly over top, then decorate with parsley and serve.

NOTE: *Makes an excellent appetizer.*

He who speaks about the future lies, even when he tells the truth.

KISHK SALAD

SERVES ABOUT 8

In the 1930s, this very healthy salad we ate almost daily during the summer months when dandelions and spinach were available.

10 oz	spinach or dandelion leaves	283 g
1	small bunch green onions, finely chopped	1
1	large tomato, finely chopped	1
½ cup	*kishk*	125 ml
½ tsp	salt	2 ml
½ tsp	black pepper	2 ml
¼ cup	olive oil	60 ml
2 tbsps	lemon juice	30 ml

1. Thoroughly wash the spinach or dandelion leaves, drain well, then chop.

2. In a salad bowl, thoroughly combine dandelions or spinach, onions, tomato, *kishk*, salt, and pepper, then stir in olive oil and lemon juice. Serve immediately.

A small house may hold a thousand friends.

KISHK WITH EGGS / KISHK MAʿ BAYD

SERVES 4

This dish can be served for any meal of the day, but is at its best when served for breakfast.

2 tbsps	butter	30 ml
2	cloves garlic, crushed	2
1	small onion, finely chopped	1
3 cups	water	750 ml
¼ cup	*kishk*, dissolved in ½ cup (125 ml) of milk	60 ml
¾ tsp	salt	3 ml
¼ tsp	black pepper	1 ml
4	eggs	4

1. Melt butter in a saucepan, then add garlic and onion and sauté over medium-low until golden. Stir in remaining ingredients, except eggs, then bring to boil. Cook for 10 minutes over low heat, stirring occasionally, then break eggs into the *kishk*. Do not stir the eggs, leave as whole. Cook for a further 5 minutes, then serve one egg in a bowl of *kishk* to each person.

Each word I utter must pass through four gates before I say it. At the first gate, the keeper asks, "Is this true?" At the second gate, the keeper asks, "Is it necessary?" At the third gate, the keeper asks, "Is it kind?" At the fourth gate, the keeper asks, "Is this something you want to be remembered for?"

KISHK PIES/ FATAAYIR BI KISHK

MAKES 12 PIES

From the Depression years until today, this has always been one of my favourite pies.

1½ lbs	frozen dough, or Dough for Pies (page 151)	680 g
1 cup	coarse or fine *kishk*	250 ml
1 cup	water	250 ml
1 cup	very small pieces of meat, fried or *qawarma* (page 75)	250 ml
1	small bunch green onions, finely chopped	1
1 tsp	salt	5 ml
½ tsp	black pepper	2 ml
½ cup	olive oil	125 ml

1. If frozen, thaw dough. Form into 12 balls and cover. Allow to rest for one hour.

2. In the meantime, make filling by mixing the *kishk* with water, then adding remaining ingredients and mixing thoroughly.

3. Roll each ball into a 5-inch (12 cm) round, then place 1 heaping tablespoon (15 ml) of filling on round. (Better still, to make all pies even, divide filling into 12 portions.) Fold dough over filling, shaping into a triangle, then close firmly by pinching the edges together. Continue until all balls are finished.

4. Place in a greased baking pan, then bake in a 400°F (200°C) preheated oven for 10 to 15 minutes or until pies turn medium brown. If a darker colour is desired, brown lightly under broiler.

OPTIONAL: *Brush the tops with butter or oil, then serve hot.*

HOT KISHK OPEN-FACED PIES / MANAQEESH KISHK

MAKES 12 PIES

When preparing these pies, the paprika and cayenne can be increased or decreased to taste.

1½ lb	frozen dough, or Dough for Pies (page 151)	680 g
1 cup	fine *kishk*	250 ml
¼ cup	flour	60 ml
1 cup	water	250 ml
1	large onion, finely chopped	1
5 tbsps	olive oil	75 ml
1 tsp	salt	5 ml
1 tsp	black pepper	5 ml
1 tsp	paprika	5 ml
⅛ tsp	cayenne	½ ml

1. If frozen, thaw dough. Form into 12 balls and cover, then allow to rest for one hour.

2. Dissolve *kishk* and flour in water, then add remainder of ingredients and thoroughly combine to make topping.

3. Roll balls into 5-inch (12 cm) rounds, then divide topping into 12 portions, placing a portion on each round. Spread evenly on rounds, then press topping evenly on dough with fingers.

4. Place on greased baking pans, then bake in a 350°F (180°C) preheated oven for 20 minutes or until the bottoms of pies are lightly browned.

5. Lightly brown under the broiler, then remove and serve hot.

KISHK POTTAGE

SERVES ABOUT 6

With no central heating, in the cold winter prairie evenings
we would often eat this dish, then the whole family would
retire for the night, sleeping around a red-hot stove.

½ cup	fine burghul, rinsed	125 ml
2½ cups	water	625 ml
½ cup	fine *kishk*, dissolved in 1 cup (250 ml) of water	125 ml
3 tbsps	butter	45 ml
½ cup	beef or lamb, cut into very small pieces	125 ml
1	medium onion, finely chopped	1
2	cloves garlic, crushed	2
1 tsp	salt	5 ml
½ tsp	black pepper	2 ml

1. Place the burghul and water in a saucepan and bring to boil, then cook over medium-low heat for 10 minutes. Turn heat to low, then stir in dissolved *kishk* and cook for further 8 minutes, stirring continually and adding a little water if necessary.

2. In the meantime, melt butter in a frying pan, then add meat and sauté over medium heat until it begins to brown. Stir in onion and garlic, then sauté further until they begin to turn golden brown.

3. Stir frying-pan contents, salt, and pepper into the burghul and *kishk*, then cook on low heat for 5 minutes, stirring a few times and adding a little more water if necessary. Serve immediately.

KISHK WITH LENTILS / MUSTOOME

In the Depression years, when there was hardly any other food around, Mother often cooked this simple yet healthy dish.

½ cup	brown or green lentils, rinsed	125 ml
7 cups	water	1.75 L
¼ cup	coarse burghul, rinsed	60 ml
2 tsps	salt	10 ml
½ tsp	black pepper	2 ml
4 tbsps	butter	60 ml
2 cups	onion, finely chopped	500 ml
3	cloves garlic, crushed	3
½ cup	fine *kishk*, dissolved in ½ cup (125 ml) of water	125 ml

1. Place lentils and 6 cups (1.5 L) of the water in a saucepan and bring to boil, then cover and cook over medium heat for 25 minutes. Stir in burghul, salt, and pepper, then cook for further 10 minutes, stirring occasionally.

2. In the meantime, melt butter in a frying pan, then add onions and garlic and sauté over medium-low heat for 10 minutes. Stir frying pan contents, remaining 1 cup (250 ml) of water, and the dissolved *kishk* into the lentils and burghul, then cook for a further 10 minutes over low heat, stirring continually and adding a little water if necessary. Serve hot.

Think of going out before you enter.

DIFFA

After a mouth-watering Moroccan meal, we sat enthralled as the Berber dancers swayed back and forth, stamping their feet in a proud fashion. Their rousing steps, which had been incorporated into the flamenco during the centuries when the Arabs were in Spain, held us spellbound. Our hosts, Muhammad el-Rafaai and his wife Souad, were entertaining us royally at their home in Khenifra—the cedar capital of Morocco. In true Berber hospitality, with food and entertainment, they were doing everything in their power to make us comfortable and happy.

The evening was coming to an end when Muhammad turned to us, saying, "It's time to rest. Tomorrow, my friend, a tribal chief near Khenifra is preparing in your honour, among the cedar trees in the nearby mountain, a *diffa*"—a Moroccan feast that gave the English the word "tiffin." That night we slept soundly for our bodies and souls were content with the food and entertainment provided by our hosts.

The cool spring breeze, perfumed with the smell of cedar, filled the air as we drove the 20 kilometres to where we were to have our picnic feast. In less than half an hour, our auto stopped in front of a huge black tent from which enticing odours filled the air. Soon we were seated around a table-sized platter, anticipating the meal to come.

Before we began to eat, a young woman went around with a jug called a *tass*, from which she poured a little water over each guest's hands.

After a towel was passed around to dry the hands, the feast commenced. With the invocation *"bismillah"* (in the name of God), our host gave the signal for the meal to begin. In typical Moroccan fashion, we dipped our right hands into the tasty, colourful communal dishes, as our host urged us on. Dozens of succulent platters, each one more appetizing than the next, appeared before us as if by magic.

Offering us the choicest of morsels, our host made certain that we partook of every dish. When it was only partially consumed, each platter was replaced by another until the main courses were finished. The leftovers were not wasted. Other members of the household were waiting for their share of the feast. ❈

—*Habeeb Salloum, "Diffa,"* City and Country Home *6.7 (1987): 126–34.*

CHAPTER 7

QAWARMA: AN ANCIENT FOOD WHICH I STILL ENJOY

Our annual *qawarma*-making time was not my favourite time of the year when I was a child. I vividly recall struggling with a pail of water, half as large as myself, through a blinding sandstorm up the hill on which our home was situated. Every day my chore was to carry water from a well, a half-mile down from our hilltop home, for two aged sheep we were fatting for the autumn kill. Exhausted, I reached the barn where my mother was feeding the sheep green vegetable leaves. "Why do I have to bring water for these sheep? Why can't I take them down to the well to drink?" I was near tears as I sat down by my mother's side.

She smiled at my childish tantrum. "It is essential that we do not tire these animals. They must be heavy with fat when we butcher them for *qawarma* in the autumn." My parents, whose emigration from Syria in the early 1920s had taken them to this southern Saskatchewan homestead, found that no sooner did they plough the land than it turned to desert. To survive, they utilized the ingenuity—and the recipes—they had inherited from their forebears.

Our ancestors, like most peasants in the lands of antiquity, had developed a variety of foods that have stood the test of centuries. My parents, too, even if they rarely had money in their new land, always had food for their numerous offspring.

Qawarma, one of the mainstays of their diet, was developed in the Middle East. In their new homeland, my parents kept up the tradition of making this time-honoured type of preserved meat. All summer long, a few aged sheep or an old cow would be hand-fed many times a day, and sometimes even at night, until they were loaded with fat.

In the autumn, after the animals were butchered, the fat was removed and melted. The meat was then cut into very small pieces and cooked in the melted fat. When the meat was well cooked, it was placed, along with the fat, in earthenware utensils or glass jars. These were stored in a cool earthen cellar, providing our supply of meat for the following year. With no refrigeration of any kind, it was an ideal way to ensure we had meat for at least twelve months. During the summer months, our neighbours could only dream of a roast or steak. As for our family, we feasted on dish after dish of tasty *qawarma*.

My favourite treats were those prepared from the intestines and the stomach. Scrubbed with soap and water until they became spotless, the intestines and stomach were then stuffed with rice (if it was available) but usually with burghul, spices, herbs, and chickpeas. Even after more than seventy years, I can still smell the inviting aroma of stuffed *karsh* (stomach) which I enjoyed so much in my boyhood years.

In the Greater Syria area, farmers of the past universally used *qawarma* in their cooking. Today, except in peasant homes, it is rarely prepared in the kitchen. The modern city Arab scoffs at it as a peasant food, best forgotten. However, in the countryside, it is still a basic food for the hard-working farmers. In the same fashion as we used *qawarma* during our Depression years, they use it as a main ingredient in their many sapid stews and stuffed vegetable dishes.

Unlike in the past, today the making of *qawarma* in a modern kitchen is a simple task. The recipe that follows is a minuscule version of our *qawarma* production in the years when it was the cornerstone of our daily menu. I have also included a few of the *qawarma* dishes we enjoyed during the Depression years. ❖

PEMMICAN

The first time I heard of pemmican was in the 1940s, when a First Nations friend in Regina invited me for a meal. Among the dishes on which we feasted was this food par excellence of the Indigenous peoples, one of the staples of life for the first inhabitants of the Great Plains. From that initial familiarization with pemmican, I developed a taste for it. Perhaps my love for qawarma led me to appreciate this Indigenous creation. In later years, I often searched for pemmican but could not find it for sale. The few times I had it in the homes of friends and acquaintances only increased my yearning for this close relative of meat jerky, the South American charqui and South African biltong. Eventually, I developed my own version of this flavoured dried meat. ❖

—*adapted from an article on pemmican, published in* Western People, *January 24, 1991, 5.*

QAWARMA

2½ lbs	melted beef fat (not suet) or margarine	1 kg
5 lbs	lean beef (any cut), cut into ¼-inch (6 mm) cubes	2.3 kg
5 tsps	salt	25 ml
2½ tsps	black pepper	12 ml

1. Place the melted fat or margarine in a saucepan and heat over low, then stir in meat, salt, and black pepper.

2. Cook uncovered over medium heat, stirring occasionally to make sure the meat does not stick to the bottom, until meat is well-cooked—that is, until meat sticks to a wooden spoon. Remove from heat.

3. Allow to cool for 1 hour. With slotted spoon (to separate it from the fat), remove *qawarma* and place in earthenware or glass jars. Pour some of the fat over *qawarma*, enough to cover it with ½ inch (1 cm) of fat. Discard the remaining fat. Cover the *qawarma* and store in cool place and always return to cool place after use.

NOTE: *Melt as much* qawarma *as needed in a recipe, then discard fat. There is no need to refrigerate the* qawarma *if it is well cooked. If the jars are sealed completely,* qawarma *will stay usable for at least a year.*

NOTE: *Mutton may be substituted for beef in this recipe.*

If you buy cheap meat, you will be sorry when you come to the gravy.

EGGS WITH QAWARMA / BAYD MAʿ QAWARMA

SERVES 4

In the past, eggs with qawarma was perhaps the most common breakfast food among the villagers of Syria and Lebanon. To me, the many modern breakfast foods cannot compare with this simple dish.

4 heaping tbsps	*qawarma*	60 ml
4	large eggs	4
¼ tsp	salt	1 ml
¼ tsp	black pepper	1 ml
1 tbsp	butter	15 ml

1. Place *qawarma* in frying pan and heat over low. Drain off fat.

2. In a bowl, thoroughly combine *qawarma*, eggs, salt, and black pepper.

3. Melt butter in a frying pan, then add *qawarma*-egg mixture. Sauté over low heat, stirring until the eggs are cooked. Serve immediately.

The ape in his mother's eyes is a gazelle.

PARSLEY SALAD WITH QAWARMA/ SALATAT SAFSOOF MAʿ QAWARMA

SERVES 6 TO 8

½ cup	dried chickpeas	125 ml
½ cup	medium burghul	125 ml
3 cups	finely chopped parsley	750 ml
1	small bunch green onions, finely chopped	1
¼ cup	finely chopped fresh mint	60 ml
2	medium tomatoes, finely chopped	2
1 cup	*qawarma*, fat removed	250 ml
1 tsp	salt	5 ml
½ tsp	black pepper	2 ml
2 tbsps	olive oil	30 ml
4 tbsps	lemon juice	60 ml
6	cabbage leaves, cut in half	6

1. Soak chickpeas overnight, then drain.

2. With a rolling pin, break chickpeas in half, then pick out and discard the skins. Place in a saucepan and cover with water, then bring to boil and cook over medium heat for 20 minutes. Remove from heat and set chickpeas aside in their cooking water.

3. While the chickpeas are cooking, soak burghul in cold water for 15 minutes, then drain by placing in a strainer and pushing water out by hand. Place in a salad bowl, then set aside.

4. Remove chickpeas from water and add to burghul (do not discard water), then stir in remainder of ingredients, except cabbage leaves.

5. Place cabbage leaves in chickpea water, then boil for a few minutes until softened. Remove, then place on top of salad. Serve immediately while the cabbage leaves are still steaming.

NOTE: *Each person should be served one or two cabbage leaves with their portion of the salad.*

A unique salad, this dish, like qawarma, is today rarely prepared in the Middle East. You will find it a delightful treat.

Remove fat from qawarma by heating it in a frying pan, then draining off the fat.

YOGURT PIES WITH QAWARMA / FATAAYIR LABNA MAʿ QAWARMA

MAKES 12 LARGE PIES

In the Middle East, there are various types of vegetarian and meat pies. This yogurt pie with qawarma *is one of my favourites.*

1½ lbs	frozen dough or Dough for Pies (page 151)	680 g
1 cup	*qawarma*, fat removed	250 ml
1½ cups	*labna* (page 50)	375 ml
1	medium onion, finely chopped	1
1 tsp	salt	5 ml
½ tsp	black pepper	2 ml

1. If frozen, thaw dough. Divide dough into 12 equal pieces. Roll into balls, then cover and allow to rest for 1 hour.

2. In the meantime, prepare a filling by thoroughly combining remaining ingredients.

3. Roll each ball to a 4- to 5-inch (10 to 12 cm) round or larger if desired. Place one heaping tablespoon (15 ml) of filling (or divide filling into 12 equal portions) on each round, then fold dough over, shaping it into a triangle and closing firmly by pinching edges.

4. Place pies on a well-greased baking pan, then bake in a 400°F (200°C) preheated oven for 15 minutes or until pies are golden brown.

OPTIONAL: *Brush the tops of pies with butter, then serve hot.*

NOTE: *Cream cheese may be substituted for the* labna.

Remove fat from qawarma *by heating it in a frying pan, then draining off the fat.*

POTATO STEW WITH QAWARMA / YAKHNIT BATAATA MAʿ QAWARMA

SERVES ABOUT 6

Qawarma may be substituted for fresh meat in almost all stews or stuffed vegetable dishes.

6	medium potatoes	6
2 tbsps	butter	30 ml
1	medium onion, finely chopped	1
4	cloves garlic, crushed	4
1 cup	*qawarma*, fat removed	250 ml
1½ tsps	salt	7 ml
½ tsp	black pepper	2 ml
½ tsp	allspice	2 ml
2 cups	stewed tomatoes	500 ml

1. Peel potatoes, then dice into ½-inch (1 cm) cubes.

2. In a saucepan, melt butter, then add onion and garlic and sauté over medium heat until golden. Add potatoes, *qawarma*, salt, black pepper, and allspice, then cover and sauté for further few minutes over very low heat. Stir in tomatoes, then barely cover with water and bring to boil. Turn heat to low, then re-cover and simmer for about 25 minutes or until potatoes are cooked, adding more water if necessary. Serve hot with cooked rice.

Remove fat from qawarma by heating it in a frying pan, then draining off the fat.

CABBAGE ROLLS WITH QAWARMA / MALFOOF MAHSHEE MA'A QAWARMA

SERVES ABOUT 8

Very tasty, this recipe my mother prepared when she had some extra time; with eight children, this did not happen very often.

1	medium cabbage, core removed	1
2 cups	*qawarma*, fat removed	500 ml
1 cup	coarse burghul, rinsed	250 ml
2 tsps	salt	10 ml
1 tsp	black pepper	5 ml
1 tsp	allspice	5 ml
½ tsp	cumin	2 ml
2 tbsps	butter, melted	30 ml
2 cups	stewed tomatoes	500 ml
6	cloves garlic	6
¼ cup	lemon juice	60 ml

Remove fat from qawarma by heating it in a frying pan, then draining off the fat.

1. Place cabbage in a saucepan, then cover with boiling water. Boil until leaves become soft. Remove cabbage from water and allow to cool. Separate softened leaves, returning cabbage to boil further if inside leaves are not soft. Scrape the thick rib of each leaf to decrease the thickness otherwise wrapping the leaf around the filling will become difficult. Place removed rib scrapings evenly at bottom of a large saucepan and set aside.

2. Prepare a stuffing by combining *qawarma*, burghul, 1 teaspoon (5 ml) of the salt, black pepper, allspice, cumin, butter, and 1 cup (250 ml) of the tomatoes.

3. Place 1 tablespoon (15 ml), more or less, of the stuffing on each cabbage leaf, then roll, making sure to tuck in ends. Continue until all leaves are rolled, then arrange rolls tightly beside each other on top of stems in pot in alternating layers with garlic cloves between.

4. Mix remaining tomatoes with remaining salt, then spread over rolls. Add lemon juice, then place inverted plate large enough to cover the top of rolls to prevent them from opening during cooking, then add enough boiling water to barely cover plate.

5. Cover the pot and bring to boil, then simmer over medium-low heat for about 1 hour or until burghul inside the rolls is cooked. Remove and place on a serving platter. Serve hot.

NOTE: *Rice may be used instead of burghul, and kohlrabi leaves, grape leaves, or Swiss chard may be substituted for cabbage. These leaves, except for the grape leaves, should be prepared by boiling for only 1 minute.*

The woman killed herself with work, yet the feast lasted only one day.

CHICKPEA STEW WITH QAWARMA / YAKHNIT HUMMUS MA'A QAWARMA

SERVES ABOUT 6

During the Depression, the spices included here were often not available and were replaced by others.

1	medium eggplant	1
1½ tsps	salt, divided	12 ml
5 tbsps	cooking oil	75 ml
1	medium onion, finely chopped	1
3	cloves garlic, crushed	3
1 cup	*qawarma*, fat removed	250 ml
2 cups	cooked chickpeas	500 ml
1 tsp	black pepper	5 ml
1 tsp	cumin	5 ml
⅛ tsp	cayenne	½ ml
2 cups	stewed tomatoes	500 ml
1½ cups	water	375 ml

Remove fat from qawarma by heating it in a frying pan, then draining off the fat.

1. Peel eggplant and dice into ½-inch (1 cm) cubes. Sprinkle ½ teaspoon (2.5 ml) of the salt on eggplant pieces, then place in a strainer with a weight on top and allow to drain for 30 to 45 minutes.

2. In a saucepan, heat oil, then sauté onion and garlic over medium heat for a few minutes. Add *qawarma* and eggplant, then sauté over high heat for a few minutes, stirring occasionally and adding more oil if necessary. Stir in chickpeas, the remaining 1 teaspoon (5 ml) of salt, black pepper, cumin, cayenne, tomatoes, and water, then bring to boil. Cover, turn heat to low and simmer for about 20 minutes or until eggplant is cooked, adding more water if necessary. Serve hot with cooked rice.

CHAPTER 8

CHICKPEAS: A WELL-KEPT SECRET AMONG THE SYRIAN IMMIGRANTS IN WESTERN CANADA

Ideal for the dry prairie climate, chickpeas, which were unknown to fellow Canadians at that time, were another of the homestead foods on which we thrived. Today, like all the other Middle Eastern foods we consumed, chickpeas are fast catching on in almost every country of the world. Although unknown to North Americans a half-century ago, this delectable legume is found today on the shelves of supermarkets and ethnic food outlets throughout Canada and the United States. Delicious as an ingredient in numerous types of dishes, this culinary delight with a nut-like flavour is fast becoming a near essential part of the North American diet.

The original home of the chickpea is believed to be in the lands touching on the eastern Mediterranean. From there, its cultivation spread eastward to the whole of Asia and westward to the Iberian Peninsula. When the Spaniards arrived in the Americas, they introduced the plant there too. In the ensuing centuries, a number of countries in South and Central America became large chickpea producers. Today, in addition to these lands, the states edging the Mediterranean and the Indian subcontinent grow most of the world's supply of this legume.

The chickpea is neither a pea nor a bean, yet it combines the best qualities of both. To thrive, chickpeas need a semi-arid sandy soil. Hence, the countries of the Middle East, North Africa, and parts of southern Europe are ideal for their cultivation. In these lands of early civilizations, they have been used in countless dishes since the dawn of history.

In Mexico and several other Latin American countries, they have been on the everyday menu from the era of the conquistadors. On the other hand, in North America, the plant was grown during the last few centuries in the southern United States as feed for cattle and hogs. It is only recently that chickpeas have become a common everyday food product in Canada and the United States.

The dry western Canadian and American prairies are also well-suited for the cultivation of this hardy Mediterranean vegetable, although this was not commonly known. Early in the twentieth century, when we homesteaded in southern Saskatchewan, year after year we planted gardens overflowing with chickpeas. In the all-encompassing drought of the Depression years when hardly any grains or vegetables grew and people went hungry, we virtually lived on our dishes of chickpeas. Today, in parts of Saskatchewan, they are now planted on a commercial scale.

The bushy chickpea plant grows to a height of two feet. It produces small white or pinkish flowers and dozens of pods, each containing one or two round seeds ranging in colour from pinkish-white to black. The shape of the plant, with the pods at the top, makes it ideal for harvesting with modern machinery. This, and the near perfect soil and climate of the prairies, guarantee it a bright future on the mechanized western farms of North America.

A pleasant change from pasta, potatoes, and rice, chickpeas can be prepared and served in numerous ways. The mature pods, when still green, can be roasted, then peeled and served as appetizers or stripped and used raw in cooking in the same manner as green peas. However, although delicious when eaten green, chickpeas are not generally eaten in this fashion. In most cases, they are harvested when fully matured and dried. Like dried beans and peas, they make an excellent ingredient in all types of soups and stews.

> *Notwithstanding the fact that their common name in the English-speaking world is chickpeas, they are also sold under their Italian name, ceci; Arabic hummus; or Spanish garbanzo.*

The peasants of the Mediterranean countries developed a series of tantalizing dishes incorporating this legume. For many centuries, chickpeas have been used as a replacement for meat in soups, stews, and stuffing. In food value, taste, and texture, these peasant dishes are unequalled in the vegetarian world. Today, these appetizing, versatile pulses are enjoyed by vegetarians in all parts of the globe.

In a number of Middle Eastern and North African countries, many benefits are attributed to chickpeas. In the North African countries where they are used extensively in cooking, many believe that chickpeas increase the energy and sexual desires of both men and women. Shaykh 'Umar Abu Muhammad, a sixteenth-century North African Arab writer, in his book *The Perfumed Garden*, suggests chickpeas as a cure for impotence and as a first-rate sexual stimulant. In the eastern Arab lands, the peasants are convinced that it has qualities which give them the essential energy necessary for their lives of toil. Even if modern people scoff at these claims and call them old folktales, they nevertheless have been firmly believed for centuries.

In North America, chickpeas are found in supermarkets and Arab, Armenian, Greek, Indian, Italian, and Spanish food stores. Notwithstanding the fact that their common name in the English-speaking world is chickpeas, they are also sold under their Italian name, *ceci*; Arabic *hummus*; or Spanish *garbanzo*. They are available packaged, canned, or in bulk. Also, they can be purchased candied or roasted for appetizers and snacks.

Chickpeas are very nourishing. There are some 350 calories in every 100 g of this ancient food. Chickpeas contain about 61 percent carbohydrates, 20 percent protein, and 5 percent fat. They are also a relatively good source of calcium, fibre, lecithin, sodium, and potassium, and contain small quantities of vitamins A, B, and C.

When compared to other legumes, chickpeas are without equal, in availability, price, food value, flexibility in cooking, and taste. There is no better way to prove this than for an uninitiated fine food explorer to plunge into the realm of the tasty and nourishing chickpea.

The following recipes from the Middle Eastern and Mediterranean countries, most of which we enjoyed during our farming days in western Canada, will ease the way into this world. ✄

CHICKPEA APPETIZER

This simple appetizer is easy, yet very tasty.

2 cups	well-cooked chickpeas	500 ml
¼ cup	olive oil	60 ml
¼ cup	lemon juice	60 ml
2	cloves garlic, crushed	2
½ tsp	salt	2 ml
2 tbsps	finely chopped green onions	30 ml
2 tbsps	finely chopped fresh cilantro	30 ml
1 tbsp	very finely chopped fresh mint	15 ml

1. Thoroughly mix all ingredients, except mint, then place in a serving bowl. Refrigerate for 1 hour, then just before serving decorate with mint.

NOTE: *Chives may be substituted for the cilantro and ½ teaspoon (2 ml) of dried mint for the fresh mint.*

Canned chickpeas may be substituted for cooked chickpeas, and vegetable oil may be substituted for the olive oil.

A promise is a cloud; fulfillment is rain.

CHICKPEA DIP / HUMMUS BI TAHINI

SERVES ABOUT *8* AS A SIDE DISH

This dish is a popular breakfast food and is served as an appetizer or side dish with almost every meal throughout the Middle East. Its consumption is fast spreading in western Europe and North America under the name "hummus"—an Arabic word which is today found in English dictionaries.

2 cups	well-cooked chickpeas	500 ml
½ cup	water	125 ml
4 tbsps	tahini	60 ml
4 tbsps	lemon juice	60 ml
2	cloves garlic, crushed	2
½ tsp	salt	2 ml
¼ tsp	cumin	1 ml
2 tbsps	olive oil	30 ml
1 tbsp	finely chopped fresh mint	15 ml

1. In a food processor, place chickpeas, water, tahini, lemon juice, garlic, salt, and cumin, then process until a smooth paste is formed, adding more water if necessary.

2. Spread on a serving platter, then sprinkle with the oil and decorate with the mint, just before serving.

   NOTE: *When served as an appetizer, it can be eaten with raw vegetables, bread sticks, or Arab bread (pita).*

Canned chickpeas may be substituted for cooked chickpeas, and vegetable oil may be substituted for the olive oil.

Tahini is sesame seed paste and can be found in Middle Eastern markets, health food stores, and in some major supermarkets.

FRIED CHICKPEAS

SERVES 4 TO 6

Can be served as an appetizer, but it also makes a delightful side dish.

3 tbsps	olive oil	45 ml
2 cups	well-cooked chickpeas	500 ml
½ tsp	salt	2 ml
½ tsp	garlic powder	2 ml
¼ tsp	black pepper	1 ml
½ tsp	paprika	2 ml
2 tbsps	finely chopped fresh cilantro	30 ml

1. Heat the oil in a frying pan, then add the chickpeas. Sprinkle with salt, garlic powder, and pepper, then gently stir-fry over medium heat for a few minutes. Spread in a flat serving platter, then sprinkle with paprika and cilantro and serve immediately.

Canned chickpeas may be substituted for cooked chickpeas, and vegetable oil may be substituted for the olive oil.

CHICKPEA AND POTATO SOUP / SHAWRABAT HUMMUS WA BATAATA

SERVES ABOUT 10

This nourishing soup, a meal unto itself, was a popular dish on our family's table during the Depression years.

1 cup	dried chickpeas	250 ml
8 cups	water	2 L
2 tbsps	olive oil	30 ml
2	medium onions, finely chopped	2
4	cloves garlic, crushed	4
4 tbsps	finely chopped fresh cilantro	60 ml
4	medium tomatoes, chopped	4
2	medium potatoes, peeled and chopped into small pieces	2
2 tsps	salt	10 ml
1 tsp	cumin	5 ml
1 tsp	black pepper	5 ml
¼ tsp	cayenne	1 ml

1. Wash and soak chickpeas overnight, then drain.

2. Place chickpeas and water in a saucepan, then bring to boil. Cover, then cook over medium heat for about 2½ hours or until chickpeas are tender.

3. In the meantime, heat oil in a frying pan, then sauté onions over medium heat until they begin to brown. Stir in garlic, cilantro, and tomatoes, then cover and cook over low heat for 15 minutes.

4. When chickpeas are tender, add the frying pan contents and remaining ingredients, then bring to a boil. Cook over medium heat for 30 minutes or until the potatoes are cooked. (Add more water if a thinner soup is desired).

CHICKPEAS AND COUSCOUS SALAD

SERVES ABOUT 8

This is an excellent Moroccan salad which can be served as the main course, or as a side dish.

1½ cups	water	375 ml
1 cup	couscous	250 ml
1 tsp	salt	5 ml
2	cloves garlic, crushed	2
1 tsp	mustard	5 ml
½ tsp	black pepper	2 ml
3 tbsps	lemon juice	45 ml
4 tbsps	olive oil	60 ml
2 cups	cooked chickpeas	500 ml
2	medium tomatoes, finely chopped	2
1	medium green pepper, seeded and finely chopped	1
2 cups	finely chopped green onions	500 ml
1 cup	finely chopped mint	250 ml
	lettuce leaves	
1 cup	crumbled feta cheese	250 ml

Canned chickpeas may be substituted for cooked chickpeas, and vegetable oil may be substituted for the olive oil.

1. Place water in a saucepan and bring to boil, then stir in couscous and ½ teaspoon (2 ml) of the salt. Remove from heat and let stand for 5 minutes, then break lumps up with fork and set aside.

2. In the meantime, make a dressing by combining remaining ½ teaspoon (2 ml) salt, garlic, mustard, pepper, lemon juice, and olive oil, then set aside.

3. Place couscous in a mixing bowl, then add chickpeas, tomatoes, green pepper, onions, and mint, then thoroughly combine. Refrigerate for about 2 hours, then stir in dressing.

4. Place lettuce leaves on a platter, then spread salad on top. Sprinkle with feta cheese and serve.

BURGHUL AND CHICKPEA SALAD / SAFSOOF

SERVES ABOUT 8

½ cup	fine burghul	125 ml
1	small bunch green onions	1
3	medium tomatoes	3
1	medium cucumber, about 5 inches (12 cm) long	1
1	large bunch parsley, finely chopped	1
1 cup	cooked chickpeas	250 ml
1½ cups	chopped fresh mint	375 ml
4 tbsps	olive oil	60 ml
4 tbsps	lemon juice	60 ml
¾ tsp	salt	3 ml
½ tsp	black pepper	2 ml
⅛ tsp	cayenne	½ ml

1. Soak burghul in cold water (enough to cover by about ½ inch or 1 cm) for 10 minutes, then drain by placing in a strainer and pushing water out by hand.

2. Finely chop the green onions, tomatoes, and cucumber.

3. Place all ingredients in a salad bowl, then thoroughly combine. Chill for about 1 hour, then serve.

Canned chickpeas may be substituted for cooked chickpeas, and vegetable oil may be substituted for the olive oil.

This salad becomes crunchier and tastier if ½ cup (125 ml) of dried chickpeas is substituted for the 1 cup (250 ml) of cooked. The dried chickpeas should be soaked overnight, then drained. The next step is to put the chickpeas, a handful at a time, in a small cloth bag, then roll with a rolling pin to break them up. Remove loose skin before using.

YEMENI-TYPE FALAFEL / FALAAFIL YAMANEE

SERVES 8 TO 10

Falafel is a vegetarian dish from the Middle East which has taken the world by storm in the last decade. It is a spicy and tasty food that can be served as part of the main course, or with Arab bread (pita) as sandwiches, or fried in little balls and served as hors d'oeuvres.

2 cups	dried chickpeas	500 ml
4	cloves garlic, crushed	4
½ cup	finely chopped fresh cilantro	125 ml
½ cup	finely chopped green onions	125 ml
½ cup	finely chopped parsley	125 ml
2 tsps	salt	10 ml
1 tsp	cumin	5 ml
1 tsp	black pepper	5 ml
⅛ tsp	cayenne	½ ml
1½ tsps	baking soda	7 ml
1	egg	1
	oil for frying	

1. Soak chickpeas overnight, then drain.

2. Place chickpeas in a food processor, then process until a semi-dough is formed. Add remaining ingredients, except oil, then process further until a smooth dough is formed. Form into small flat patties (or into small balls if for hors d'oeuvres), then set aside.

3. Heat oil in a saucepan, then fry patties or balls over medium heat until golden brown. Remove and drain on paper towels, then serve hot.

   NOTE: *When served in sandwiches, the patties should be placed in Arab bread (pita) half-loaves in a bed of tomato and lettuce salad.*

If pots did not break, the potter would have no work.

CHICKPEAS WITH MACARONI

SERVES ABOUT *6*

When one of our neighbours told Mother that macaroni was available at the Ponteix grocery store, she made sure Dad would bring some back each time he made his biannual trips there. With this she created a number of simple macaroni dishes, including this tasty and nourishing one.

2 tbsps	olive oil	30 ml
2	medium onions, finely chopped	2
3	cloves garlic, crushed	3
¼ cup	finely chopped fresh cilantro	60 ml
1	small hot pepper, seeded and very finely chopped	1
2 cups	stewed tomatoes	500 ml
2 cups	well-cooked chickpeas	500 ml
1½ cups	macaroni	375 ml
1 cup	water	250 ml
1 tsp	salt	5 ml
½ tsp	black pepper	2 ml
½ tsp	allspice	2 ml
½ tsp	cumin	2 ml

1. Heat oil in a frying pan, then sauté onions and garlic over medium heat until they begin to brown. Stir in cilantro and hot pepper, then sauté for a further few moments. Transfer the frying pan contents to a casserole, then stir in remaining ingredients.

2. Cover, then bake in a 350°F (180°C) preheated oven for about an hour or until macaroni is cooked.

Canned chickpeas may be substituted for cooked chickpeas, and vegetable oil may be substituted for the olive oil.

CHICKPEAS WITH SWISS CHARD

SERVES 4 TO 6

Kohlrabi leaves, cabbage, or spinach may be substituted for the Swiss chard.

4 tbsps	olive oil	60 ml
2	medium onions, finely chopped	2
4	cloves garlic, crushed	4
4 cups	finely chopped Swiss chard	1 L
¼ cup	finely chopped fresh cilantro	60 ml
2 cups	cooked chickpeas	500 ml
2 cups	stewed tomatoes	500 ml
1 tsp	salt	5 ml
1 tsp	tarragon	5 ml
½ tsp	black pepper	2 ml
⅛ tsp	cayenne	½ ml

1. Heat oil in a saucepan, then sauté onions and garlic over medium heat until onions turn limp. Stir in Swiss chard and cilantro, then stir-fry for a few minutes. Stir in remaining ingredients, then simmer over low heat for 30 minutes. Serve either hot or cold.

Canned chickpeas may be substituted for cooked chickpeas, and vegetable oil may be substituted for the olive oil.

STUFFED TOMATOES WITH CHICKPEAS / MAHSHEE BANADOORA BI HUMMUS

SERVES 6

12	medium tomatoes, ripe but slightly firm	12
¼ cup	olive oil	60 ml
2	medium onions, chopped	2
4	cloves garlic, crushed	4
¼ cup	pine nuts or slivered almonds	60 ml
¼ cup	finely chopped fresh cilantro	60 ml
2 cups	well-cooked chickpeas	500 ml
½ tsp	allspice	2 ml
½ tsp	cumin	2 ml
⅛ tsp	cayenne	½ ml
2 tsps	salt	10 ml
1 tsp	black pepper	5 ml
2 tbsps	butter	30 ml
1 cup	water	250 ml

1. Cut off tomato tops, then scoop out the pulp with a spoon. (Reserve both cut tops and pulp.) Set aside.

2. Heat oil in a frying pan, then sauté onions and garlic over medium heat until they begin to brown. Stir in pine nuts or slivered almonds and cilantro, then stir-fry for 5 minutes. Remove from heat, then stir in remaining ingredients, except 1 teaspoon (5 ml) of the salt and ½ teaspoon (2 ml) of the pepper, butter, and water. Fill tomatoes with this mixture, then replace tops.

3. Place tomatoes, tops up, in a casserole. Combine reserved tomato pulp with remaining salt and pepper, and water, then pour in, between tomatoes. Place a little of the butter on each of the tomatoes, then cover and bake in a 350°F (180°C) preheated oven for 30 minutes or until tomatoes are cooked.

4. Serve tomatoes hot with some of the juice spooned on top. (Excellent served with mashed potatoes or cooked rice.)

In the Mediterranean lands vegetables are usually stuffed with meat. However, chickpeas make a healthy substitute.

Canned chickpeas may be substituted for cooked chickpeas, and vegetable oil may be substituted for the olive oil.

Alternate recipes for stuffed tomatoes are on pages 224 and 271.

BRAZIL'S ARABIAN DELIGHTS

The culinary contributions that the Arabs gave Portugal were later to be brought by the Portuguese to Brazil. This historical base of the Brazilian cuisine with its Arab connection was further buttressed in the last one hundred years by the immigration occurring from the area of Greater Syria to all parts of that land of the Amazon. Today, in every large Brazilian town, the Arab delights of *hummus* (Arabic *Hummus*—chickpea appetizer), *sfeehah* (*Safeeha*—open meat pies), *taboulah* (*tabbula*—parsley salad) and, above all, *kubbah* (*kubba*—burghul and meat patties known in Brazil as *kibbe*) are offered in many homes and public eating places.

The first time I entered a restaurant in Recife—Brazil's major northeastern resort—I was astonished to see featured on the menu *kibbe*, a delicious dish whose original home is the Middle East. In the ensuing days, I discovered that this famous Middle Eastern dish had become a Brazilian food. Served in a great number of eating places throughout the country, it was prepared in a much tastier fashion than in its land of origin. ◈

—*Habeeb Salloum, "Arabian Delights of Brazil,"* Américas, *52.4 (2000): 56-58.*

CHAPTER 9

LENTILS: PART OF OUR DAILY MENU

Exhausted from working in the fields, my father and I looked forward to finally sitting down to eat a good and hearty dinner. That day, in the mid-1930s, the south Saskatchewan heat had been especially aggravating as we summer-fallowed the land. Now with the dust washed from my face and hands, I felt relaxed and hungry. As we sat down around the table, my mother brought out a steaming pot of stew.

The aroma filling the air was mouth-watering. I lifted the lid, "What are we having this evening?" My mother smiled, "*Yakhnat ʿAdas* (lentil stew). Eat! It's a healthy-tasty dish."

"Oh! no! Not lentils again! We just had a lentil salad yesterday." I was angry. It seemed to me in these Depression years that our diet consisted, in the main, of burghul and lentils.

According to historians, the lentil was one of the first food plants to be brought under cultivation by humans in the Middle East. In that part of the world where civilization began, this legume has been a part of the diet for millennia. As a food, only bread and rice are believed to have been on the human menu for a longer period.

Lentils have been found in ancient Egyptian tombs and have, since the Pharaonic era, been the main staple of Egyptian and other Middle Eastern peasants. The Bible mentions that David received from Sheba a gift of lentils, and this legume formed a part of the bread of Ezekiel. In the same vein, the Holy Qur'an states that lentils were a food the Jews in Sinai asked Moses to provide.

A few hundred years before the birth of Christ, the cultivation of lentils spread to eastern Asia, East Africa, and the countries around the Mediterranean basin. In ancient Egypt and Greece it became one of the favourite pulses. However, the Romans never acquired a fondness for this ancient food. A number of chroniclers have written that, since the Romans had little use for the plant, its cultivation did not spread in Europe. It was only in Spain, after the Arab occupation, that lentils became a common food in that part of Europe.

The plant was introduced by the Spaniards when they arrived in the Americas. However, only in the countries of Central and South America have lentils become an everyday ingredient. In North America, this indispensable legume in the diet of many peoples is surprisingly neglected. Although it has recently been cultivated extensively in parts of the northwest United States and western Canada, it has never caught on as a popular food here. Only in the last few years are lentils beginning to enter the American and Canadian culinary worlds.

During the 1930s on the western Canadian prairies, this ancient pulse was not known to the vast majority of our fellow farmers. However, my parents' ancestors in Syria had cultivated this tasty legume, one of the world's oldest foods, for untold centuries. When our family immigrated to Canada, they brought their love for lentils with them. It was for this reason, that lentils were the mainstay of our hand-watered garden every year.

In the dry soil of the prairies, this hardy plant, which had adapted to the arid conditions of the Middle East, grew and thrived. None of our fellow farmers were familiar with lentils, and we, like other Arab immigrants, kept the knowledge of cultivating lentils well hidden. We ate our delicious

> *None of our fellow farmers were familiar with lentils, and we, like other Arab immigrants, kept the knowledge of cultivating lentils well hidden. We ate our delicious lentil soups, salads, and stews hidden in our home, safe from the prying eyes of our neighbours.*

lentil soups, salads, and stews hidden in our home, safe from the prying eyes of our neighbours.

Now, when I look back to those years, I think to myself how foolish we were. Instead of acquainting others with this ancient healthy food, we were ashamed to mention its very name. In fact, as children, my siblings and I thought that our parents were forcing us to eat inferior food.

All this has changed in the last few decades. In the late 1970s, I visited my sister's family who, at that time, were farmers in Saltcoats, near Yorkton, Saskatchewan. To my suprise, I found that lentils had become one of the major crops in Saskatchewan, and many people were talking about this pulse as a health food. It was then that I realized how unwise I was in my youthful years.

Today, Canada is one of the world's top lentil-producing countries, with most of the crops grown in Saskatchewan. Even though India produces half of the world's supply, most of its production is consumed locally. Canada is the second-largest exporter of this pulse, exceeded only by Turkey.

Lentils tolerate a wide range of soil. Nevertheless, to thrive they need a light sandy land and sunny climate. They are one of the few plants which enrich the soil. This is common knowledge among the Mediterranean farmers who, when they rotate their crops, always include lentils. The nitrogen-fixing bacteria harboured in their roots have made them a preferred peasant crop in the Middle East. For thousands of years, these bacteria have aided in the revitalization of the soil and kept the land productive.

A member of the bean family, the lentil grows to a bushy plant 10 to 16 inches high. It produces oblong flat pods containing usually two lens-shaped seeds the size of a small pea. The seeds are allowed to mature and dry on the plant before harvesting.

These ovules, which are the edible part, come in a variety of colours: brown, grey, green, yellow, red, and other cross shades. No matter what colour, every shade is tasty and has its own unique flavor.

In the Mediterranean countries, their wide cultivation and storage qualities make lentils available at all times of the year and at almost every food outlet. However, it is only the peasants and labourers who consume this vegetable on a regular basis. Many of the well-to-do eat it secretly in their homes and deny with great fervour the idea that they enjoy this ancient food.

In my many journeys to the Middle East, I have never been served lentils, even in village homes. No peasant or labourer will admit they are so poor that they must serve lentils to their guests. Yet, for the daily fare, hardly a day passes without the cook of the house preparing a type of lentil dish for the family.

Little did I know in our farming years that the fare that my mother cooked from lentils was, perhaps, one of the reasons why our family members rarely had to see a doctor. They are low-fat, containing about 116 calories in half a cup of cooked lentils. Highly nutritious, this legume is chock-full of minerals such as folacin, iron magnesium, phosphorus, and potassium, and rich in calcium, carbohydrates, vitamin B_6, and especially protein.

Lentils have one of the highest protein contents of any vegetable, containing more protein than an equal amount of meat. To get the full punch of this protein content and create a complete and tasty vegetarian meal, lentils should be combined with a grain like rice or burghul.

In addition to their nutritional value, lentils are recommended for anemia, emaciation, hemorrhoids, low blood pressure, and ulcerated digestive tracts. A boon to diabetics, they assist the body in controlling blood sugar and insulin levels. However, they have one

drawback: they tend to produce gas, an irritant which can be somewhat relieved by adding turmeric as an ingredient in the cooked dishes.

Cheap and wholesome, lentils are climbing the social ladder in North America, appearing more regularly on household menus. It is possible that in the foreseeable future they will become one of the basic foods in the Western Hemisphere. Should this happen, then many will understand the Biblical story of how Esau sold his birthright to his twin brother Jacob for a bowl of pottage made from this legume.

One of the simplest foods to prepare, most lentils take only about 35 minutes to cook. The red type, sometimes sold as Egyptian lentils, are usually retailed with the outer skin removed and split. They become ready for the table much more quickly than the other varieties. Unlike many other pulses, all types of lentils do not require soaking, but if placed in water for a few hours, they take half the time to cook.

Lentils are delicious when prepared with almost any grain, meat, or vegetable and even, simply, boiled with spices. In salads, soups, stews, and as a vegetable side dish, they are delightful, satisfying, and highly appetizing. In the lands where lentils have been consumed for centuries,

the number of soups and stews made from this vegetable are legion.

With their meaty flavour and healthful qualities, lentils make any dish in which they are an ingredient appetizing and nourishing. There is no question that lentils must have contributed greatly to the health of our family during the Depression years.

These few lentil dishes, made by my mother from a repertoire of hundreds, will open the door for the uninitiated into the culinary possibilities of one of the oldest foods in the world. ✺

CHICKPEA AND LENTIL APPETIZER

SERVES ABOUT 8

The early homestead years did not provide for a huge variety of ingredients. But Mother was always creative with what she had and could produce the best of dishes for her growing family. This dish makes an excellent appetizer when scooped up with crackers or Arab bread (pita).

½ cup	brown or green lentils, rinsed	125 ml
3 cups	water	750 ml
2 cups	cooked chickpeas	500 ml
2	cloves garlic, crushed	2
1 tsp	oregano	5 ml
½ tsp	salt	2 ml
¼ tsp	cumin	1 ml
¼ tsp	black pepper	1 ml
⅛ tsp	cayenne	½ ml
5 tbsps	lemon juice	75 ml
2 tbsps	finely chopped parsley	30 ml
½	medium tomato, finely chopped	½
2 tbsps	olive oil	30 ml

1. Place lentils and water in a saucepan, then bring to boil. Cover and cook over medium heat for 30 minutes or until lentils are cooked but still whole, then drain and allow to cool.

2. Place in a food processor with remaining ingredients, except parsley, tomato, and olive oil, then process into paste.

3. Spread on a flat serving plate, then decorate with parsley and tomato pieces. Sprinkle with oil just before serving.

He who has his hand in the water is not like him who has his hand in the fire.

LENTIL AND CHICKPEA SOUP /
SHAWRABAT ʿADAS WA HUMMUS

SERVES ABOUT 8

The ancients in the Middle East believed that the herbs and spices in the broth, besides enriching the soup, stimulated the appetite, helped in the circulation of the blood, alleviated rheumatic disorders, and eased diabetic problems. Even if these claims were only myths, these hearty and nourishing concoctions make an appetizing and gratifying meal.

¾ cup	brown or green lentils	175 ml
2 tbsps	olive oil	30 ml
½ cup	finely chopped fresh cilantro	125 ml
1 tsp	paprika	5 ml
2 cups	cooked chickpeas	500 ml
2 tbsps	rice	30 ml
2 tsps	salt	10 ml
1 tsp	black pepper	5 ml
1 tsp	cumin	5 ml
¼ tsp	chili powder	1 ml
2 tbsps	flour, dissolved in ½ cup (125 ml) water	30 ml
¼ cup	lemon juice	60 ml
2 tbsps	butter	30 ml

1. Wash lentils and soak overnight in 7 cups (1750 ml) of water.

2. Place lentils with their water, olive oil, cilantro, and paprika in a saucepan, then bring to boil. Cover and cook over medium heat for 25 minutes, then add remaining ingredients, except dissolved flour, lemon juice, and butter. Re-cover and cook for further 15 minutes or until rice grains are tender but still whole.

3. Remove from heat, then slowly stir in flour paste, lemon juice, and butter. Return to heat and bring to a boil, then serve immediately.

LENTIL AND RICE SOUP / SHAWRABAT ʿADAS MAʿA RUZ

SERVES 8

If desired, after the soup is cooked, it can be puréed in a blender, then the coriander and lemon juice added.

4 tbsps	olive oil	60 ml
2	large onions, finely chopped	2
2	cloves garlic, crushed	2
1 cup	split brown or green lentils	250 ml
1½ tsps	salt	7 ml
½ tsp	black pepper	2 ml
½ tsp	cumin	2 ml
¼ tsp	cayenne	1 ml
pinch	saffron	pinch
7 cups	boiling water	1750 ml
2 tbsps	rice, rinsed	30 ml
2 tbsps	very finely chopped fresh cilantro	30 ml
8 tsps	lemon juice	40 ml

1. Heat oil in a saucepan, then sauté onions over medium heat until they begin to brown. Add garlic and stir-fry for a further 3 minutes, then add remaining ingredients, except cilantro and lemon juice. Bring to boil, then cover and cook over medium heat for 25 minutes or until lentils are tender. Remove from heat, then stir in cilantro.

2. Place into 8 soup dishes, then stir 1 teaspoon (5 ml) lemon juice into each dish.

LENTIL AND NOODLE SOUP / SHAWRABAT ʿADAS MAʿA SHI ʿIREEYA

SERVES 8

4 tbsps	olive oil	60 ml
2	medium onions, finely chopped	2
4	cloves garlic, crushed	4
½ cup	finely chopped fresh cilantro	125 ml
7 cups	water	1750 ml
1 cup	brown or green lentils, rinsed	250 ml
1½ tsps	salt	7 ml
½ tsp	black pepper	2 ml
½ tsp	cumin	2 ml
⅛ tsp	cayenne	½ ml
½ cup	vermicelli	125 ml

1. Heat oil in a saucepan, then sauté onions over medium heat until they begin to brown. Add garlic and cilantro, then stir-fry for 3 minutes. Add remaining ingredients, except vermicelli, then bring to boil. Cover and cook for 20 minutes over medium heat, then stir in vermicelli and bring to boil. Re-cover and simmer for about 15 minutes on medium heat or until the lentils and vermicelli are well cooked.

The wound that bleedeth inwardly is the most dangerous.

LENTIL AND TOMATO SOUP / SHAWRABAT ʿADAS MAʿA BANADOORA

SERVES 8

1 cup	brown or green lentils, rinsed and drained	250 ml
7 cups	water	1750 ml
4 tbsps	butter	60 ml
2	medium onions, chopped	2
4	cloves garlic, crushed	4
4	medium tomatoes, finely chopped	4
2 tsps	salt	10 ml
1 tsp	black pepper	5 ml
1 tsp	cumin	5 ml
1 tsp	ground coriander	5 ml
⅛ tsp	cayenne	½ ml
¼ cup	rice, rinsed	60 ml
3 tbsps	lemon juice	45 ml

1. Place lentils and water in a saucepan, then bring to boil. Cover and cook over medium heat for 20 minutes.

2. In the meantime, melt butter in a frying pan, then sauté onions and garlic over medium heat until they begin to brown. Stir in tomatoes and sauté for 5 minutes, then add frying pan contents to lentils.

3. Stir in remaining ingredients, except lemon juice, cover, and simmer over low heat about 30 minutes or until lentils and rice are well cooked, adding more water if necessary. Stir in lemon juice, then serve hot.

LENTIL SALAD / SALATAT ʿADAS

SERVES 8 TO 10

Due to Syria's rich history, Damascus and Aleppo developed a gourmet cuisine, not yet well-known in other lands. In the following centuries, other Middle Eastern cities only copied the foods of these historic urban centres. What is known today as Lebanese, Syrian, Jordanian, or Palestinian food was originally developed in the kitchens of these historic cities in their days of splendour. It is said that new dishes are not created by peasants but by those with time to spare and those who have the money to experiment with new ideas.

Visitors need only to have entered the old quarters of Aleppo or Damascus and breathed deeply the aroma of exotic spices to feel that they were in a medieval world of action and colour—a vestige from the days when these cities were literally at the centre of the world. In the labyrinth of narrow ancient streets, a bewildering mixture of people at work or on the move, one could see artisans hand-pounding their brass, copper, iron, and precious metals and merchants offering their endless food products. Dishes such as this likely were carried from the peasants to the opulent.

1 cup	brown or green lentils, rinsed	250 ml
6 cups	water	1.5 L
6 tbsps	olive oil	90 ml
½ cup	lemon juice	125 ml
1 bunch	green onions, finely chopped	1 bunch
3	large tomatoes, diced	3
1 cup	cooked chickpeas	250 ml
½ cup	finely chopped parsley	125 ml
1 tsp	salt	5 ml
½ tsp	black pepper	2 ml

1. In a saucepan bring lentils and water to boil. Cover and cook over medium heat until tender but still intact and slightly firm (about 20 minutes), then allow to cool. Drain lentils, then combine thoroughly with remaining ingredients in a salad bowl just before serving.

LENTILS WITH YOGURT / 'ADAS MA'A LABAN

SERVES 4

Lentils with Yogurt was probably one of the most refreshing meals we enjoyed during our farm days. With homemade yogurt and lentils almost always on hand, this was an invigorating dish. especially on Saskatchewan's hot summer days. This tasty delight may be served as an appetizer or as a side dish.

½ cup	brown or green lentils, rinsed	125 ml
3 cups	water	750 ml
1 quart	plain yogurt, chilled	1 L
2 tbsps	finely chopped fresh mint	30 ml
1	clove garlic, crushed	1
½ tsp	salt	2 ml
¼ tsp	black pepper	1 ml
¼ tsp	chili powder	1 ml

1. Place lentils and water in a saucepan, then bring to boil. Cover, then cook over medium heat for 30 minutes or until the lentils are tender but not mushy. Drain lentils, then allow to cool.

2. Place in a serving bowl with remaining ingredients, then combine well just before serving.

   NOTE: *The fresh mint in this recipe can be replaced by 1 teaspoon (5 ml) dried mint.*

BEAN AND LENTIL STEW / YAKHNIT FASOOLIYA WA LAHAM

SERVES ABOUT 8

½ cup	navy beans	125 ml
9 cups	water	2.25 L
1 cup	brown or green lentils, rinsed	250 ml
4 tbsps	olive oil	60 ml
2	medium onions, chopped	2
4	cloves garlic, crushed	4
1	hot pepper, seeded and finely chopped	1
¼ cup	long-grain rice, rinsed	60 ml
1 tsp	cumin	5 ml
1 tsp	oregano	5 ml
1½ tsps	salt	7 ml
½ tsp	black pepper	2 ml
3 tbsps	finely chopped fresh cilantro	45 ml

1. Soak navy beans overnight and drain.

2. Place beans and water in a saucepan, then bring to boil. Cover, then cook over medium heat for 1¼ hours. Add lentils, then cook for a further 20 minutes, adding more water if necessary.

3. In the meantime, heat oil in a frying pan, then sauté onions over medium heat until they begin to brown. Stir in garlic and hot pepper, then stir-fry for a further 3 minutes.

4. Add the frying pan contents and remaining ingredients, except cilantro, to lentils and beans, then cover and simmer over low heat for 30 minutes or until lentils and beans are cooked, adding more water if necessary. Stir occasionally to prevent stew from sticking to the bottom of the pot. Stir in cilantro, then serve hot.

VEGETARIAN LENTIL DELIGHT / MUJADDARA

SERVES 4 TO 6

Mujaddara, suspected to be the dish for which Esau sold his birthright, is made in numerous ways. Although this is one of the preferred dishes the Arab immigrant peasants brought with them to North America, they never served it to their guests. The old country tradition of not serving this hearty dish to visitors because it costs so little to make was carried on even in southern Saskatchewan.

1 cup	brown or green lentils, rinsed	250 ml
5 cups	water	1250 ml
¼ cup	burghul, rinsed	60 ml
6 tbsps	butter	90 ml
3	medium onions, finely chopped	3
1 tsp	salt	5 ml
½ tsp	black pepper	2 ml
½ tsp	cumin	2 ml
¼ tsp	chili powder	1 ml

Rice may be substituted for the burghul.

1. Place lentils and water in a saucepan, then bring to boil. Cover, then cook over medium heat for 15 minutes or until lentils are half-cooked. Add burghul, then bring to boil. Reduce heat to low, cover, then cook for a further 20 minutes or until both lentils and burghul are tender but still intact and slightly firm, stirring occasionally and adding more water if necessary.

2. In the meantime, melt butter in a frying pan, then sauté onions over medium heat until golden.

3. Stir frying pan contents and remaining ingredients into saucepan, and cook for a further 3 minutes. Serve hot.

LENTIL AND MEAT STEW / YAKHNIT ʿADAS

SERVES 8

4 tbsps	butter	60 ml
½ lb	beef or lamb, cut into ½-inch (1 cm) cubes	227 g
2	medium onions, chopped	2
4	cloves garlic, crushed	4
1	small hot pepper, seeded and finely chopped	1
1 cup	brown or green lentils, rinsed	250 ml
5 cups	water	1.25 L
4	medium potatoes, peeled and diced into ¾-inch (2 cm) cubes	4
4	medium tomatoes, chopped	4
1½ tsps	salt	7 ml
1 tsp	cumin	5 ml
1 tsp	black pepper	5 ml
½ tsp	turmeric	2 ml

1. Melt butter in a saucepan, then add meat and sauté over medium heat for 5 minutes. Add onions, garlic, and hot pepper, then stir-fry for a further 10 minutes. Add remaining ingredients, cover, then cook over medium heat until meat and lentils are well done, about 50 minutes, stirring occasionally and adding more water if necessary. Serve hot with cooked rice.

Tire out your body but not your mind.

LENTILS AND SPINACH

SERVES 8 TO 10

4 tbsps	butter	60 ml
1 cup	rice, rinsed	250 ml
6 cups	boiling water	1.5 L
1 tsp	salt	5 ml
1 cup	brown or green lentils, rinsed	250 ml
4 tbsps	olive oil	60 ml
10 oz	spinach, thoroughly washed and chopped	283 g
4	cloves garlic, crushed	4
2 tbsps	finely chopped fresh cilantro	30 ml
1 tsp	oregano	5 ml
½ tsp	black pepper	2 ml
½ tsp	cumin	2 ml
1 tsp	sumac *	5 ml

1. Melt butter in a frying pan, then stir-fry the rice over medium heat for 2 minutes. Add 2 cups (500 ml) of the water, then bring to boil. Stir in ½ teaspoon (2 ml) of the salt, then cover and turn heat to low. Cook for 15 minutes, then turn heat off, stir, re-cover, and allow to cook in its own steam for 30 minutes. Set aside.

2. In the meantime, place lentils and remaining 4 cups (1 L) of water in a saucepan, then bring to boil. Cover and cook over medium heat for 30 minutes or until lentils are cooked but not mushy, adding more water if necessary, then drain and set aside.

3. Heat oil in another frying pan, then add spinach and garlic and stir-fry over medium heat until spinach wilts. Add lentils, remaining salt, cilantro, oregano, pepper, and cumin, then sauté for 8 minutes, stirring occasionally. Place frying pan contents on a flat serving platter, then spread rice evenly on top and sprinkle with sumac, just before serving hot.

* Sumac can be purchased from Middle Eastern grocery stores.

One of the ingredients in this dish is sumac, a spice popularly used in Syria, Lebanon, Palestine, and Jordan to give a tart flavour to foods. It was also a spice that we never had on the farm. To compensate for its taste, Mother used fresh lemon juice.

Years later, Mother was able to add sumac to her cooking ingredients thanks to a wholesaler/retailer in Montreal, Abusamra Al-Khoury. My parents would go through the company's catalogue and order what was needed, or rather, what had been missing when making Syrian food from the day they had first arrived to the prairies of Saskatchewan.

LENTIL PIES / FATAAYIR BI 'ADAS

MAKES 16 PIES

1½ lbs	frozen dough, thawed, or Dough for Pies (page 151)	680 g
1 cup	brown or green lentils, rinsed	250 ml
4 cups	water	1 L
3	medium onions, finely chopped	3
4	cloves garlic, crushed	4
1	small hot pepper, seeded and very finely chopped	1
5.5 oz	tomato paste (small can)	156 ml
4 tbsps	butter	60 ml
4 tbsps	lemon juice	60 ml
1 tsp	ground coriander	5 ml
1 tsp	salt	5 ml
½ tsp	black pepper	2 ml
½ tsp	cumin	2 ml

1. Form dough into 16 balls, then cover and allow to rest for 1 hour and 30 minutes.

2. In the meantime, place lentils and water in a saucepan, then bring to boil. Cover, then simmer over medium heat for 40 minutes or until lentils are soft. Drain lentils and allow to cool, then mash and combine with remaining ingredients to make filling.

3. Roll each dough ball into 5-inch (13 cm) circles, then place 2 heaping tablespoons (30 ml) of the filling on the centre of each circle. Fold dough over and press the edges firmly to seal, in the process shaping the pie into a triangle, then continue until all balls are finished. Place on well-greased trays, then bake in a 350°F (180°C) preheated oven for 20 minutes. Brown under broiler for a minute or two until golden.

4. Remove from oven, then brush with oil or butter and serve hot.

LENTIL LOAF

SERVES 8 TO 10

Dec. 24/19

2 cups	brown or green lentils, rinsed	500 ml
6 cups	water	1500 ml
2	medium onions, chopped	2
5	cloves garlic, crushed	5
1	hot pepper, seeded and chopped	1
4 tbsps	finely chopped fresh cilantro	60 ml
1 cup	bread crumbs	250 ml
5.5 oz	tomato paste (small can)	156 ml
4 tbsps	butter	60 ml
3	eggs	3
1½ tsps	salt	7 ml
1 tsp	thyme	5 ml
1 tsp	black pepper	5 ml
1 tsp	cumin	5 ml
2 tbsps	olive oil	30 ml

 — panko crumbs

1. Place lentils and water in a saucepan, then bring to boil. Cover and cook over medium heat for 40 minutes or until lentils are soft but still whole, adding more water if necessary. Drain, then place in a food processor and process until lentils are crushed. Remove, then transfer to a mixing bowl. Place remaining ingredients, except oil, in the food processor and process for 2 minutes.

2. Transfer to the mixing bowl, and thoroughly combine with lentils. Place in two 8- × 4-inch (20 × 10 cm) greased loaf pans. Sprinkle with oil, then cover with aluminum foil. Bake in a 350°F (180°C) preheated oven for 45 minutes, then remove the aluminum foil. Bake uncovered for a further 10 minutes, then allow to slightly cool. Serve hot or cold, but preferably hot.

Meat was a luxury when we were young. It was usually reserved for special occasions and holidays. Although we did have our fair share, Mother could successfully improvise certain dishes by substituting lentils for the meat. Lentil Loaf was one of these dishes.

THE PLEASURES OF DAMASCUS

After a full day of touring Damascus, the oldest inhabited city in the world, we were seated in Abo Alez Restaurant, which is housed in an old, renovated, beautifully tiled Arab home across the street from the renowned Umayyad Mosque. Here, surrounded by groups of tourists, we dined on the tastiest food in all Damascus—a city known for its fine dishes.

Endless *mazzas* (appetizers) were followed by *harrack isbouaau* (lentil dumplings), *waraq cinab* (stuffed grape leaves), *kubbah* (meat and burghul patties), and numerous other dishes. As we enjoyed our *maamuneeya* (semolina dessert), the melodies of the *muwashshahat* (classical music and song developed in Arab Spain) playing in the background soothed our nerves, creating an atmosphere conducive to friendly conversation. The captivating music of these classical songs from Andalusia were like sirens calling us to come and enjoy the pleasures of life. ✺

—adapted from Habeeb Salloum, "Do Nations Express Themselves in Their Foods?" published in Contemporary Review, *278.1621 (2001): 107-11.*

CHAPTER 10

BROAD BEANS: DELICIOUS WHEN COOKED BY MY MOTHER

S ince the dawn of recorded history, broad beans, also known as fava, vicia, Windsor, English dwarf or horse beans, have been grown in western Asia and North Africa. From there, through the centuries, they have spread to every corner of the globe. However, during our home-steading days in Saskatchewan, it was a different story. Not one of our neighbours was familiar with this tasty bean loved by the inhabitants of the Middle East for centuries.

Broad beans were known in the classical Greek world, but they were not much appreciated. The Greeks believed that broad beans made them listless and caused them to have horrible dreams. On the other hand, in the Egypt of the Pharaohs it was a different story. Both rich and poor loved the taste of broad beans, and since that time this vegetable has continued to grace the tables of the inhabitants of the Nile Valley.

The peoples of the Indian sub-continent have enjoyed the culinary advantages of broad beans for thousands of years. Today, rare is the garden in India or Pakistan that does not have at least one patch of this historic vegetable.

The cool climate of Europe is ideal for the growth of this bean, and from Roman times to the arrival in the Americas, broad beans were the only edible beans known to the inhabitants of that continent. In pre-Columbus Europe, this legume, which some have labelled the "bean of history," nourished all strata of society. It was only after Europeans arrived in the Americas that it was replaced by newly introduced beans from these newly explored lands.

Why broad beans, which are more delicious than others, lost favour is still a mystery. Perhaps, the long period required for growth had something to do with their replacement. Other types of beans need a much shorter time period from seeding to harvest. To produce a good crop, broad beans must be planted in very early spring. Perhaps another reason for their demise is the susceptibility of the plant to a type of garden worm. Only by spraying or hand picking the worms can the plant be saved.

Even though in Europe this legume was replaced by other beans, its cultivation did not fade away. Farmers continued to plant it as a food for animals. As feed for livestock the plant is prepared in a number of ways. The seeds are sometimes ground and mixed with grain. At other times, the plant is harvested when almost full-grown, then made into silage. Also, at the same stage of growth, the plant can be utilized as forage. Many cattle are prepared for market by having them graze in rich broad bean fields.

In the Western Hemisphere, after the seeds had been introduced by the conquistadors, broad beans thrived. Mexico and Brazil became the largest producers. The high protein and carbohydrate content, along with some calcium, fiber, sodium, and traces of fat and vitamin C, made this legume an ideal food for the peasants and labourers in these countries. Today, the largest grower in the United States is California; and in Canada, the Maritime provinces. However, initially, in both countries broad beans were not grown for human consumption, but as feed for animals.

There are a number of types of broad beans. The most common grow from two to four feet high and produce large thick pods with flat angular seeds. The size of the seeds vary from the size of a pea to over an inch long and half an inch wide. Nevertheless, no matter what size or type, the pods are delicious when picked green and still tender. Harvested at this stage, the whole pods, including the shells and seeds, are tasty and pleasant to eat.

The tender pods are excellent when served as snacks or *hors d'oeuvres*. In the Arab East, where broad beans are known as *fool*, rare is an evening banquet or a gourmet meal when delectable tender *fool* is not served as an appetizer. During our farming years, I always looked to the time when our *fool* ripened and we children would gorge ourselves for days on their succulent, tender pods.

More common than harvesting the broad beans when they are green and tender is harvesting them when they are mature, but still green. The seeds are then removed from the shells and served as snacks or as a vegetable ingredient in preparing various dishes. At this stage, the shelled beans can be frozen or canned and are offered for sale in this form in Mediterranean stores and many large supermarkets.

Although frozen or canned green broad beans are used to some extent in cooking, in most cases the beans are allowed to dry on the plant before harvesting. The dry broad bean is at this stage brown in colour. Like chickpeas, lentils, or peas, they are sold either in bulk or packaged in plastic bags.

The culinary potential of this cholesterol-free vegetable is endless. With these few recipes, most of which our family enjoyed in our farm days in southern Saskatchewan, the newcomer to this type of bean can sample these delicious dishes from the Middle East and North Africa.

BROAD BEAN SALAD / SALATAT FOOL

SERVES ABOUT 4

This salad, which can be served as an appetizer or a side dish, is simple to prepare, yet tasty.

1 lb	fresh or frozen shelled green broad beans, cooked	454 g
½ cup	finely chopped parsley	125 ml
4 tbsps	chopped green onions	60 ml
2	cloves garlic, crushed	2
¼ cup	olive oil	60 ml
2 tbsps	lemon juice	30 ml
	salt and black pepper to taste	

1. Combine all ingredients well, then place on a platter and serve.

Give the guest food even though you yourself are starving.

BROAD BEAN SALAD WITH EGGS / FOOL MA'A BAYD

SERVES ABOUT 4

During the hot summer months when our garden flourished, we often enjoyed this dish.

1 lb	fresh or frozen shelled green broad beans, cooked	454 g
4 tbsps	finely chopped parsley	60 ml
2	cloves garlic, crushed	2
¾ tsp	salt	3 ml
½ tsp	black pepper	2 ml
3 tbsps	lemon juice	45 ml
¼ cup	olive oil	60 ml
3	hard-boiled eggs	3
¼ tsp	paprika	1 ml

1. Combine all ingredients, except hard-boiled eggs and paprika, in a serving dish, then set aside.

2. Chop hard-boiled eggs, then carefully stir into broad bean mixture, making sure that the egg pieces do not become mashed. Sprinkle with the paprika, then serve.

Have faith in a stone, and you will be healed.

SYRIAN BROAD BEAN PURÉE / FOOLEEYA

SERVES 6 TO 8

Perhaps more popular than green broad bean appetizers and salads are the purées made from the dried broad beans. They can be served as breakfast dishes, salads, appetizers, side dishes or for snacks. These two recipes, the first from the Greater Syria area and the other from Morocco, are common dishes in these lands.

1 cup	large, dry broad beans, soaked overnight, then drained	250 ml
6	small onions, cut into halves	6
6 cups	water	1.5 L
¼ cup	olive oil	60 ml
2 tsps	salt	10 ml
1 tsp	black pepper	5 ml
2 tbsps	lemon juice	30 ml
4 tbsps	finely chopped green onion	60 ml
4 tbsps	finely chopped parsley	60 ml
2 tbsps	pomegranate seeds	30 ml

1. Place broad beans, onions, and water in a saucepan, cover, then cook over medium heat until all the water has been absorbed and broad beans are well cooked, adding more water if necessary.

2. Place saucepan contents in a food processor, then process until broad beans are well puréed. Add 2 tablespoons (30 ml) of the olive oil, salt, pepper, and lemon juice, then process for a further few moments.

3. Allow to cool, then place on a flat serving platter. Sprinkle with remaining oil. Garnish with green onions, parsley, and pomegranate seeds just before serving.

Every moustache has its scissors.

MOROCCAN BROAD BEAN PURÉE / BISSAARA

SERVES 8 TO 10

2 cups	large, dry broad beans, soaked overnight, then drained	500 ml
4	cloves garlic, crushed	4
2 tsps	salt	10 ml
½ cup	olive oil	125 ml
8 cups	water	2 L
5 tbsps	lemon juice	75 ml
2 tsps	cumin	10 ml
1 tsp	paprika	5 ml
½ tsp	chili powder	2 ml
½ cup	chopped parsley	125 ml

1. Place broad beans, garlic, salt, 4 tablespoons (60 ml) of the olive oil, and water in a saucepan, cover, then cook over medium heat until broad beans are well done, adding more water if necessary.

2. Place saucepan contents in a food processor, then process until broad beans become paste-like. Return to saucepan, then stir in lemon juice and cumin. Simmer over low heat for 5 minutes, stirring a few times, then spoon onto a serving platter. Spread remaining olive oil evenly over top, then sprinkle with paprika and chili powder. Garnish with parsley and serve.

If you conduct yourself properly, fear no one.

BROAD BEANS IN OIL / FOOLEEYEE

SERVES 4 TO 6

No one who has tasted fresh cilantro, one of the oldest condiments known to man and today the most widely consumed fresh herb, will doubt that it inspires some to ecstasy. However, for others, it is an offensive herb. Strange as it may seem, there are some who despise its taste and abhor its smell. On the other hand, the vast majority who use it in their cuisine are addicted to its very name.

¼ cup	olive oil	60 ml
3	cloves garlic, crushed	3
1	large onion, finely chopped	1
1 tsp	salt	5 ml
½ tsp	black pepper	2 ml
¼ tsp	allspice	1 ml
4 tbsps	finely chopped fresh cilantro	60 ml
3 cups	shelled fresh or frozen green broad beans	750 ml
3 tbsps	lemon juice	45 ml

1. Place olive oil in a saucepan, then heat. Add garlic, onion, salt, pepper, allspice, and cilantro, then sauté over medium heat until onions begin to brown. Stir in broad beans, then cover with water. Bring to boil, cover, then cook over medium heat for approximately 30 minutes or until broad beans are tender. Stir in lemon juice, then cook for a few more minutes. Serve either hot or cold.

BROAD BEANS WITH RICE / FOOL MA'A RUZ

SERVES 4 TO 6

Broad beans have a long history in the Middle East. The oldest seeds have been found in northwest Syria dating back to the tenth millennium. With such a long history, it is no wonder that there are so many varieties of broad bean dishes.

4 tbsps	butter	60 ml
2	large onions, finely chopped	2
3	cloves garlic, crushed	3
2 tsps	salt	10 ml
½ tsp	black pepper	2 ml
¼ tsp	allspice	1 ml
2 cups	fresh or frozen green broad beans	500 ml
1 cup	rice, rinsed	250 ml
3 cups	boiling water	750 ml
2 tbsps	finely chopped fresh cilantro	30 ml

1. Melt butter in a saucepan, then add onions, garlic, salt, pepper, and allspice. Stir-fry over medium heat until onions begin to brown. Add broad beans, rice, and water, then stir. Cover saucepan, then cook for 30 minutes over medium-low heat. Turn off heat, stir, re-cover, and allow to cook in own steam for another 30 minutes.

2. Place on a serving platter, then sprinkle with cilantro and serve hot.

FEZ-STYLE BROAD BEANS / FOOL FAS

SERVES ABOUT 4

2 cups	fresh or frozen broad beans	500 ml
¼ cup	olive oil	60 ml
1	large sweet red pepper, seeded and finely chopped	1
4	cloves garlic, crushed	4
1½ tsps	salt	7 ml
1 tsp	cumin	5 ml
½ cup	finely chopped fresh cilantro	125 ml
¼ tsp	chili powder	1 ml

1. Place all ingredients in a saucepan, then cover with water. Cover and cook over medium heat until broad beans are tender. Serve hot or cold as appetizer, snack, or side dish.

If you come back from a journey, offer your family something, though it only be a stone.

EGYPTIAN FALAFEL / TA'MIYYA

MAKES FROM 40 TO 50 PATTIES

Today, this tasty vegetarian delight is the hamburger of the Middle East and is fast replacing the meat hamburger in North America. The simplest way to make this dish is to purchase the falafel or ta'miyya powder, ready-made, in markets selling Arab or Middle Eastern foods.

Directions are on the packages on how to prepare this dish, known as "the hamburger of the poor." However, even though ready-made falafel is simple to prepare, it is not as tasty as falafel made from scratch. This recipe, common in Egypt, is how true falafel, or ta'miyya, is made.

1	large bunch parsley	1
4 cups	dried broad beans, soaked overnight and drained	1 L
3	large onions, chopped into large pieces	3
1	head of garlic, peeled	1
2	green, small, hot peppers, seeded	2
4 tsps	salt	20 ml
2 tsps	cumin	10 ml
2 tsps	ground coriander seeds	10 ml
1½ tsps	black pepper	7 ml
1 tsp	baking soda	5 ml
1 tsp	baking powder	5 ml
	oil for frying	

Dwell not upon thy weariness; thy strength shall be according to the measure of thy desire.

1. Wash parsley and remove stems.

2. Place parsley, broad beans, onions, garlic, and hot peppers in a food processor, then process until broad beans are very finely ground—to the consistency of flour. Add salt, cumin, coriander, black pepper, baking soda, and baking powder, then process for a further minute. Remove from processor and form into patties. If patties tend to crumble, add a little flour, then return to the processor and process further.

3. Heat the oil in a deep fryer or saucepan, then deep-fry the patties over medium heat, turning them over once or twice, until they turn golden brown and crisp on the outside. Drain on paper towels.

4. Serve patties in sandwiches in half rounds of Arab bread (pita), in a bed of tossed salad, or as an entrée with tossed salad.

FALAFEL

Falafel is spreading like wildfire throughout the world. In Egypt, it is known as ta'miyya and is one of the country's national dishes. It is equally enjoyed by everyone. In the days of my youth, I never heard of ta'miyya since it was unknown to my mother. It seems strange that this food, eaten in Egypt for thousands of years, was not known to the peasants in Syria, where my parents lived.

In Egypt, fool mudammas is the common breakfast food for 90 percent of Egyptians. In the early morning hours, streets of the cities in the Nile Valley are lined with vendors selling this tempting dish from copper or earthenware pots. Although in North America there are no vendors with pots of steaming broad beans, with little effort anyone can produce delicious fool mudammas by following this recipe.

BROAD BEAN POTTAGE / FOOL MUDAMMAS

SERVES 4

Mother would often make this dish during the winter months and serve it along with pickles. In summer, when our garden flourished, she would serve it along with a salad—usually safsoof.

1 cup	small, dried broad beans, soaked overnight and drained	250 ml
¼ cup	olive oil	60 ml
1½ tsps	salt	7 ml
¾ tsp	black pepper	3 ml
¾ tsp	ground coriander	3 ml
¾ tsp	cumin	3 ml
4 tbsps	lemon juice	60 ml
2	cloves garlic, crushed	2
4	hard-boiled eggs, with shells removed	4
2 tbsps	finely chopped cilantro	30 ml

1. Place broad beans in a saucepan and cover with water, then cover saucepan and cook over medium heat for about 2 hours or until beans are very tender, adding more water if necessary.

2. Drain broad beans and place in a mixing bowl, then add 2 tablespoons (30 ml) of the olive oil, salt, pepper, coriander, cumin, lemon juice, and garlic. Mix well until some of broad beans break.

3. Transfer to four soup bowls, then place an egg in centre of each bowl. Sprinkle each bowl with remaining oil, then garnish with cilantro and serve.

CHAPTER 11

GARLIC: A NATURAL MEDICINE

One of the herb-vegetables which dominated our garden during our farming years was garlic—a food that was part of almost every meal. Even though many times our fellow school children taunted us as "garlic eaters" or "smelly garlic," my mother was adamant that we were healthy because we ate garlic.

I am sure my mother had never read an article about the medicinal benefits of garlic, but the oral traditions of the people in her village, which had been handed down for untold generations, all pointed to garlic as a natural medicine for many ailments. As I was to find later in life, these traditions were not fantasies. Garlic is truly one of the healthiest foods known to humankind.

Through the centuries, people have either believed that garlic was divine or with fanatical aversion have detested its very name. This well-known condiment with a unique flavour not found in any other vegetable has caused, and is still arousing, much controversy. To admirers who adore the taste of garlic, it is the king of seasonings. However, those who have a deep dislike for this pungent herb often quote an old proverb which says, "garlic makes men wink and drink and stink."

An all-round flavouring and medical herb, garlic was one of humankind's earliest foods—believed to have been first cultivated in the Euphrates and Nile valleys over five thousand years ago. In Middle Eastern mythology, when Satan sat triumphant in the Garden of Eden, onions sprang from his right footprint and garlic from the left.

The ancient Egyptians, who listed twenty-two garlic prescriptions for a variety of ailments, placed garlic as an offering on the altars of the gods. They believed it to be so healthy that they tried to take it with them to the afterlife. Not surprisingly, then, garlic was found in King Tutankhamen's tomb. Later in history, the classical Greek athletes were fed this vegetable-herb to give them strength, and the Romans believed that it could cure over sixty diseases.

In India and Sri Lanka, the time-honoured ayurvedist physicians employed it to lower the cholesterol level, and, in China, which today consumes half the garlic in the world, it has been used for centuries in the treatment of high blood pressure, gangrene, heart problems and meningitis.

The inhabitants of Asia and the countries surrounding the Mediterranean have employed garlic in their cooking since the dawn of recorded history. For centuries, these people, from which almost all the known civilizations sprung, knew the gourmet and medicinal benefits of garlic, and, hence, used it extensively in their cuisines. Even today, Egypt, China, India, Thailand, and Spain remain the largest garlic-growing and -consuming countries in the world.

Garlic contains water, carbohydrates, protein, fats, thiamine, riboflavin, niacin, and ascorbic acid. Its essential volatile oil has antiseptic properties which prevent the formation of bacteria and, hence, aid in the healing process of many diseases.

Medieval doctors and health writers in the Eastern lands have long attributed many benefits to garlic. Long before modern medicine,

Long before modern medicine, in China, India, and the Arab lands, the herb doctors in these countries prescribed garlic as a remedy for the common cold, senility, menstrual disorders, impotence, and cancer.

in China, India, and the Arab lands, the herb doctors in these countries prescribed garlic as a remedy for the common cold, senility, menstrual disorders, impotence, and cancer. According to medieval Arab herbalists, garlic gives strength, beautifies the complexion, acts as an aphrodisiac, and helps cure countless diseases.

In 1858, Louis Pasteur found that garlic had antibacterial qualities; Albert Schweitzer used it for the curing of gastrointestinal disorders. Morton Walker, author of forty-two books on alternative medicine, calls garlic "nature's gift to mankind" and maintains that all the ancient myths about its power to heal are not folkloric stories. Rather, they truly describe its healthful qualities.

Recent scientific research indicates that garlic indeed does have health benefits. A study in the Monell Chemical Senses Center in Philadelphia found that if mothers eat garlic before they begin breast-feeding, it can help to kindle the newborn's appetite for breast milk. Experiments held at the Hamburg Institute of Pharmaceutical Biology have found that garlic contains a colourless compound called allicin, also known as Russian penicillin, which acts like a fungicide in killing bacteria. In a study published in 1981 in the *American Journal of Clinical Nutrition*, Dr. Arun Brodia confirms that garlic has a cholesterol-lowering effect.

According to Lloyd Harris in *The Book of Garlic*, allicin is a great help in fighting bacterial infections and acts as a heavy-duty antibiotic. In the same vein, Dr. J. Martyn Baily, a member of a research team in Washington, has found that this ageless natural medicine inhibits clot formation, thereby reducing the risk of heart attacks and strokes.

Called by many a medical super-food, garlic contains a high amount of sulphur compounds, which could very well account for its healing properties. It is considered by many to be the most potent remedial herb—a fine gift of nature.

Some benefits of this herbal food are that it normalizes the body's blood pressure, helps in the prevention of cancer and tumors, protects the body from toxins, aids in the digestion of food, enhances the immune system, strengthens white blood cells, kills intestinal worms and aids in the removal of boils and pimples, assists sufferers of asthma and arthritis, and acts as an anti-diabetic and superb expectorant—an unmatched cough medicine. In addition, for those leaning towards a low-salt diet, garlic is a healthy alternative to that seasoning.

Yet, in spite of all its medical qualities, the true kingdom of garlic is the kitchen where, as a tasty, aromatic condiment, it reigns supreme, producing culinary gems. To the peoples of the Mediterranean basin, most basic foods cooked without garlic are considered bland and not worthy to be eaten. Only when cooks in these countries use the right amount of this vegetable-condiment in their cuisine are they considered praiseworthy.

In North America, where California is the largest garlic-producing state in the United States, the consumption of this ancient herb has spread like wildfire in the last few decades. Almost 500 million pounds of garlic were produced in this state in 1994. Gilroy, California, claims the title of "Garlic Capital of the World." Annually, during the last weekend in July, a "Garlic Festival" is held, where a myriad of garlic dishes from sauces to desserts are offered.

The innumerable qualities of this vegetable-herb—with its distinctive odour and sharp flavour, antagonizing to some but enticing to others—work miracles in the preparation of food. The finer that garlic is chopped, the more flavour it will have. However, due to its odour, some call it a destroyer of romance, an enchanted poison, or the fare of the poor. Yet, this offensive smell, which is produced after garlic has been eaten, can be eliminated by chewing a handful of parsley or, better still, by having all members of the household eat food prepared with garlic. No one will be annoyed with the offensive odour if this pungent vegetable is eaten by all.

The quality of the dishes cooked with garlic are immensely enhanced by its subtle use. Like my mother, the women in the Asiatic and Mediterranean countries who flavour appetizers, salads, soups, stews and all other types of meat and vegetable dishes with garlic know the culinary pleasures of this condiment. Fresh, cooked or utilized as an extracted oil, garlic is a delicious and healthy addition to myriad dishes.

GARLIC SAUCE / SALSAT AL-THUUM

There is no place in the world where garlic is more employed and enjoyed than in the Middle East. A simple, fiery garlic sauce called taratoor *is a common dish of the peasants. They use it as a condiment with fowl, meat, fish or vegetables in the manner of mint sauce, horseradish or ketchup.*

2	heads of garlic	2
½ cup	olive oil	125 ml
½ cup	lemon juice	125 ml
¾ tsp	salt	3 ml

1. Peel the two heads of garlic and place the garlic cloves in a food processor. Process for a few moments. Add remaining ingredients, then continue blending until a creamy-looking sauce is formed.

2. Place in a container with a tight-fitting lid, then refrigerate until ready to use.

NOTE: *It is easier to peel garlic cloves if they are lightly tapped, or soaked overnight in cold water before peeling.*

And, most dear actors, eat no onions nor garlic, for we are to utter sweet breath.

—WILLIAM SHAKESPEARE, *A Midsummer Night's Dream*

SESAME SAUCE / SALSAT TAHINI

Garlic used raw is at its most potent. It is much milder when cooked. This Middle Eastern dish can be eaten as an appetizer, scooped in pita bread, or used as a sauce with other food.

½	head of garlic, peeled	½
½ cup	tahini (sesame seed paste)	125 ml
¼ cup	water	60 ml
3 tbsps	lemon juice	45 ml
1 tbsp	finely chopped seeded hot pepper	15 ml
¼ tsp	salt	1 ml
¼ cup	finely chopped parsley	60 ml
1 tbsp	olive oil	15 ml

1. In a food processor, place garlic, then process for a few moments. Add tahini, water, lemon juice, hot pepper, and salt, then purée, adding more water, a little at a time, until sauce becomes light in colour and the same consistency as mayonnaise.

2. Place on a serving platter, then garnish with parsley.

3. Refrigerate for half an hour, then sprinkle with oil just before serving.

Ignorance is not a disgrace. The disgrace is in refusing to learn.

GARLIC AND BREAD SAUCE

This is a very hot sauce which should be used in moderation
when cooked meats and vegetables are dipped into it.

4 slices	white bread	4 slices
1	small head of garlic, peeled and crushed	1
1	small hot pepper, seeded and finely chopped	1
6 tbsps	olive oil	90 ml
4 tbsps	finely chopped fresh cilantro	60 ml
3 tbsps	vinegar	45 ml
½ tsp	salt	2 ml

1. Soak bread in water for a few minutes, then squeeze out water with hands. Place in a food processor, then add remaining ingredients and process into soft paste. Use immediately or store in refrigerator in a container with a tight-fitting lid for future use.

GARLIC BARBECUE SAUCE

A great barbecue enhancer, this spicy, hot garlic sauce goes
well with all types of barbecued meats and vegetables.

1	head of garlic, peeled and crushed	1
4 tbsps	olive oil	60 ml
4 tbsps	lemon juice	60 ml
½ tsp	salt	2 ml
¼ tsp	cayenne	1 ml

1. Place all ingredients in a food processor, then process for 1 minute.

2. Serve with barbecued meats and vegetables, or place in a container with a tight-fitting lid and store in a refrigerator for future use.

GARLIC BREAD

After being seduced by garlic, it is difficult to imagine food without this herb's flavour.

1 loaf	French bread	1 loaf
4 tbsps	butter	60 ml
2	cloves garlic, crushed	2
1 tbsp	very finely chopped fresh cilantro	15 ml

1. Cut the French loaf into ¾-inch (2 cm) slices without cutting through the bottom crust (in order to keep the loaf together).

2. Combine butter, garlic, and cilantro, then spread on both sides of the cut slices of bread.

3. Wrap in aluminum foil, then bake in a 350°F (180°C) preheated oven for 10 minutes or until toasted. Serve hot.

ROASTED GARLIC

Roasted garlic cloves have a mild nutty taste and are delicious eaten on toast.

1 to 2 heads garlic
oil
salt

1. Peel garlic, then place in a casserole. Brush with oil, then lightly sprinkle with salt. Roast in a 350°F (180°C) preheated oven for 15 minutes or until cloves turn light brown. Serve immediately on toast or as a snack.

GARLIC-ZUCCHINI APPETIZER

SERVES *6 TO 8*

*For a healthy, but not as tasty, version of this
recipe the zucchini can be baked.*

4 tbsps	olive oil	60 ml
1	small head of garlic, peeled and sliced	1
1½ lbs	zucchini, cut into	680 g
	¼-inch (6 mm) thick slices	
4 tbsps	vinegar	60 ml
2 tbsps	finely chopped green onions	30 ml
2 tbsps	finely chopped fresh cilantro	30 ml
¾ tsp	salt	3 ml
½ tsp	black pepper	2 ml
⅛ tsp	cayenne	½ ml

1. Heat oil in a frying pan, then sauté garlic slices over medium heat until they turn light brown. Remove garlic slices with a slotted spoon and set aside.

2. In same oil, sauté zucchini slices over medium heat until golden brown, turning them over once and adding more oil if necessary. Remove, then set aside, allowing to drain on paper towels.

3. Combine remaining ingredients to make a sauce, then set aside.

4. Place zucchini on a serving platter. Sprinkle sauce over zucchini, then evenly top with garlic slices. Allow to stand for at least 4 hours before serving.

GARLIC SOUP / SHAWRABAT THOOM

SERVES ABOUT 8

Healthy and tasty, this dish can make one addicted to garlic.

4 tbsps	olive oil	60 ml
1	large onion, chopped	1
1	head of garlic, peeled and chopped	1
2	medium sweet peppers, seeded and finely chopped	2
1	small hot pepper, seeded and finely chopped	1
2 cups	stewed tomatoes	500 ml
4 tbsps	chopped fresh cilantro	60 ml
2 tsps	salt	10 ml
1 tsp	black pepper	5 ml
1 tsp	cumin	5 ml
6 cups	water	1.5 L
2	eggs, beaten	2

1. Heat oil in a saucepan, then sauté onion, garlic, and both sweet and hot peppers over medium heat for 10 minutes. Stir in tomatoes and cilantro, then cover and cook over medium-low heat for 10 minutes, adding a little water if necessary. Add remaining ingredients, except eggs, then bring to boil. Re-cover, then cook over medium heat for 20 minutes. Stir in eggs and serve immediately.

Let trouble alone, and trouble will let you alone

CHICKEN-GARLIC-NOODLE SOUP / SHAWRABAT DAJAAJ MA'A SHI'IREEYA

SERVES 10

Nutmeg has often been regarded highly as an aphrodisiac. According to R. Hendrickson in his book Lewd Food, *the Chinese favour nutmeg as a love spice in teas, and the Yemenites consume large amounts to increase fertility.*

2 to 3 lbs	chicken bones with a little meat	1 to 1.5 kg
1 cup	broken fine noodles	250 ml
½	head of garlic, peeled and crushed	½
2 tbsps	finely chopped fresh cilantro	30 ml
1 tsp	salt	5 ml
1 tsp	black pepper	5 ml
1 tsp	thyme	5 ml
½ tsp	nutmeg	2 ml
⅛ tsp	cayenne	½ ml
4 tbsps	finely chopped green onions	60 ml
2 tbsps	finely chopped fresh mint	30 ml

1. Place chicken bones in a pot and cover with water to about 3 inches (8 cm) over bones, then bring to boil. Cover, then cook over medium heat for 2½ hours. Strain into another saucepan to remove bones, then add water to make 8 cups (2 L).

2. Add remaining ingredients, except onions and mint, then bring to boil. Cover, then cook over medium heat for 25 minutes. Stir in onions and mint, then serve immediately.

A man with one intention goes out to fulfill it; a man with two plans becomes perplexed.

TOMATO-TAHINI SALAD / SALATAT TAHINI

SERVES *6 TO 8*

It is thought that the sesame plant originated in Africa and, at the dawn of civilization, spread through the Middle East to India and China. It was grown as a food crop by the Sumerians, Babylonians, Egyptians, Persians, Greeks, Romans, and Arabs, who all used its seeds for food, medicine, and for making liquor. In Babylon, the oil from its seeds was the only oil used for cooking, and, as it was with all the other Mesopotamian civilizations, it was prized as an offering for the gods. In the Biblical era, the ancient Egyptians and Persians made bread from its flour, and the Romans consumed its oil as we use butter.

During the eighth century, the Arabs introduced the seeds into European cooking and gave us their name, sesame, which is derived from the Arabic simsim. After the arrival of Europeans in the Americas, the Portuguese and Spaniards brought the plant to Central and South America, and the African slaves carried it with them to the United States under the name benne.

3 tbsps	tahini (sesame seed paste)	45 ml
¼ cup	lemon juice	60 ml
5	cloves garlic, crushed	5
½ tsp	salt	2 ml
¼ tsp	black pepper	1 ml
pinch	cayenne	pinch
5	medium tomatoes, finely diced	5
1	medium cucumber, finely diced	1
½ cup	finely chopped parsley	125 ml
1 tbsp	finely chopped fresh mint	15 ml

1. In a serving bowl, thoroughly combine the tahini, lemon juice, garlic, salt, pepper, and cayenne. Add tomatoes, cucumber, and parsley, then toss. Garnish with fresh mint just before serving.

If you have much, give from your wealth; if you have little, give from your heart.

POTATO-GARLIC SALAD

SERVES 8

Middle Eastern salads can be appetizers to start a meal, entrées, or accompaniment (side dishes) to the main courses. They are never monotonous, since they can be altered in many ways. Perhaps, more than any of the other cultures of the world, the people of the Middle East have, through the centuries, refined their edibles such as salads into a tasty, healthy fare. Indeed, it is no wonder, then, that these tasty dishes with a history going back to early Egyptian and Mesopotamian civilizations are today found on the health menus of Europe and North America.

This salad goes well with all types of meats.

2½ lbs	potatoes	1 kg
2 tbsps	finely chopped fresh cilantro	30 ml
½ cup	green garlic leaves	125 ml
4 tbsps	olive oil	60 ml
4 tbsps	lemon juice	60 ml
½ tsp	salt	2 ml
½ tsp	black pepper	2 ml
½ tsp	powdered mustard	2 ml
⅛ tsp	cayenne	½ ml

1. Peel potatoes. Boil until tender but firm, drain, and allow to cool. Dice into ½-inch (1 cm) cubes.

2. Place potatoes in a salad bowl, then stir in cilantro and set aside.

3. Place remaining ingredients in a blender, then blend for a minute. Pour over potatoes.

4. Refrigerate for an hour or more, then toss just before serving.

GARLIC-CUCUMBER-YOGURT SALAD /
KHIYAAR BI LABAN MA'A THOOM WA KHALL

SERVES 8

In summer this salad is a very refreshing dish. But summer also brings around some very nasty insects—bees. The old Syrian method for dealing with a bee sting is to cut a garlic clove in half and rub it over the stung area to relieve the pain of the bee sting.

2	cucumbers, each 8 inches (20 cm) long	2
4 tbsps	finely chopped green garlic leaves	60 ml
2 tbsps	finely chopped fresh mint	30 ml
2 tbsps	olive oil	30 ml
2 tbsps	vinegar	30 ml
½ tsp	salt	2 ml
¼ tsp	black pepper	1 ml
1 cup	plain yogurt	250 ml

1. Peel cucumbers, halve lengthwise, and slice into thin half-rounds. Place cucumber slices in a salad bowl, then set aside.

2. Combine remaining ingredients. Pour over cucumber slices, then toss. Chill before serving.

    NOTE: *The garlic leaves can be replaced by 2 cloves garlic, crushed.*

It is as sinful to use a knife to cut bread as it is to raise a sword against God.

GARLIC RICE PILAF

SERVES 4

4 tbsps	butter	60 ml
1	medium onion, finely chopped	1
4	cloves garlic, crushed	4
1 cup	rice, rinsed	250 ml
1 tsp	dried oregano flakes	5 ml
¼ tsp	salt	1 ml
¼ tsp	black pepper	1 ml
¼ tsp	ground ginger	1 ml
2 cups	boiling water	500 ml
2 tbsps	finely chopped fresh cilantro	30 ml

1. Melt butter in a saucepan, then sauté onion over medium heat until golden. Add garlic, then sauté for a further few minutes. Add rice, then stir-fry for about 2 minutes. Stir in remaining ingredients, except cilantro, then bring to boil and cover. Cook for 20 minutes over low heat, then turn off heat, stir, re-cover, and allow the rice to cook in its own steam for 30 minutes.

2. Place on a serving platter, then decorate with cilantro and serve immediately.

Be cheerful and eat bread while you are alive.

GARLIC MASHED POTATOES
/ BATAATA BI THOOM

SERVES 6 TO 8

Excellent when served as an entrée or with stews.

3 cups	mashed potatoes	750 ml
½	head of garlic, peeled and crushed	½
½ cup	pistachios	125 ml
4 tbsps	lemon juice	60 ml
2 tbsps	olive oil	30 ml
½ tsp	salt	2 ml
½ tsp	black pepper	2 ml
½ tsp	nutmeg	2 ml
6 tbsps	water	90 ml

1. Place potatoes in a bowl, then set aside.

2. Place remaining ingredients in a food processor, then process for 1 minute. Thoroughly combine the processor's contents and the potatoes. Place on a platter and serve.

GARLIC OMELET / BAYD MA'A THOOM

SERVES 4

In the villages of Syria and Lebanon, Bayd Ma' Thoom, a tasty garlic omelet, is served to a mother who has just given birth. It is believed that the garlic will purify the blood and speed the recovery after childbirth. Whether it purifies the blood or not, this dish makes an excellent breakfast treat.

4 tbsps	olive oil	60 ml
1	large head of garlic, peeled and finely chopped	1
6	eggs	6
¼ tsp	salt	1 ml
¼ tsp	black pepper	1 ml

1. Heat oil in a frying pan, then stir-fry garlic over medium heat until golden. Remove from heat, then remove garlic with a slotted spoon, but reserve oil in frying pan.

2. In a bowl, beat eggs with fork, then add fried garlic, salt, and pepper and thoroughly mix. Pour into frying pan, then stir-fry over low heat until eggs are cooked.

*My brother and I against my cousin;
my cousin and I against a stranger.*

GARLIC AND SPINACH CASSEROLE

SERVES 6

A very tasty main course and an ideal dish for light lunches.

20 oz	spinach, thoroughly washed	560 g
2 tbsps	olive oil	30 ml
2	medium onions, finely chopped	2
1	head of garlic, peeled and chopped	1
1	small hot pepper, seeded and finely chopped	1
2 tbsps	finely chopped fresh cilantro	30 ml
½ tsp	black pepper	2 ml
½ tsp	cumin	2 ml
½ cup	water	125 ml
½ cup	crumbled feta cheese	125 ml

1. Half fill a large saucepan with water, then bring to boil. Add spinach, then cook for 2 minutes. Drain and set aside.

2. Heat oil in a frying pan, then sauté onions, garlic, and hot pepper over medium heat for 10 minutes. Stir in drained spinach and remaining ingredients, except cheese, then sauté for 3 minutes. Transfer frying pan contents to a casserole, then sprinkle cheese over top. Bake uncovered in a 350°F (180°C) preheated oven for 25 minutes, then serve hot from casserole.

GARLIC CHICKEN / DAJAAJ MA'A THOOM

SERVES 6

This is one version of a Spanish recipe inherited from the Moors. Although we enjoyed several versions of this dish in our travels throughout Spain, it is Mother's recipe that evokes the best of memories.

3 tbsps	olive oil	45 ml
2 lbs	boned chicken breasts, cut into 1-inch (2.5 cm) cubes	907 g
1	head of garlic, peeled and crushed	1
1 tsp	tarragon	5 ml
1 tsp	salt	5 ml
½ tsp	black pepper	2 ml
½ tsp	thyme	2 ml
⅛ tsp	cayenne	½ ml
1 cup	water	250 ml

1. Heat oil in a frying pan, then sauté chicken cubes over medium heat for 10 minutes. Add garlic, then stir-fry for a further 5 minutes. Transfer to a casserole.

2. Combine remaining ingredients, then stir into casserole. Cover, then bake in a 350°F (180°C) preheated oven for 30 minutes. Uncover, then bake for another 30 minutes or until chicken is tender. Serve hot from casserole with mashed potatoes or cooked rice.

He married the monkey for its money; the money went and the monkey remained a monkey.

FRIED LIVER WITH GARLIC / KABID MIQLEE MA'A THOOM

SERVES 4

This is one of the best methods for preparing liver. The delicious taste of the stir-fried liver is unequalled when compared to other methods for cooking liver.

5	cloves garlic, crushed	5
1	small hot pepper, seeded and very finely chopped	1
4 tbsps	very finely chopped fresh cilantro	60 ml
½ tsp	salt	2 ml
½ tsp	black pepper	2 ml
½ tsp	allspice	2 ml
4 tbsps	oil	60 ml
1 lb	calf or baby beef liver	454 g

1. Thoroughly combine garlic, hot pepper, fresh cilantro, salt, pepper, and allspice, then set aside.

2. Cut liver into ¾-inch (2 cm) cubes.

3. Heat oil in a frying pan, then sauté liver cubes over fairly high heat until liver barely begins to brown. Stir in garlic mixture, then stir-fry for a few moments. Serve sizzling hot.

Call someone your lord and he will sell you in the slave market.

GARLIC MEATBALLS / MUTHAWWIM

SERVES ABOUT 10

*Once you try this North African dish, you will
know the culinary delight of garlic.*

4 tbsps	butter	60 ml
1	large onion, finely chopped	1
1 lb	beef, cut into ½-inch (1 cm) cubes	454 g
1	head of garlic, peeled and crushed	1
2 tsps	salt	10 ml
1 tsp	black pepper	5 ml
1 tsp	cinnamon	5 ml
⅛ tsp	cayenne	½ ml
5 cups	water	1250 ml
1 lb	ground beef	454 g
¼ cup	rice, rinsed	60 ml
1	bunch parsley, finely chopped	1
1	egg, beaten	1
4 tbsps	tomato paste	60 ml
19 oz	canned chickpeas (with water)	540 ml

1. Melt butter in a saucepan, then sauté onions over medium heat until they begin to brown. Add cubed meat, half the garlic, 1 teaspoon (5 ml) of the salt, ½ teaspoon (2 ml) of the pepper, ½ teaspoon (2 ml) of the cinnamon and the cayenne, then sauté for a few minutes. Add water, then bring to boil. Cover, then simmer over medium heat for 45 minutes, adding more water if necessary.

2. In the meantime, thoroughly combine ground beef, rice, parsley, egg, and the remaining garlic, salt, pepper, and cinnamon. Form into small meatballs then gently place meatballs in simmering saucepan. Bring to a boil, then simmer for about 15 minutes. Add tomato paste and chickpeas, then simmer over medium heat until meatballs are well cooked, adding more water if necessary.

CURRIED GARLIC-FISH

The medley of spices used in this dish gives it its 'curried' flavour.

SERVES 6

4 tbsps	olive oil	60 ml
1	large onion, chopped	1
½	head of garlic, peeled and chopped	½
1	small hot pepper, seeded and finely chopped	1
1 tsp	grated fresh ginger	5 ml
2	medium tomatoes, chopped	2
4 tbsps	tomato paste	60 ml
½ tsp	salt	2 ml
½ tsp	black pepper	2 ml
½ tsp	turmeric	2 ml
¼ tsp	ground cardamom	1 ml
¼ tsp	cumin	1 ml
¼ tsp	cinnamon	1 ml
¼ tsp	nutmeg	1 ml
pinch	cayenne	pinch
1 cup	water	250 ml
2 lbs	fish fillets, cut into pieces	907 g

1. Heat oil in a large frying pan, then add onion, garlic, hot pepper, and ginger. Sauté over medium heat until onions begin to brown. Add tomatoes and tomato paste, then stir-fry for about 3 minutes. Add remaining ingredients, except fish pieces, then cover and simmer over low heat for 30 minutes. Turn heat to medium, then add fish pieces and cover. Simmer for about 20 minutes or until fish is cooked. Serve hot.

NOTE: *Chicken may be substituted for the fish but should be cooked for about 15 minutes longer or until tender.*

TAHINI

Similar in consistency and appearance to peanut butter but more subtle in taste, tahini has been a choice food in the countries that edge the eastern Mediterranean since time immemorial. The product of hulled and crushed sesame seeds, this delectable, nourishing, wholesome thick paste with a nutty flavour is the mayonnaise of the Middle East.

Tahini, also spelled *taheeni, taheneh,* or *tahineh,* which comes from the Arabic word *tahana* (to grind), is very nutritious, containing many of the food values needed by the human body. It has no cholesterol, is relatively sodium-free, and is made of approximately 50 percent fat, 20 percent protein, 16 percent carbohydrates, 5 percent fibre, and a good amount of calcium, iron, potassium, phosphorus, and vitamins C and E. In the Middle Eastern lands, it has long been believed that when combined with legumes tahini becomes the ultimate human edible. In past ages, this sesame seed product, besides being employed as a tasty food enhancer in the kitchen, was eaten to restore vitality and sex appeal, and as a bowel movement stimulant. Today, modern science has established that these ancient attributes have some merit, finding that sesame seeds have some anti-aging qualities helpful in the improvement of skin capillaries and the smooth movement of food through the body. Versatile in all types of cooking, tahini is utilized in a wide variety of everyday dishes. However, it is chiefly used as a basic vehicle in many sauces and dips and as a healthy substitute for butter on bread. ✣

—*Habeeb Salloum, "Tahini—A Health Food Par Excellence,"* Backwoods Home Magazine, 89 (2004): 77–79.

CHAPTER 12

VEGETARIAN PIES: DELICIOUS, NUTRITIOUS, AND EASY TO PREPARE

Pies or turnovers are found among the traditional foods of every culture. They are delicate, flavourful, and very satisfying, and many think that if all snack foods were ranked in order, these would, without question, lead the list.

I will always remember the aroma flowing out of the kitchen when, after returning from school as a child, I opened the door to our home. The mouth-watering smell of baking vegetarian or meat pies would increase my hunger pangs a hundredfold. No matter what type of pie Mother was making that day, the smell from the kitchen was captivating.

My mother seemed to have a never-ending storehouse of ideas for new pies. This was especially true in summer and autumn when our garden overflowed with vegetables. With no type of refrigeration at our disposal, during the warm months we ate very little meat. Hence, her vegetarian pies were a welcome addition to our diet. For lunch, snacks, or main courses, they were always delicious and unforgettable. The memory of these pies has always lingered with me. I have never tired of replicating my mother's pies and developing numerous other versions.

Known in the eastern Arab-speaking lands as *sambousak*, *fataayir*, or *lahma bi 'ajeen*, they were often packed for school lunches, enjoyed as snacks at home, or a meal my mother carried to Dad while he worked in the fields. When leaving their homelands, the emigrants from the Middle East, like our family, never forget their pies, especially those freshly baked, perfuming the home with their seductive aroma.

In that part of world, from the tiny *sambousak* to the larger *fataayir* or *lahma bi ʿajeen*, they are often offered as a savoury and appetizing "fast food." While North Americans munch on hot dogs, hamburgers, or pizza to satisfy the hunger pangs in our fast-paced lives, the peoples of the Greater Syria area turn instead to their delectable variety of pies. Partakers of these delights enjoy munching them on the streets—their enticing aromas flow from small bakeries and restaurants, too overpowering to resist. The first thing I do when I reach Damascus, Beirut, or any other urban centre in the Middle East is search for a bakery—and there are many—and the tempting fragrance of its pies.

Traditionally, pies are stuffed with meats or a combination of vegetables and meats. However, innovative cooks throughout the Middle East have, like my mother, often replaced the meats with almost every kind of vegetable. In the process they have created a great number of appetizing and succulent vegetarian pies and these have for centuries been an important food in the kitchens of these lands.

Pies can be made very small, medium-sized, or large enough for a one-person meal. The petite and medium versions can be served as appetizers, for snacks, as part of buffet meals, or as supplements to soups and salads. Large ones make a filling all-in-one entrée. Also, excellent for lunches and as picnic fare, they add much to the culinary world of sandwich-type foods.

Vegetarian pies can be stuffed with a wide variety of meatless ingredients, and most are simple to prepare. They can be made in advance and frozen, then removed and allowed to thaw half an hour before being baked. More flavourful when served hot, they lose only a little of their mouth-watering taste if eaten cold.

The following vegetarian pies are some of the ones Mother used to bake, and a number are my own creations.

DOUGH FOR PIES

FOR 12 TO 16 PIES

1 tbsp	sugar	15 ml
1 package	dry yeast	1 package
¼ cup	lukewarm water	60 ml
3 cups	flour	750 ml
½ tsp	salt	2 ml
⅛ tsp	ground ginger	½ ml
¾ cup	lukewarm milk	175 ml
4 tbsps	butter, melted	60 ml

1. Dissolve sugar and yeast in the lukewarm water, then allow to stand until yeast begins to froth—about 20 minutes.

2. In the meantime, combine flour, salt, and ginger in a mixing bowl, then make a well in the middle. Add yeast, milk, and butter. Knead into a dough, adding more flour or milk if necessary (do not allow the dough to become sticky). Shape into ball, then brush the outside with oil. Place on a floured tray or pan, then cover with a cloth. Allow to rest in warm spot until it becomes double in size.

NOTE: *An equal amount of frozen dough (1½ lbs or 680 g) will serve equally well for all of the following recipes.*

SPINACH PIES / FATAAYIR BI SABAANIKH

1	Dough for Pies recipe (page 151)	1
10 oz	spinach, thoroughly washed, drained and finely chopped	280 g
2	medium onions, chopped	2
½ cup	crumbled feta cheese	125 ml
1 tbsp	pine nuts or slivered almonds	15 ml
4 tbsps	olive oil	60 ml
2 tbsps	lemon juice	30 ml
¾ tsp	salt	3 ml
½ tsp	black pepper	2 ml
½ tsp	nutmeg	2 ml
⅛ tsp	cayenne	½ ml

1. Prepare dough for pies, then set aside.

2. Make a filling by thoroughly combining all remaining ingredients, then set aside.

3. Form dough into 12 to 16 balls, then place them on a floured tray. Cover with a cloth, then allow to stand in a warm place for 30 minutes.

4. Roll balls into 5- to 6-inch (12 to 15 cm) rounds, then place 2 heaping tablespoons (about 30 ml) of filling on each round, stirring the filling each time. (Alternatively, the filling can be divided into 12 to 16 equal parts.) Fold dough over the filling, then close by firmly pinching edges together into half-moon or triangle shape.

5. Place pies on well-greased baking trays, then bake in a 350°F (180°C) preheated oven for 20 minutes or until pies turn golden brown. Remove from oven, then brush with olive oil. Serve hot or cold.

The farm days allowed us only a handful of greens, such as green onions, lettuce, the occasional dandelion, and a certain type of mallow. It was only later, when I travelled to the larger cities, that I got my first taste of spinach, and luckily it was in a pie, prepared by my future wife!

FETA CHEESE PIES / FATAAYIR BI JIBN

Made with Syrian cheese, a product my mother made at home, these creamy pies became one of her signature best. Bringing the skill of cheese-making from her village, she continued the tradition on our Saskatchewan homestead. After the cheese had set, we would have it for breakfast, scooping it up with Mother's homemade Arab bread. My version of her recipe uses feta. With its tart salty nature, it works well with these cheese pies.

1	Dough for Pies recipe (page 151)	1
3 cups	crumbled feta cheese	750 ml
2	large onions, finely chopped	2
2 tbsps	finely chopped fresh cilantro	30 ml
4 tbsps	olive oil	60 ml
¾ tsp	black pepper	3 ml
¼ tsp	salt	1 ml
⅛ tsp	cayenne	½ ml

1. Prepare the dough for pies, then set aside.

2. Make a filling by thoroughly combining all remaining ingredients, then set aside.

3. Form dough into 12 to 16 balls, then place them on a floured tray. Cover with a cloth and allow to stand in a warm place for 30 minutes.

4. Roll balls into 5- to 6-inch (12 to 15 cm) rounds, then place 2 heaping tablespoons (about 30 ml) of filling on each round, stirring the filling each time. (Alternatively, the filling can be divided into 12 to 16 equal parts.) Fold dough over the filling, then close by firmly pinching edges together into half-moon or triangle shape.

5. Place pies on well-greased baking trays, then bake in a 350°F (180°C) preheated oven for 20 minutes or until pies turn golden brown. Remove from oven, then brush with olive oil. Serve hot or cold.

When I think back on the days on our homestead, the kitchen brings up the best memories. The wonderful aromas rising from Mother's oven were proof enough of her baking skills and her creative ideas to reproduce old country favourites with what was available on the farm. However, it was her cheese pies that remained authentic to the core.

Almost anything that came out of our garden Mother could use as an ingredient in fataayir. Leeks were not available during that period but green onions were. Mother put them to use in a variety of ways, fresh from the garden, accompanying labna, or in salads and stews. But it was her genius in preparing them for stuffing fataayir that especially satisfied her hungry family, particularly after a hard day's work. It was years and years later that I had my first taste of leeks and chose to use them in place of our garden's green onions in making her fataayir recipe.

LEEK PIES / FATAAYIR BI KURATH

1	Dough for Pies recipe (page 151)	1
4	heaping cups chopped leeks, thoroughly washed	1 L
4	medium onions, finely chopped	4
4	cloves garlic, crushed	4
1	small hot pepper, seeded and very finely chopped	1
2 tbsps	sumac *	30 ml
2 tbsps	finely chopped fresh cilantro	30 ml
¼ cup	olive oil	60 ml
¼ cup	lemon juice	60 ml
1 tsp	salt	5 ml
½ tsp	black pepper	2 ml

1. Prepare the dough for pies, then set aside.

2. Make a filling by thoroughly combining all remaining ingredients, then set aside.

3. Form dough into 12 to 16 balls, then place them on a floured tray. Cover with a cloth and allow to stand in a warm place for 30 minutes.

4. Roll balls into 5- to 6-inch (12 to 15 cm) rounds, then place 2 heaping tablespoons (about 30 ml) of filling on each round, stirring the filling each time. (Alternatively, the filling can be divided into 12 to 16 equal parts.) Fold dough over the filling, then close by firmly pinching edges together into half-moon or triangle shape.

5. Place pies on well-greased baking trays, then bake in a 350°F (180°C) preheated oven for 20 minutes or until pies turn golden brown. Remove from oven, then brush with olive oil. Serve hot or cold.

   * Sumac can be purchased from Middle Eastern grocery stores.

POTATO AND TOMATO PIES / FATAAYIR BI BATAATA WA BANADOORA

1	Dough for Pies recipe (page 151)	1
4 cups	shredded potatoes	1 L
2	medium tomatoes, finely chopped	2
1	large onion, finely chopped	1
1	small hot pepper, seeded and very finely chopped	1
2	cloves garlic, crushed	2
2 tbsps	finely chopped fresh cilantro	30 ml
2 tbsps	melted butter	30 ml
1	egg, beaten	1
1 tsp	salt	5 ml
1 tsp	cumin	5 ml
½ tsp	black pepper	2 ml

1. Prepare dough for pies, then set aside.

2. Make a filling by thoroughly combining all remaining ingredients, then set aside.

3. Form dough into 12 to 16 balls, then place them on a floured tray. Cover with a cloth and allow to stand in a warm place for 30 minutes.

4. Roll balls into 5- to 6-inch (12 to 15 cm) rounds, then place 2 heaping tablespoons (about 30 ml) of filling on each round, stirring the filling each time. (Alternatively, the filling can be divided into 12 to 16 equal parts.) Fold dough over the filling, then close by firmly pinching edges together into half-moon or triangle shape.

5. Place pies on well-greased baking trays, then bake in a 350°F (180°C) preheated oven for 20 minutes or until pies turn golden brown. Remove from oven, then brush with olive oil. Serve hot or cold.

Even during the rough years of the drought of the 1930s, our family survived well, thanks to our hand-watered garden, which produced essential vegetables that fed our family of ten.

Mother's potato and tomato fataayir were the result of the bounty of our garden. We would sit in anticipation as Mother placed them on the table, piping hot from the oven. No need for niceties as our hands overtook the tray, grabbing these delicious pies.

EGGPLANT AND TOMATO PIES / FATAAYIR BI BAADHINJAAN WA BANADOORA

In the spirit of Mother's culinary resourcefulness, I created this fataayir stuffing simply because nothing tastes so good as a medley of eggplant, tomatoes, and onions in a freshly baked piece of bread.

1	Dough for Pies recipe (page 151)	1
1 lb	eggplant	454 g
1 tsp	salt	5 ml
6 tbsps	olive oil	90 ml
2	medium onions, finely chopped	2
1	small hot pepper, seeded and finely chopped	2
4 cloves	garlic, crushed	2 cloves
2	large tomatoes, finely chopped	2
1 tsp	oregano	5 ml
½ tsp	black pepper	2 ml
2	eggs, beaten	2

1. Prepare dough for pies then set aside.

2. Peel eggplant and cut into ¼-inch (6 mm) cubes. Lightly sprinkle eggplant cubes with salt, then place in a strainer over a pot. Place heavy weight atop eggplant cubes, then allow to drain for 1 hour.

3. Heat oil in a frying pan, then sauté onions over medium heat for 10 minutes. Add eggplant, hot pepper, and garlic, then stir-fry for 5 minutes, adding more oil if necessary. Make filling by stirring in remaining ingredients, then stir-fry for a few more minutes. Allow to cool.

4. In the meantime, form dough into 12 to 16 balls, then place them on a floured tray. Cover with a cloth and allow to stand in a warm place for 30 minutes.

5. Roll balls into 5- to 6-inch (12 to 15 cm) rounds, then place 2 heaping tablespoons (about 30 ml) of filling on each round, stirring the filling each time. (Alternatively, the filling can be divided into 12 to 16 equal parts.) Fold dough over the filling, then close by firmly pinching edges together into half-moon or triangle shape.

6. Place pies on well-greased baking trays, then bake in a 350°F (180°C) preheated oven for 20 minutes or until pies turn golden brown. Remove from oven, then brush with olive oil. Serve hot or cold.

If your messenger tarries, expect good.

PEA AND ZUCCHINI PIES / FATAAYIR BI BIZILLA WA KOOSA

1	Dough for Pies recipe (page 151)	1
2½ cups	unpeeled zucchini, cut into ¼-inch (6 mm) cubes	625 ml
1½ cups	fresh or thawed frozen peas	375 ml
1	large onion, finely chopped	1
4	cloves garlic, crushed	4
½ cup	grated Parmesan cheese	125 ml
2	eggs, beaten	2
1 tsp	salt	5 ml
1 tsp	oregano	5 ml
½ tsp	black pepper	2 ml
½ tsp	paprika	2 ml
⅛ tsp	cayenne	½ ml

1. Prepare dough for pies, then set aside.

2. Make a filling by thoroughly mixing all remaining ingredients, then set aside.

3. Form dough into 12 to 16 balls, then place them on a floured tray. Cover with a cloth and allow to stand in a warm place for 30 minutes.

4. Roll balls into 5- to 6-inch (12 to 15 cm) rounds, then place 2 heaping tablespoons (about 30 ml) of filling on each round, stirring the filling each time. (Alternatively, the filling can be divided into 12 to 16 equal parts.) Fold dough over the filling, then close by firmly pinching edges together into half-moon or triangle shape.

5. Place pies on well-greased baking trays, then bake in a 350°F (180°C) preheated oven for 20 minutes or until pies turn golden brown. Remove from oven, then brush with olive oil. Serve hot or cold.

MUSHROOM AND COTTAGE CHEESE PIES

1	Dough for Pies recipe (page 151)	1
3 cups	thinly-sliced mushrooms, thoroughly washed	750 ml
1 cup	cottage cheese	250 ml
1 cup	chopped green onions	250 ml
1	medium sweet green pepper, seeded and finely chopped	1
¼ cup	finely chopped parsley	50 ml
2	cloves garlic, crushed	2
1	egg, beaten	1
3 tbsps	butter	45 ml
1 tsp	salt	5 ml
1 tsp	marjoram	5 ml
½ tsp	black pepper	2 ml
⅛ tsp	cayenne	½ ml

1. Prepare dough for pies, then set aside.

2. Make a filling by thoroughly combining all remaining ingredients, then set aside.

3. Form dough into 12 to 16 balls, then place them on a floured tray. Cover with a cloth and allow to stand in a warm place for 30 minutes.

4. Roll balls into 5- to 6-inch (12 to 15 cm) rounds, then place 2 heaping tablespoons (about 30 ml) of filling on each round, stirring the filling each time. (Alternatively, the filling can be divided into 12 to 16 equal parts.) Fold dough over the filling, then close by firmly pinching edges together into half-moon or triangle shape.

5. Place pies on well-greased baking trays, then bake in a 350°F (180°C) preheated oven for 20 minutes or until pies turn golden brown. Remove from oven, then brush with olive oil. Serve hot or cold.

There are plenty of people who will give you advice, but very few who will give you bread.

CORN AND PEPPER PIES

1	Dough for Pies recipe (page 151)	1
4 tbsps	butter	60 ml
1	medium sweet pepper, seeded and finely chopped	1
1	medium onion, finely chopped	1
1	small hot pepper seeded and finely chopped	1
4	cloves garlic, crushed	4
4½ cups	fresh corn or thawed frozen corn	1125 ml
½ cup	finely chopped parsley	125 ml
2	eggs, beaten	2
1 tsp	salt	5 ml
½ tsp	black pepper	2 ml
½ tsp	powdered mustard	2 ml
½ tsp	cumin	2 ml

1. Prepare dough for pies, then set aside.

2. In the meantime, prepare filling. Melt butter in a frying pan, then sauté sweet pepper, onion, hot pepper, and garlic over medium heat for 5 minutes. Add corn, then stir-fry for further 5 minutes. Stir in remaining ingredients, then remove from heat and allow to cool.

3. Form dough into 12 to 16 balls, then place them on a floured tray. Cover with a cloth and allow to stand in a warm place for 30 minutes.

4. Roll balls into 5- to 6-inch (12 to 15 cm) rounds, then place 2 heaping tablespoons (about 30 ml) of filling on each round, stirring the filling each time. (Alternatively, the filling can be divided into 12 to 16 equal parts.) Fold dough over the filling, then close by firmly pinching edges together into half-moon or triangle shape.

5. Place pies on well-greased baking trays, then bake in a 350°F (180°C) preheated oven for 20 minutes or until pies turn golden brown. Remove from oven, then brush with olive oil. Serve hot or cold.

EGG AND TOMATO PIES

1	Dough for Pies recipe (page 151)	1
4 tbsps	olive oil	60 ml
2	large onions, finely chopped	2
2	cloves garlic, crushed	2
2 tbsps	finely chopped fresh cilantro	30 ml
2 lbs	tomatoes, finely chopped	907 g
5	eggs, beaten	5
4 tbsps	chopped green olives	60 ml
1 tsp	salt	5 ml
1 tsp	dry basil	5 ml
½ tsp	black pepper	2 ml
⅛ tsp	cayenne	½ ml

1. Prepare dough for the pies, then set aside.

2. In the meantime, prepare the filling. Heat oil in a frying pan, then sauté onions, garlic, and cilantro over medium heat for 5 minutes. Stir in tomatoes and continue sautéing for another 5 minutes. Add remaining ingredients, then stir-fry for a minute or until eggs begin to gel. Remove from heat, then allow to cool.

3. Form dough into 12 to 16 balls, then place them on a floured tray. Cover with a slightly damp cloth and allow to stand in a warm place for 30 minutes.

4. Roll balls into 5- to 6-inch (12 to 15 cm) rounds, then place 2 heaping tablespoons (about 30 ml) of filling on each round, stirring the filling each time. (Alternatively, the filling can be divided into 12 to 16 equal parts.) Fold dough over the filling, then close by firmly pinching edges together into half-moon or triangle shape.

5. Place pies on well-greased baking trays, then bake in a 350°F (180°C) preheated oven for 20 minutes or until pies turn golden brown. Remove from oven, then brush with olive oil. Serve hot or cold.

These pies were one of my favourites, especially when we would take a break from working in the fields. Mother would bring them to us freshly baked and steaming hot—one of the good memories of doing my tedious chores on the farm.

THYME AND SUMAC PIES / MANAQEESH BI ZA'TAR

Perhaps it was za'tar, a spice-and-dried-herb mixture, that my parents missed most from Syria. So essential and basic was za'tar to the Syrian diet, and so beloved by my parents, that my mother made the mixture herself. My children and grandchildren were raised with it too. Indeed, no breakfast is complete without it, whether served on its own mixed with olive oil or by way of Manaqeesh Bi Za'tar. And now my great-grandchildren, when asked what they would like for breakfast, in near-unison respond, "za'tar!"

There is nothing closer to the eternal in this world than the baking of bread.

1	Dough for Pies recipe (page 151)	1
½ cup	olive oil	125 ml
3 tbsps	thyme	45 ml
3 tbsps	sumac *	45 ml
2 tbsps	sesame seeds	30 ml
1 tsp	marjoram	5 ml
¼ tsp	salt	1 ml
⅛ tsp	cayenne	½ ml

1. Prepare dough for pies, then set aside.

2. In the meantime, thoroughly mix all remaining ingredients, then set aside.

3. Form dough into 20 balls, then place them on a floured tray. Cover with a cloth, then allow to stand in a warm place for 30 minutes.

4. Roll balls into ⅛-inch (3 mm) thick rounds, then place on well-greased cookie tray. Spread the mixed ingredients evenly over top of rounds, then with fingertips make a few impressions in the dough. Bake in a 350°F (180°C) preheated oven for 15 minutes or until edges of pies turn light brown, then serve hot or cold.

* Sumac can be purchased from Middle Eastern grocery stores.

CHICKPEA PIES / MANAQEESH BI HUMMUS

Often prepared by my mother, chickpea pies are believed to have been eaten by the peasants in the Middle East since pre-Roman times.

1	Dough for Pies recipe (page 151)	1
4 tbsps	olive oil	60 ml
½ tsp	salt	2 ml
½ tsp	black pepper	2 ml
1 cup	chickpeas, soaked overnight and drained	250 ml

1. Prepare dough for pies, then set aside.

2. In the meantime, combine remaining ingredients, then set aside.

3. Form dough into 20 balls, then place them on a floured tray. Cover with a cloth, then allow to stand in a warm place for 30 minutes.

4. Roll balls into ⅛-inch (3 mm) thick rounds, then place on well-greased cookie tray. Stir chickpea mixture, then place about 1 tablespoon (15 ml) of mixture on each round. Press chickpeas evenly and firmly on rounds.

5. Bake in a 350°F (180°C) preheated oven for 15 minutes or until edges of pies turn light brown. Place under broiler until tops brown, then serve hot.

CHAPTER 13

THE DANDELION: A HEALTHY WEED RELISHED DURING THE PIONEERING YEARS

"Come! Get a pail and let's go! The *silq* [a colloquial Syrian-Arabic word meaning 'wild greens'] are at their prime today," my mother urged as she put on her boots. It had rained overnight, and the south Saskatchewan prairie land was soggy, but it smelled fresh after the night's rain.

The atmosphere felt invigorating as we made our way up a hill across the valley from our homestead abode. Trailing behind with a pail competing with my size, I was irritated, thinking, "Why are we picking weeds that our neighbour's children told me were poisonous even for animals?"

Little did I or our neighbour's kids know that these wild greens were among the healthiest foods in the world. There is no doubt that dandelions had a large hand in adding variety to our diet and keeping our family healthy during the years when the south Saskatchewan plains were turning into a desert of blowing sand.

In spring and early summer, the tender wild shoots of lamb's quarters or pig weed, sorrel, dandelion and a host of other prairie greens were part of our daily meals. Without question, they were responsible, to a great extent, for not one of us children ever needing to see a doctor during our growing years. Of course, there were other factors that helped to keep us away from medical facilities, such as the lack of money and the fact that the nearest doctor was twenty-five miles away—a considerable distance in the horse-and-buggy days.

With a sharp-pointed knife, my mother cut a few inches underground to the roots of tender dandelion and other plants with which the prairie land teemed. I shook the soil off before putting them in my pail. Back home, I felt relief after I left my mother to clean the greens while I joined my brother and sister in our daily play.

During late spring and early summer, year after year, we children would accompany our mother on the weekends through the unploughed prairie land to pick wild greens—and there were innumerable types. The Indigenous peoples of these lands traditionally have utilized over sixty types of these prairie edibles in their cooking.

In the Middle East, many of these weeds were well-known, and so my parents continued the tradition of using them in their daily cuisine. Hence, every year our kitchen overflowed with endless dishes made from these tasty and nutritious wild greens. However, as children, we never appreciated the delightful foods resulting from these wild plants. To

us, helping to pick them was only another of our boring farm tasks.

Of all the prairie greens, dandelion leaves were our favourite. Versatile and tasty before they

During late spring and early summer, year after year, we children would accompany our mother on the weekends through the unploughed prairie land to pick wild greens—and there were innumerable types.

flower and before the leaves become bitter and tough, they were excellent as ingredients in our omelets, salads, stews, and soups. I have fond memories of the many

dandelion dishes we ate during our homestead days.

Although North Americans generally view the dandelion as a bothersome weed, culinary artists in many parts of the world welcome it as one of the tastiest and most nourishing of foods, even with its slightly bitter taste.

Indeed, dandelions were part of the spring larder of some of the early settlers in Canada and the United States. Their tender new leaves with a distinct flavour were one of springtime's eagerly awaited treats and were likely responsible to some degree for the generally good health of these early pioneers. However, in the ensuing years dandelions were somewhat forgotten. Today, people spend hours digging them out of lawns, then change clothing and rush to the supermarket to buy similar greens.

A naughty perennial herb, dandelions derive their name from the French *dent de lion* (lion's tooth). They are believed to be native to Eurasia but are now found wild in open fields and backyards in almost every country of the world.

Most of the twenty-five species of dandelion grow from 2 to 12 inches (5 to 30 cm) high with long thick roots and rich-green, shiny, oblong toothed leaves, thickly clustered at the base. In the centre, leafless hollow stems topped by golden yellow flowers that mature to puffballs give the plant its character.

In the wild, the leaves must be picked when tender, in the early spring before flowers develop. As growth progresses and the blossoms appear, the leaves become bitter and tough, making them useless for salads. However, they can still be used as a food if they are soaked for 24 hours in a solution of one gallon (3.75 L) water, 2 tablespoons (30 ml) lemon juice, and 2 teaspoons (10 ml) salt, then drained and cooked in the same fashion as tender leaves.

In the larger cities of North America there is no need to worry about the tough leaves. Commercially grown dandelions, picked when tender, are on sale in specialty markets, and more recently, in some of the larger supermarkets. The leaves of the cultivated plant are larger, milder, and lighter green than those growing wild, and somewhat less nutritious. Nevertheless, cooks prefer the commercially grown variety, which requires much less work in its preparation.

Every bit of the dandelion plant can be used. The roots, which are reputed to have saved populations from starvation during famines, can be dug out, then trimmed, thoroughly washed, and cooked in the same manner as vegetables like carrots and parsnips, or made into a delicious coffee substitute.

This coffee-like drink is made by roasting the cleaned roots in a low-heat oven until they turn crisp and dry. These should then be stored in airtight containers and ground just before use. Some health food stores carry this coffee substitute, closely related to chicory, in powdered form. Both the homemade and purchased products contain the stimulant properties of coffee but without the caffeine.

The blossoms taste like mushrooms when batter fried and can also be made into an invigorating beer, mead, or wine. A great food for bees in early spring, these flowers known as "emblems of the sun" are associated with lovers eager to know their romantic fate. According to an old tradition, if one can blow all the seeds from a downy dandelion head, they are loved with passion. Another folkloric tale states that if one whispers a phrase of love before blowing off the fluff, the message will be carried to the beloved.

The leaves are without question the main part of the dandelion plant used in cooking. They are used as salad greens, cooked as vegetables, or made into tea. When cooking dandelion greens you need not add water. The moisture from the rinsing is enough for the cooking. They should be placed in a pot, covered, and cooked for 8 to 15 minutes. In all types of dishes they are excellent as a spinach substitute and are one of the healthiest foods known.

The Greek botanical name *taraxacum*, meaning "remedy for disorders," indicates that dandelions have been used as a medicine for many centuries. In the Middle Ages, Arab physicians prescribed them as a tonic for eye remedies and stomach ailments. Also, European medieval herbalists made fantastic claims about their medicinal qualities. They used the flowers, juice, leaves, and roots for improving eyesight, cleansing wounds, relieving skin afflictions, curing jaundice, removing obstructions of the liver, gall bladder and spleen, and cleansing ulcers from the urinary tract.

Modern medicine has scientifically proven that most of the medieval prescriptions were not figments of the imaginations of medieval doctors. Dandelions are indeed rich in minerals and nutrients. They are one of the vegetable kingdom's richest sources of vitamin A, calcium, iron, and potassium, and also contain small amounts of carbohydrates, fibre, magnesium, protein, fat, and vitamin C. The leaves have as much iron as spinach. They have 50 times more vitamin A than asparagus; 25 times more than tomato juice; 7 times more than lettuce or carrots; and 5 times more than broccoli.

Beverages made from the leaves or roots aid in the cure of kidney and liver infections, and are valuable in the treatment of arthritis, colds, diabetes, and rheumatism. The juice strengthens the teeth and gums, and the cooked leaves help alleviate dermatitis, eczema, and other skin diseases. In addition, they are recommended for acidosis, anemia, constipation, emaciation, low blood pressure, and poor circulation.

For preservation, the leaves must be washed and re-washed, preferably every leaf separately under running water. They can then be stored in perforated plastic bags in the refrigerator where they will remain crisp and fresh for about five days. If to be kept for a longer period, they should be blanched for one minute in boiling water, then drained, placed in plastic bags, and frozen.

In taste and nutritional value, it matters not if dandelions are frozen or fresh. Grown in the wild or cultivated as a garden plant, every part of this much-maligned green can be used in cooking. In fact, one can prepare an entire meal from dandelions alone: the leaves can be made into a delicious salad; the roots, after being thoroughly cleaned, steamed, and buttered, can be served as a main dish; while a wine made from dandelion flowers can accompany the meal. Finally, a coffee made from roasted dandelion roots could serve as a conclusion to this healthy and hearty culinary spread.

For those not familiar with dandelion greens, perhaps these simple recipes, the majority of which we enjoyed during our homesteading days, will serve as an introduction to the exotic dandelion world. ✄

DANDELION WITH ONIONS / ʿASSOORA

SERVES 4

Because of the abundance of dandelions on our homestead in early spring, this traditional Syrian dish was presented as our vegetable serving with many a meal. ʿAssoora means 'squeezed out', referring to the process of squeezing out the excess water from the dandelion and squeezing fresh lemon juice over it. When dandelions were not available, Mother would use beet greens. Nothing went to waste.

This and all of the following dandelion recipes call for commercially grown dandelions. However, an equal amount of the wild plant may be substituted.

1 lb	dandelion leaves, thoroughly washed and chopped	454 g
4 tbsps	olive oil	60 ml
2	medium onions, finely chopped	2
2	cloves garlic, crushed	2
2 tbsps	finely chopped fresh cilantro	30 ml
½ tsp	salt	2 ml
¼ tsp	black pepper	1 ml
pinch	cayenne	pinch
1	lemon, halved	1

1. Fill a large saucepan with water and bring to boil. Add dandelion and boil for 5 minutes. Drain dandelion in a sieve and when somewhat cooled, press with a wooden spoon to squeeze out the water. Set aside.

2. Heat the oil in a saucepan, then sauté the onions and garlic for 12 minutes over medium heat. Stir in cilantro, salt, pepper, and cayenne, then stir in the dandelion and mix well. Squeeze juice of half a lemon over the mixture, then cover and cook over low heat for 3 to 5 minutes.

3. Transfer saucepan contents to serving dish and let cool. Serve at room temperature. Squeeze remaining lemon over individual servings if desired.

DANDELION AND CHEESE APPETIZER

This is my creation of an absolutely delicious dip using dandelions and cream cheese as the main ingredients. While growing up we had the same dip, except labna *was used in place of the cream cheese. We also enjoyed it best scooping it up with freshly baked thin Arab bread* (marqūq).

3 packed cups	finely chopped dandelion leaves	750 ml
8 oz	cream cheese	227 g
½ cup	blanched almonds	125 ml
3 tbsps	lemon juice	45 ml
2 tbsps	olive oil	30 ml
1	clove garlic, crushed	1
½ tsp	salt	2 ml
¼ tsp	black pepper	1 ml
⅛ tsp	cayenne	½ ml
1	small tomato, finely chopped	1

1. Place all the ingredients, except tomato, in a food processor and process into smooth paste. Place on a serving platter, then decorate with tomato. Chill for a few hours before serving.

One man's weed is another man's treasure.

SCRAMBLED EGGS WITH DANDELION

SERVES 4

This recipe makes an excellent breakfast dish.

4 tbsps	butter	60 ml
4 packed cups	finely chopped dandelion leaves	1 L
1 tbsp	finely chopped fresh cilantro	15 ml
½ tsp	salt	2 ml
¼ tsp	black pepper	1 ml
6	eggs, beaten	6

1. Melt butter in a frying pan, then add dandelion and cilantro. Cover, then cook over low heat for 15 minutes.

2. In the meantime, combine salt and pepper with eggs, then pour over dandelions and stir-fry until the eggs are cooked. Serve immediately.

When your son is young, discipline him; when he grows older, be a brother to him.

DANDELION-LENTIL SOUP / SHAWRABAT HINDBA WA 'ADAS

SERVES 10 TO 12

In the spring, after coming in from the fields, we would often be greeted by this soup, piping hot, ready on the table.

1 cup	brown or green lentils, rinsed	250 ml
9 cups	water	2250 ml
4 tbsps	cooking oil	60 ml
1	large onion, finely chopped	1
4	cloves garlic, crushed	4
1	small hot pepper, seeded and finely chopped	1
1 tbsp	finely grated fresh ginger	15 ml
1 lb	dandelion leaves, thoroughly washed and chopped	454 g
¼ cup	rice	60 ml
4 tbsps	lemon juice	60 ml
1½ tsps	salt	7 ml
1 tsp	cumin	5 ml
½ tsp	black pepper	2 ml

1. Place lentils and water into a saucepan, then bring to boil. Cover, then cook over medium heat for 30 minutes.

2. In the meantime, heat oil in a frying pan, then sauté onion, garlic, hot pepper, and ginger over medium heat for 12 minutes. Transfer frying pan contents to the lentils, then stir in remaining ingredients. Bring to boil, then cover and cook over medium heat for 20 minutes. Serve hot.

Once someone has had a bad experience, he will always be cautious.

DANDELION AND CHEESE SALAD

SERVES 6 TO 8

*In Syria and Lebanon, a similar salad is served
with* kishk *instead of the feta cheese.*

1 lb	dandelion leaves, thoroughly washed and finely chopped	454 g
3	medium tomatoes, diced into ½-inch (1 cm) cubes	3
1 cup	finely chopped green onions	250 ml
1 cup	crumbled feta cheese	250 ml
1	clove garlic, crushed	1
4 tbsps	olive oil	60 ml
4 tbsps	lemon juice	60 ml
1½ tsps	oregano	7 ml
½ tsp	salt	2 ml
½ tsp	black pepper	2 ml

1. Toss dandelion, tomatoes, onions, and cheese in a salad bowl, then set aside.

2. Combine remaining ingredients in a separate bowl, then pour over salad bowl contents and toss just before serving.

*Whoever gets between
the onion and its skin will
get nothing but its stink.*

CORNED BEEF AND DANDELION SALAD

SERVES 4 TO 6

In my search for new ideas for salads, I decided to use my homestead prowess and combine it with one of my favourite processed meats. The final result—a great salad that provides both meat and greens in one dish!

1 lb	dandelion leaves, thoroughly washed, drained well, and finely chopped	454 g
4 tbsps	cooking oil	60 ml
¼ lb	uncooked corned beef, cut into very small pieces	113 g
2	cloves garlic, crushed	2
4 tbsps	lemon juice	60 ml
1 tsp	ground mustard	5 ml
¾ tsp	salt	3 ml
½ tsp	black pepper	2 ml
⅛ tsp	cayenne	½ ml

1. Place dandelions in a salad bowl, then set aside.

2. Heat oil in a frying pan, then stir-fry corned beef over medium heat for 10 minutes. Add frying pan contents to dandelions, then toss.

3. Combine remaining ingredients in a separate bowl, then pour over salad bowl contents. Toss and serve.

Even paradise is no fun without people.

DANDELION AND YOGURT

SERVES 4 TO 6

*For my mother, this dish was a new take on Cucumber and
Yogurt Salad (page 186) since dandelions were always around.
Her motto?—"Use them rather than waste them."*

1 lb	dandelion leaves, thoroughly washed and finely chopped	454 g
¼ cup	water	60 ml
2 cups	plain yogurt	500 ml
2	cloves garlic, crushed	2
2 tbsps	finely chopped fresh cilantro	30 ml
½ tsp	black pepper	2 ml
½ tsp	salt	2 ml

1. Place dandelion and water in a frying pan, then cover. Cook over low heat for 15 minutes, then allow to cool.

2. Place the remaining ingredients in a serving bowl, then thoroughly mix. Stir in the frying pan contents, then serve.

*Why should a man die
who grows sage in his garden?*

DANDELION AND RICE

SERVES 6 TO 8

Another one of my mother's great creations, Dandelion and Rice was a great way for Mother to enforce her rule on us children—that we needed to eat vitamin-rich greens to be strong and healthy. Knowing that we all loved rice, she incorporated dandelions in it so that we couldn't help but eat our necessary greens.

5 tbsps	butter	75 ml
2	medium onions, finely chopped	2
2	cloves garlic, crushed	2
½	small hot pepper, seeded and finely chopped	½
1 lb	dandelion leaves, thoroughly washed and finely chopped	454 g
½ tsp	salt	2 ml
¼ tsp	black pepper	1 ml
1 cup	rice, rinsed	250 ml
2½ cups	water	625 ml

1. Melt butter in a frying pan, then sauté onions, garlic, and hot pepper over medium heat for 10 minutes. Add dandelion, then cover and cook over low heat for 10 minutes. Stir in remaining ingredients, then bring to a boil. Cover and cook over medium-low heat for 20 minutes, then shut off heat and allow to cook in its own steam for a further 20 minutes. Serve hot.

*They said to the mule,
"Who is your father?"
He said,
"The horse is my uncle."*

FROM DEODORANTS TO
ASPARAGUS TO TABLE
ARRANGEMENTS

*Ziryab, one of the greatest
teachers of musicians
and singers of all time,
arrived in Andalusia
under the patronage of
Abd al-Rahman II in
821 CE from the court
of Baghdad....Ziryab's
contribution in the field
of music was great, but he
was also credited with the
introduction into Europe
of: deodorants and the
spraying of rosewater
on garments; new
types of dishes,*

(continued on next page...)

DANDELION PIES / FATAAYIR BI HINDBA

MAKES 12 TO 16 PIES

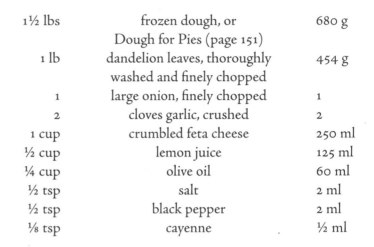

1½ lbs	frozen dough, or Dough for Pies (page 151)	680 g
1 lb	dandelion leaves, thoroughly washed and finely chopped	454 g
1	large onion, finely chopped	1
2	cloves garlic, crushed	2
1 cup	crumbled feta cheese	250 ml
½ cup	lemon juice	125 ml
¼ cup	olive oil	60 ml
½ tsp	salt	2 ml
½ tsp	black pepper	2 ml
⅛ tsp	cayenne	½ ml

1. If frozen, thaw dough.

2. Cut dough into 12 to 16 pieces, then roll into balls. Cover with a cloth, then allow to rest for 30 minutes.

3. In the meantime, thoroughly combine remaining ingredients to make a filling, then set aside.

4. Roll out the dough balls on a floured board to between 5- and 6-inch (13 to 15 cm) rounds—one at a time. Place 2 heaping tbsps (30 ml) of filling on a round, then pinch closed into triangle shape with fingers dipped in flour. Stir filling before placing filling on each round.

5. Place pies on a greased baking pan, then bake in a 350°F (180°C) preheated oven for 20 minutes or until pies turn golden brown.

6. Remove from oven, then brush with oil and serve hot or cold.

DANDELION AND MEATBALLS

SERVES *6 TO 8*

Meatballs are usually associated with spaghetti. Because spaghetti is not one of my favourites, I put together this meatball dish, a type of tajine to prove to the world that those thin long noodles are good, but dandelions and chickpeas cooked with meatballs taste even better.

1 lb	ground lean beef	454 g
1	medium onion, very finely chopped	1
4	cloves garlic, crushed	4
2 tbsps	finely chopped fresh cilantro	30 ml
2	eggs, beaten	2
⅓ cup	fine bread crumbs	75 ml
½ tsp	cumin	2 ml
½ tsp	black pepper	2 ml
⅛ tsp	cayenne	½ ml
4 tbsps	butter	60 ml
1 lb	dandelion leaves, thoroughly washed and chopped	454 g
2 cups	cooked chickpeas	500 ml
1 tsp	ground ginger	5 ml
1 tsp	salt	5 ml
1½ cups	water	375 ml

1. In a mixing bowl, combine beef, onion, garlic, cilantro, eggs, bread crumbs, cumin, pepper, and cayenne, then form into marble-sized balls and set aside.

2. Melt butter in a saucepan, then sauté meatballs over medium heat until golden brown. Add remaining ingredients and cover, then simmer over low heat for 1 hour, stirring occasionally and adding more water if necessary. Serve hot.

(...continued)

including asparagus; finely made leather cloaks; drinking out of glass instead of plate; eating snacks between meals; and the correct arrangement of meals. There are not many today who know that the method of how food is served in the Western world was established by Ziryab over 1100 years ago.

—from Habeeb Salloum's Journeys Back to Arab Spain, *Toronto: Middle East Studies Centre, 1994, 174.*

DANDELION TEA / SHAY HINDBA

Sometimes I find it ironic that the foods and beverages on which we were raised, and which, in many cases, were frowned upon by others, have now reached the status of health foods.

4 cups	water	1 L
1½ cups	dandelion leaves, packed	375 ml
1 tsp	orange or rose blossom water	5 ml

1. Pour water into a metal teapot, then bring to boil. Add dandelion leaves and orange or rose blossom water, then steep for 5 minutes before serving.

Let experts or professionals do things for you, however expensive it may be. In the long run, it pays.

CHAPTER 14

MINT BROUGHT FLAVOUR AND FRAGRANCE TO OUR FOOD IN THE DEPRESSION YEARS

"Why are you growing these smelly weeds in your garden?" Our neighbour's wife was walking with my mother, praising our thriving garden, until they stopped at a patch of mint edging our homestead well. As my mother explained to her how we used mint almost every day—in spring and summer fresh, and during the remainder of the year dried—I, a lad of perhaps ten, listened to their conversation as I drew buckets of water from the well. I could not believe that our neighbour did not use this fragrant herb which I loved.

In Mother and Dad's "old country," mint leaves are used in every course of the meal, from appetizers to desserts and drinks, especially tea. They added much to the taste of my mother's jellies, salads, sauces, and soups as well as giving a tang to a wide variety of yogurt and stuffed vegetable dishes.

This inherited tradition of including mint almost daily helped immensely in perking up our meals during the Depression years. With no money to buy other herbs and spices, mint was our top food enhancer. Going well with beans, burghul, carrots, eggplant, lentils, peas, potatoes, and tomatoes, it was a lifesaver when it came to preparing tasty dishes.

Of course, as we enjoyed our mint-flavoured foods, none of our family had any idea about the folklore of mint or its history. Yet, this ancient herb, besides being appetizing and aromatic, has had a long and illustrious history.

To the ancient Greeks, this herb was once Mentha, the nymph who was kidnapped by Pluto, ruler of the underworld, to be his lover. Pluto's wife Persephone, finding Mentha in his arms, flew into a jealous rage and trampled the nymph into the ground. Pluto could not undo his wife's spell, but to soften it a little and protect his love, he transformed her into the herb that we know as mint. Ovid, the Roman poet, assures us that Mentha lives on as mint, destined to be stomped on in order to give out her sweet fragrant smell.

Aristotle claimed that mint was an aphrodisiac, and according to some early writers mint leaves left potential lovers in "mint" condition, stirring up the mind and taste to greedy desire. Alexander the Great felt that mint so erotically aroused his soldiers that it took away their desire to fight.

The Pharisees paid their tithes in mint, and the Romans crowned themselves with this fragrant herb. According to the Roman scholar Pliny, the smell of mint stirs up the mind and appetite to an avaricious desire for food.

Of course, these historic attributes only add to the merits of mint—one of the most popular herbs, commonly garden-grown, but also found in the wild. Native to the Mediterranean, but now cultivated worldwide, mint comes in over 2,000 species—all labeled simply as "mint." However, the *Mentha* species, which includes 25 to 40 types, is the true mint. From among these are apple mint, Bergamot mint, lemon mint, pineapple mint, and water mint, but the three types most often cultivated are pennyroyal, peppermint, and spearmint or garden mint. Pennyroyal is bitter tasting and not usually used in cooking, but is the top source of the medically important menthol; peppermint, distinguished by its purple stems, defuses a strong odour and taste of menthol; and spearmint, the oldest of all mints is believed to be the one mentioned in the Bible. The latter, a favourite of the Greeks and Romans, is, to many,

According to the Roman scholar Pliny, the smell of mint stirs up the mind and appetite to an avaricious desire for food.

the best all-purpose variety. Even though most mints can be used interchangeably, only peppermint and spearmint are usually retailed.

Like all other mints, spearmint is a perennial that sprouts from quickly spreading roots or cuttings. It grows easily, but not from seeds. Instead, it is spread rapidly by way of wandering deep-reaching roots which, if not checked, quickly become an unwanted garden weed. Valued for its qualities as an insect repellent, it matures into a green, square-stemmed plant with bright lance-shaped leaves and lilac or pink flowers. Its leaves can be picked at any time, but are at their best when young and tender, before the plant flowers.

Cultivated since the dawn of history in the Middle East and the Far East, this herb has always been highly valued for its refreshing scent and pleasant taste. In the Middle Ages, its aromatic volatile oil, menthol, which all types of mint contain, made it ideal to strew around kitchens and sick rooms to freshen the air. Nevertheless, through the centuries, it has been, above all, renowned for its use in the culinary arts and medicine.

In the ancient and medieval worlds, mint was used to: repress the curdling of a mother's breast milk; stop bad breath, hiccoughing, and vomiting; aid with child-bearing and digestion; and as a relief for difficult menstruation, sore gums, stomach disorders, and gonorrhea.

Modern research has established that most of the ancient uses of mint in the medical field have a firm base. Today, mint is noted for giving medicine a pleasant taste, and for its anti-flatulent, anti-spasmodic, and stimulant attributes. Experimentation has established that it helps in relieving both nausea and diarrhea, and stimulates the menstrual flow. A few drops of mint oil mixed with water helps to alleviate the common cold or flu, colic in babies, insomnia, and headaches or toothaches.

Oil extracted from the leaves is used to flavour alcoholic and soft drinks, chewing gums, confections, cosmetics, detergents, soaps, and toothpastes. Yet, in spite of all its medical and other attributes, mint's main use is for culinary purposes.

Throughout Europe and North America, mint is the essential ingredient in a sauce for roast lamb and to enhance the roast itself. Mint leaves wrapped around whole garlic cloves, then placed in incisions throughout the leg of lamb, are used to heighten the flavour of the meat.

The flavour of mint leaves is best when they are picked fresh. If wrapped with a damp towel and refrigerated, they will keep for about a week. The leaves can be dried, but they lose some of their flavour and aroma. One teaspoon of dried, finely crushed mint leaves may be substituted for 4 tablespoons of fresh mint. Last, but not least, mint is one of the great decorating herbs for the plate. In the Middle East and North Africa, mint is an essential ingredient for embellishing all types of food. My parents always understood during their homesteading years that mint was a gourmet garden green, rather than a weed.

The following dishes are a small sample of how mint spices up food and gives it an enticing aroma. ⌘

MINT-FLAVOURED LENTIL SOUP / SHAWRABAT 'ADAS MA'A NA'NA'

SERVES 6 TO 8

In the Depression years during the 1930s, our family often enjoyed this dish. However, in those days, ginger and cumin were unknown in Saskatchewan grocery stores. Mother made do without these exotic spices, but her soups, no matter what, were the best. As the years went by and more international food products became available, Mother continued to cook delectable meals using the now available condiments from the Middle East and other lands. During the forty years of my mother's life in Canada, she never ceased to prepare the foods of the "old country."

4 tbsps	olive oil	60 ml
2	medium onions, chopped	2
4	cloves garlic, crushed	4
1	small hot pepper, seeded and finely chopped	1
1 tbsp	grated fresh ginger	15 ml
2 cups	stewed tomatoes	500 ml
7 cups	hot water	1750 ml
1 cup	brown or green lentils	250 ml
2½ tsps	salt	12 ml
1 tsp	cumin	5 ml
1 tsp	black pepper	5 ml
4 tbsps	finely chopped fresh mint	60 ml

1. Heat oil in a saucepan, then sauté onions, garlic, hot pepper, and ginger over medium heat for 10 minutes. Stir in remaining ingredients, except mint, then bring to boil. Cover and cook over medium heat for 45 minutes or until lentils are well cooked, adding more water if necessary. Stir in mint, then serve.

MINT AND CARAWAY SOUP / SHAWRABAT NA'NA' WA KARAAWIYA

SERVES 6

During the Depression years, my mother substituted other herbs or spices that we had on hand for the caraway. She used to say, "If I only had caraway, then you would see how tasty this soup can be."

6 cups	water	1500 ml
2 tbsps	flour, dissolved in ½ cup (125 ml) water	30 ml
2 cups	very finely chopped fresh mint leaves	500 ml
1 tbsp	ground caraway seeds	15 ml
3 tbsps	butter	45 ml
1 tsp	salt	5 ml
1 tsp	black pepper	5 ml
¼ cup	lemon juice	60 ml

1. Heat water in a saucepan, but before it comes to boil, slowly stir in flour-water mixture. Add remaining ingredients, except lemon juice, then bring to boil, stirring constantly. Remove from heat, then stir in lemon juice. Serve immediately. If soup is not served at once, it will lose much of its taste.

Live together like brothers and do business like strangers.

TOMATO-MINT SALAD / SALATAT BANADOORA MA'A NA'NA'

SERVES 4

There is no better way to begin a meal than with this refreshing mint-enhanced salad.

4	medium tomatoes	4
1	small onion	1
4 tbsps	chopped fresh mint	60 ml
3 tbsps	olive oil	45 ml
2 tbsps	vinegar	30 ml
½ tsp	salt	2 ml
¼ tsp	black pepper	1 ml

1. Quarter tomatoes and slice thinly. Halve the onion, and slice thinly. Place tomatoes and onion in a salad bowl. In another bowl, thoroughly combine remaining ingredients, then stir into tomato and onion mixture just before serving.

He who craves heights must stay up nights.

BREAD AND VEGETABLE SALAD / FATTOOSH

SERVES 8 TO 10

One of the most popular and healthy salads in the Middle East, Fattoosh can be served as a main course—perfect for a summer lunch.

	large loaf Arab bread (pita) or 4 thin slices white bread	
1	medium cucumber, peeled and chopped	1
½	head of lettuce, chopped	½
1	medium sweet red pepper, seeded and finely chopped	1
4	medium firm ripe tomatoes, chopped	4
1	small bunch parsley, finely chopped	1
2 cups	finely chopped green onions	500 ml
½ cup	finely chopped fresh mint	125 ml
2	cloves garlic, crushed	2
5 tbsps	olive oil	75 ml
5 tbsps	lemon juice	75 ml
1 tsp	salt	5 ml
½ tsp	black pepper	2 ml
2 tbsps	sumac *	30 ml

1. Toast the pita or bread until brown, then break into small pieces. Set aside.

2. Place all vegetables in a salad bowl, then toss.

3. Combine remaining ingredients, except bread, then pour over vegetables. Add bread, toss again, then serve immediately, before bread becomes soft.

   * Sumac can be purchased from Middle Eastern grocery stores.

You can substitute 2 teaspoons (10 ml) dried crushed mint for the fresh mint in this recipe.

CUCUMBER AND YOGURT SALAD / KHIYAAR BI LABAN

SERVES 6

3	cloves garlic, crushed	3
1 tsp	salt	5 ml
½ tsp	black pepper	2 ml
1 quart	plain yogurt	1 L
2	medium cucumbers, peeled and diced	2
2 tbsps	dried mint	30 ml

1. Place garlic, salt, pepper, and yogurt in a serving bowl, then combine thoroughly. Stir in cucumbers and mint, then mix. Chill before serving.

MINT-FLAVOURED FRUIT SALAD

SERVES 6 TO 8

1	small cantaloupe, diced into ½-inch (1 cm) cubes	1
2 cups	½-inch (1 cm) cubes of papaya	500 ml
2 cups	½-inch (1 cm) cubes of pineapple	500 ml
2	medium bananas, cut in halves, then sliced into ¼-inch (6 mm) thick half-rounds	2
½ cup	finely chopped fresh mint	125 ml
2 tbsps	sugar	30 ml

1. Combine all fruit in a serving bowl, then sprinkle with mint and sugar. Gently stir then serve immediately.

NOTE: *Other fruits can be used interchangeably with the ingredients indicated. This dish may be served as a salad or dessert.*

MINTED PEAS

SERVES 4

*This simple-to-prepare recipe gives taste and colour to
a meal, especially when served as a side dish.*

2 cups	fresh or frozen peas	500 ml
2 tbsps	finely chopped fresh mint	30 ml
2 tbsps	olive oil	30 ml
½ tsp	salt	2 ml
¼ tsp	black pepper	1 ml

1. Place peas in a saucepan, then barely cover with water. Bring to boil, then cover and cook over medium heat for 10 minutes. Stir in remaining ingredients, then serve.

MINTED POTATOES

SERVES 4 TO 6

Mint goes well with potatoes cooked any way.

2 lbs	potatoes	907 g
6 tbsps	olive oil	90 ml
½ cup	finely chopped fresh mint	125 ml
4 tbsps	vinegar	60 ml
1 tsp	salt	5 ml
½ tsp	black pepper	2 ml

1. Peel potatoes and dice into ½-inch (1 cm) cubes.

2. Heat oil in a frying pan, then sauté potato cubes over medium-low heat until they turn light brown, stirring a few times. Sprinkle with remaining ingredients, then thoroughly combine and serve.

HONEY-MINTED PEACHES

SERVES 4

This tasty dessert can be made by substituting a variety of fruits like apricots or mangos for the peaches.

5 tbsps	honey	75 ml
5 tbsps	lemon juice	75 ml
2 tbsps	chopped fresh mint leaves	30 ml
3 cups	sliced peaches	750 ml
	a few extra mint leaves	

1. Place honey, lemon juice, and mint in a saucepan, then bring to boil to make syrup. Strain, then set aside to cool.

2. Place peaches in a serving bowl, then stir in syrup. Garnish with mint leaves and serve.

MINT HONEY DRINK

Simple to prepare, this pleasant drink can be used to relieve a whole series of stomach ailments and headaches.

½ cup	fresh mint leaves, firmly packed	125 ml
1 tbsp	honey	15 ml
2 cups	boiling water	500 ml

1. Place mint and honey in a teapot, then pour in boiling water. Cover and allow to steep for 1 hour before serving.

MINT TEA / SHAY NA'NA'

SERVES 4

Mother often prepared this tea on the farm, especially when we children had stomach aches. In Morocco, where it is the country's national drink, it is consumed at all times of the day by people from every stratum of society. Whether served in a humble café, an elaborate restaurant, or at home, this special mint tea is the refreshment most loved by the Moroccans and the other peoples of North Africa. The only difference between Moroccan tea and our tea is that on the farm we used a little or no sugar while in Morocco a good amount of sugar is used. Morocco is known for its special tea ceremony where the beverage is poured from a silver teapot high above the serving tea glass in order to form bubbles.

1½ tbsps	green tea leaves	25 ml
4½ cups	boiling water	1125 ml
½ cup	firmly packed fresh mint leaves with stalks	125 ml
4 tsps	sugar	20 ml

1. Rinse teapot with hot tap water; then add green tea. To remove bitterness, pour in ½ cup (125 ml) boiling water and swish around in pot quickly. Discard water, but make sure not to throw away tea. Stuff mint leaves with their stalks in pot, then add sugar and remainder of boiling water. Allow to steep for 5 minutes, checking occasionally to make sure mint does not rise above water. Stir and taste, adding more sugar if necessary before serving.

   NOTE: *For second helpings, leave mint and tea in the pot; then add 1 teaspoon (5 ml) of tea, several mint leaves, and some sugar. Add again the same amount of boiling water. When mint rises to surface, the tea is ready. Stir and taste for sugar; then serve. The same process can be repeated for the third pot. Also, tea can be served by omitting the sugar, allowing diners to add sugar to suit their own taste.*

If green tea is not available, Indian tea may be substituted.

If fresh mint is not available, dried mint leaves may be used (but are not as good). Use 2 teaspoons (10 ml) finely crushed dried mint leaves.

CHAPTER 15

OLIVES: A CULINARY JOY DISCOVERED IN MY EARLY YEARS

The spring of 1935 was a memorable time that I will always cherish. It all began on one particular day when my father had just returned from town with our friend and neighbour Albert Hattum. With them they brought untold varieties of Middle Eastern foods and ingredients which I had never dreamed existed. Now as I helped them bring the groceries into the house from our wagon, I was giddy with delight.

For days my parents had talked about the *ḥalāwà* (halvah), *qaḍāma* (roasted chickpeas), *mulabbas* (candy-coated almonds), and olives they had ordered from Abusamra Al-Khouri, a wholesaler-retailer of Middle Eastern groceries in Montreal. I had never heard of, let alone tasted, these foods, and my parents had not enjoyed them since they left Syria some eleven years before. All these delights had been paid for jointly by my father and Albert Hattum, but it was my father who had ordered them since, unlike Albert Hattum, he could read and write.

Now it was time to evenly divide what were then, to me, strange foods. We children stood amazed, watching them divide the cartons of halvah, roasted chickpeas, and almond candies. Of course, as they worked, they would every once in while give us a taste of these Middle Eastern treasures.

The last to be divided was the small barrel of black olives. After they had filled two large tubs, Albert took the small pail they were using and, after filling it with olives from his portion, gave it to my father. Even though illiterate, he still preserved the Arab virtues of his ancestors—from among these, generosity. Since my father had done the ordering, he wanted to thank him.

Strangely, I liked the first olive that I ever tasted, and this fondness for olives has always remained with me. The next day we enjoyed for our lunch at school Arab bread sandwiches stuffed with olives. One of my schoolmates, seeing that I had something different for lunch, asked what I was eating. Taking one of the olives from the sandwich, I gave it to him to taste. Quickly he spit it out, commenting, "How can you eat this horrible foreign food!"

I was stunned. I had loved my first taste of an olive, and this was long before I came to know of its many health and culinary benefits. Through the years and until now, many times when I have olives for breakfast, I recall that incident with my schoolmate, thinking of how much he had missed in life by rejecting one of the oldest foods known to humankind.

The olive tree is one of the most useful plants in the world; its by-products have always been employed in myriad ways. In ancient times, a single olive tree provided a family with a year-round supply of food, oil for healing, fuel for cooking, and wood for housing, furniture, and jewellery. Hence, for

millennia, it has been a symbol of wealth, stability, and the tranquility of a self-sufficient farming society.

In Greek mythology, the goddess Athena created the olive tree to win a dispute with Poseidon, the god of the sea. The olive tree is said to have been first grown in the Garden of Eden. The Bible makes at least 140 references to olives and their oil. In the story of Noah, the dove that heralds the new era after the deluge appears carrying an olive branch. In the Qur'an, the olive tree, referred to as blessed, has sacred associations. Even today its mystical lure continues. An olive branch, a token of peace since Biblical times, graces the flag of the United Nations.

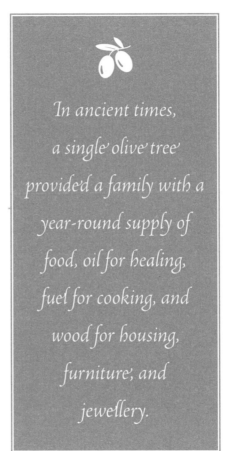

In ancient times, a single olive tree provided a family with a year-round supply of food, oil for healing, fuel for cooking, and wood for housing, furniture, and jewellery.

In our time, the olive tree remains a very valued plant to the farmers of the Mediterranean countries, accounting for 98 percent of the olives grown in the world. Worldwide, Spain is the largest producer of olives, while Italy is the second largest; beyond the Mediterranean, olives are also grown in parts of Australia, California, and South America.

Olives are the fruit of an evergreen tree with small greenish-silvery leaves that bear clusters of fragrant white flowers. The plant, started from a cutting, grows to a height of 10 to 40 feet (3 to 12 metres) and begins to bear fruit when four to eight years old. It takes about fifteen years to fully mature, but will bear fruit for hundreds of years. Some trees in the eastern Mediterranean are believed to be over two thousand years old.

Olives are harvested by hand or by striking the tree with long sticks to bring the fruit down to the ground. They come in dozens of shapes and colours, varying in size from half an inch to 2 inches (1 to 5 cm). About 40 percent are picked green before they mature; the remainder are harvested as they ripen in various shades ranging from purple-blue to black, at which time they reach their maximum oil content—100 kg of olives will produce 25 kg of oil.

The oil comes in at least five grades. The top grade is *extra-virgin*, obtained from pressed green olives picked by hand; *virgin*, from the first pressing of black olives; *refined*, from the second pressing; *pure*, a mixture of virgin and refined; and *sulphide*, extracted with solvents from the third pressing.

Olives and their oil are, in the main, consumed as a food, especially by people living in the countries which border on the Mediterranean. However, despite the fact that olives are cultivated principally for the table, their oil has always been used as a medicine.

In the times of the Prophets, it was believed that olive oil would cure every malady except the illness of death. There is a legend that Adam, suffering with pain, complained to God who sent Gabriel down from heaven with an olive tree. He presented it to Adam, telling him to plant it, then to pick the fruit and extract the oil, using it whenever he had pain—assuring him that it would cure all ills.

Today's Middle Eastern farmers believe that if they drink half a cup of olive oil before breakfast, it will clear their system, and they will live a long life free from disease. Their cure for an infected ear is a little heated olive oil dropped into the ear in a number of doses; for sore muscles, the remedy is a massage of olive oil. In these countries, many people even maintain, as did their ancestors in ancient times, that olive oil is a powerful sexual stimulant.

And they have a point. Olives are characterized by high nutritional and health values. Dried olives contain 51.9 percent fat, 30.07 percent water, 10.45 percent carbohydrates, 5.24 percent protein, and 2.33 percent mineral matter, being exceptionally rich in potassium. Olive oil, rich in monounsaturated fat, has the ability to reduce the LDL (bad) cholesterol without reducing the HDL (good) cholesterol in the blood.

The energy-giving properties in olives are more than that contained in any other fruit or vegetable, and the calcium content is greater than in other fruit, vegetables, fish, shellfish, or cockle-fish. Fresh cow's milk contains the same quantity of calcium as olives, but olives have more vitamin A than that contained in milk. Thus, olives are an excellent food for pathological cases which require intensified quantities of calcium.

Scientifically, even though olive oil will not make a sick person well, it may help keep one from becoming sick. The oil is excellent for sufferers from a debility or those who are underweight. Drunk pure, 2 ounces (4 tablespoons or 60 ml) per day makes a superb laxative. Soothing for insect bites, itching, and bruises, the oil also contains vitamin E, a powerful antioxidant which plays a role in reducing the risk of cancer and heart diseases. This has led the World Health Organization to recommend olive oil for cardiovascular diseases and to promote bone growth.

The last pressing of the oil is often utilized in the manufacture of soap, while virgin olive oil is used as a hair conditioner. There is no oil as good for the skin. Olive oil is easily absorbed into the subcutaneous layers, keeping the skin supple and the body flexible and pliant.

In ancient Greece, pure olive oil was a highly prized luxury for anointing the body. Mediterranean beauties have, through the ages, used undiluted olive oil as a massage ingredient to soften their delicate skin and to enhance their flowing black tresses which have inspired many a romantic Arabic and Latin-speaking poet. It is believed that Cleopatra always had an olive oil massage before her trysts with Caesar and Anthony.

At times, after the olives are crushed to produce the oil, the pulverized pits are then made into firebricks which make excellent fuel material. Many family meals in the Mediterranean Basin are cooked over the glowing embers of olive-pit bricks. These are augmented by the trimmed dead branches of the trees—another source of cooking material which the olive tree adds to the meagre energy resources of the Mediterranean peasant farmers.

In the Middle East, the many fine pieces of furniture in the homes of peasants which have been passed down from generation to generation and the beautiful artifices that for hundreds of years have helped keep the tourist industry alive are made from the wood of the olive tree. Although not as prevalent now as in ancient times, necklaces made from the polished pits of the olives adorn the necks of many maidens, especially tourists from the West coming to enjoy the exotic Mediterranean lands.

Nevertheless, it is as a food that olives reach their epitome of usefulness. Their highly digestible oil can be drizzled on toast and ripe tomatoes or brushed on grilling chicken or fish. The oil is used in all types of cooking and in countless salad dressings, adding an appetizing gusto to food. Olive oil keeps well but should be stored in jars or covered containers. When exposed to sunlight it becomes rancid and develops an offensive odour.

As for olives themselves, they are eaten as appetizers, form part of the ingredients in many dishes, and are often used for decoration. No breakfast in the Middle Eastern countries is complete without at least one type of olive being served; and no morning, afternoon, or evening snack is offered without a few types of this ancient vegetable-fruit.

In the Mediterranean countries, olives are usually pickled in brine or oil, but there are many varieties of olives, and the type of pickling is purely a matter of taste. Green ones are picked unripe and usually pickled in brine; black ones are left to ripen on the tree and are often preserved in oil, but may also be pickled in brine. Both types can be stuffed with almonds, garlic, pimentos, or anchovies; or embellished with hot pepper, lemon peel, sumac, thyme, and other herbs or spices.

Pickled olives are usually sold in bulk in food markets throughout most of the world. Unlike the tasteless canned olives on many North American supermarket shelves, these prepared olives are very tasty, adding flavour to any dish in which they are used as an ingredient. As they have for millennia, olives remain today a healthy and nourishing food for millions.

I am very pleased that I relished my first olive in those Depression years. I give them much of the credit for keeping me healthy as I was growing up. ✸

SEASONED OLIVES / ZAYTOON MUTABBAL

In the Middle East, this is one of the most common ways of flavouring olives.

1 lb	black olives, washed	454 g
1 tsp	dried thyme	5 ml
½ cup	olive oil	125 ml
½ tsp	marjoram	2 ml
2 tsps	sumac *	10 ml
½ tbsp	salt	7 ml
⅛ tsp	cayenne	½ ml
1 tsp	toasted sesame seeds	5 ml

1. Combine all ingredients, then place in a covered jar and top with water. Serve as needed, but stir olives before each serving.

* Sumac can be purchased from Middle Eastern grocery stores.

LEMON AND OLIVE OIL SALAD DRESSING

FOR SALADS THAT SERVE FROM 6 TO 8

This is the traditional salad dressing of the Middle East. At times, vinegar is substituted for the lemon juice.

4 tbsps	olive oil	60 ml
1	clove garlic, crushed	1
4 tbsps	lemon juice	60 ml
2 tbsps	finely chopped fresh mint or cilantro	30 ml
	salt and black pepper to taste	

1. Thoroughly combine all ingredients, then stir and pour over salad. Toss and serve immediately.

GARLIC BREAD IN OLIVE OIL

SERVES 4

Very tasty, this dish is common in many Mediterranean lands.

	olive oil for frying	
4	slices of bread, smeared with Garlic Sauce (page 130)	4
4	small cucumbers, sliced	4
4	small tomatoes, sliced	4
	salt and black pepper to taste	

1. Heat oil in a frying pan, then fry bread slices over medium until they begin to brown, turning them over once. Drain on paper towels, then place on 4 plates. Place cucumbers and tomatoes evenly over top, then sprinkle with salt and pepper and serve.

Wheat and oil are the pillars of the house.

Although tahini was not available to my family during the early years on the homestead, Mother always talked about it as a staple for making dips in Syria. Thanks to Canadian importers, tahini eventually hit the shelves of almost all of the larger grocery outlets. Its versatility is evident in this Olive Dip, a recipe that I developed out of my love for olives.

OLIVE DIP

SERVES 6 TO 8

2 cups	green olives, pitted and washed to remove the salt	500 ml
1 tbsp	lemon juice	15 ml
2	cloves garlic, crushed	2
4 tbsps	tahini (crushed sesame seeds)	60 ml
⅛ tsp	cayenne	½ ml
2 tbsps	chopped fresh cilantro	30 ml
1	small tomato, finely chopped	1
1 tbsp	olive oil	15 ml

1. Place all ingredients, except tomato and olive oil, in a food processor, then process until smooth. Spread on a serving platter; then refrigerate for 1 hour. Garnish with the chopped tomato, then sprinkle with oil and serve.

OLIVE AND CARROT SALAD / SALATAT ZAYTOON WA JAZAR

SERVES ABOUT 6

2	medium carrots, peeled then thinly sliced	2
½	head of medium lettuce, chopped into small pieces	½
½ cup	pitted black olives, sliced in half	125 ml
	Lemon and Olive Oil Salad Dressing (page 194)	

1. Place carrots, lettuce, and olives in a salad bowl, then thoroughly mix. Pour in salad dressing, then toss and serve.

OLIVE AND ORANGE SALAD /
SCHLADA ZAYTOON BI LITCHEEN

SERVES 4

The following Moroccan dish makes an unusual and vividly coloured salad which also can be served as an appetizer. We did not have the pleasure of enjoying this dish during our homesteading years; this is one of the many olive recipes I have collected in my world travels.

½ cup	black olives, pitted and halved	125 ml
4	large seedless oranges, peeled, sectioned, and cut into small pieces	4
½ tsp	cumin	2 ml
pinch	cayenne	pinch

1. Combine olives and oranges in a salad bowl. Cover and refrigerate for at least 1 hour.

2. Thoroughly mix cumin and cayenne in a separate dish then set aside.

3. Just before serving, sprinkle cumin-cayenne combination over olive-orange mixture and toss.

The olive is the sultan of the table.

ZUCCHINI AND EGGS

SERVES ABOUT *6*

In all the Arab countries, olive oil has been, through the centuries, the most commonly used oil in cooking. Although less expensive vegetable oils have, in our modern age, made inroads into the lands of olives, olive oil is still the most important ingredient used to cook a daily meal.

½ cup	olive oil	125 ml
2	medium onions, finely chopped	2
3	cloves garlic, crushed	3
4 cups	finely chopped zucchini	1 L
3	medium tomatoes, finely chopped	3
1 tsp	salt	5 ml
½ tsp	black pepper	2 ml
½ tsp	crushed dried basil	2 ml
3	eggs	3

1. Heat oil in saucepan, then sauté onions over medium heat until they begin to brown. Add garlic and zucchini and sauté for 10 minutes or until zucchini is cooked. Stir in tomatoes, salt, pepper, and basil, then simmer over medium-low heat for 10 minutes, stirring occasionally. Break in eggs, then stir-fry for a few more minutes. Serve hot.

Hide the honey in the jars until the price gets higher.

CHICKEN WITH LEMONS AND OLIVES/ DAJAAJ ZAYTOON BI LAYMOON

SERVES 4 TO 6

1	lemon	1
3 to 4 lbs	chicken	1.5 to 2 kg
5 tbsps	olive oil	75 ml
1	large onion, finely chopped	1
1 tbsp	paprika	15 ml
1 tsp	ground ginger	5 ml
¼ tsp	turmeric	1 ml
2 tsps	salt	10 ml
1 tsp	black pepper	5 ml
1½ cups	water	375 ml
½ cup	small green olives	125 ml

1. Cut lemon lengthwise into quarters and remove seeds. Set aside.

2. Cut chicken into serving-size pieces. In a frying pan, heat oil over medium-high heat, then fry chicken, turning frequently, until pieces begin to brown. Drain chicken pieces on paper towels, then set aside.

3. Pour out fat from frying pan, except for 4 tablespoons (60 ml), then add onion and sauté over medium heat until limp, about 8 minutes. Add paprika, ginger, turmeric, salt, pepper, lemon, water, and chicken. Stir, then bring to boil over high heat. Reduce heat to low, then simmer covered for about 30 minutes or until the chicken is tender, adding a little more water if necessary. Add olives, then re-cover and simmer for 3 minutes.

4. Remove chicken pieces and arrange on a platter. Spoon sauce with lemon quarters and olives over chicken pieces and serve immediately.

OLIVES

In North Africa, one's choice in olives is not limited to black or green; olives vary in colour and type of curing. Particularly favoured are the ripe black olives that have been cured in salt and then dried; or the pale grey-green ones cured in oil and a little salt. The latter are frequently combined with lemon and used in chicken dishes, as in this recipe, another dish that I discovered during my North African travels.

HERB-STUFFED FISH

SERVES 4 TO 6

This delightful Moroccan dish is much spicier than the one Mother used to make. Its taste and texture are smooth and unforgettable.

4 to 5 lbs	fresh whitefish, scaled and cleaned	1.8 to 2.3 kg
1 cup	finely chopped fresh cilantro	250 ml
1	medium head of garlic, peeled and crushed	1
2 tsps	salt	10 ml
½ cup	lemon juice	125 ml
½ cup	tomato juice	125 ml
⅛ tsp	cayenne	½ ml
2 tsps	paprika	10 ml
5	medium tomatoes, thinly sliced	5
4	medium potatoes, thinly sliced	4
4	medium carrots, thinly sliced	4
1 cup	olive oil	250 ml
1 cup	water	250 ml
½ cup	pimento-stuffed olives	125 ml

1. Place fish in an oiled roasting pan, then set aside.

2. In a small bowl, combine cilantro, garlic, salt, lemon juice, tomato juice, cayenne, and paprika.

3. Using half the mixture, spread inside the fish, then rub remaining half of mixture all over the outside of the fish. Arrange tomatoes, potatoes, and carrots over fish. Pour oil and water evenly over vegetables. Bake covered in a 350°F (180°C) preheated oven for 30 minutes. Remove from oven, then spread olives over fish. Return to oven and bake uncovered for an additional 10 minutes.

4. Serve fish hot with juices and vegetables.

CHAPTER 16

ZUCCHINI: ONE OF OUR COMFORT FOODS

The vegetarian reception food stand was crammed full of delicious tidbits. Each looked more appetizing than the last. Yet the guests seemed to be crowding around a colourfully decorated dish near the end of the table. "It's an eggplant dip." "No, I think it's puréed potatoes." "I'm sure it's a pumpkin concoction." Each one who was gathered around the food had a different opinion as to what they were eating as they scooped with their crackers bits of puréed zucchini. The conflicting ideas about what they were enjoying truly demonstrates the versatility of this vegetable, known in Arabic as *koosa*.

The evening reception reminded me of my mother's vegetable marrow dishes—a related species of zucchini. In late summer and early autumn, meat (with the exception of chicken) was scarce, but our garden overflowed with vegetable marrow. During these months, Mother served the family a never-ending series of dishes, many her own creations, prepared from this vegetable which has today been replaced to a great extent by its relative, the zucchini—now more commonly found throughout North America. Only the immigrants from the Middle East and some parts of Europe still hold on to vegetable marrow, claiming it to be more scrumptious.

The late discovery of both vegetable marrow and zucchini in North America is somewhat strange since they, as with all other types of squash and pumpkins, originated in the Mexico of the Aztecs. Taken back to Europe and Asia by the Spaniards, these vegetables soon

ARAB COOKING ON A PRAIRIE HOMESTEAD 201

became part of the cuisine in almost every country of the "Old World."

Subsequently, in England, vegetable marrow became popular, and in Italy a darker green version was developed and became known as zucchini. In the latter country, it became a favourite vegetable, and, later, the Italian immigrants were largely responsible for its introduction into the Western Hemisphere. There is no doubt that its wide cultivation in North America is due to the love for this summer squash by these immigrants. This is attested to by its name, zucchini, which in Italian means "little squash"—a name by which it is now known throughout Canada and the United States.

Resembling cucumbers, both zucchini and vegetable marrow are some of the simplest of all vegetables to cultivate. They thrive in all types of soil and are easy to grow. Their plant is very prolific and bumper crops are almost always guaranteed. If attended to with care, each plant produces up to three dozen fruits.

Zucchini, which has now almost erased vegetable marrow from the field, is very colourful—dark green with specks of grey. When picked before they mature, they are tender-skinned with firm, light-green flesh. If they are left on the vine, they can grow to the size of a large pumpkin.

However, they are at the maximum of flavour when harvested at 4 to 6 inches (10 to 15 cm) long. If picked at this stage, the plant continues to bear fruit for many weeks. On the other hand, if the fruit is allowed to mature the plant ends its productive cycle.

Both vegetable marrow and zucchini have a very low calorie count and, when eaten raw, they have a fair amount of calcium, iron, and vitamins A and C. Their sodium content is very low, making them ideal for people who are on a low-sodium diet.

A very versatile vegetable, zucchini can be prepared with any type of vegetable, pulse, or meat. It can be cooked in countless ways, and, by whatever method it is prepared, it is always delectable. Raw, baked, fried, puréed, stewed, or stuffed, it gives a tasty and appetizing appeal to any dish.

When harvested and prepared during their tender stage, zucchini cook very quickly. This is why they should be cooked only briefly, allowing them to retain their crisp and delicate flesh. If they are overcooked they tend to lose much of their flavour.

For those who enjoy the adventure of new dishes, the blossoms of the zucchini vine make an exotic dish. After being washed, the flowers are dipped in an egg-and-flour batter, then deep fried to a golden brown. They have a tantalizing taste and make excellent appetizers.

Another delicacy are the seeds of the mature fruit. After the zucchini is allowed to fully mature on the plant, the seeds are removed and the flesh discarded. These are roasted and salted and then served as snacks in the same fashion as peanuts. In the cold winter evenings during our homesteading days, night after night we snacked on these seeds that Mother prepared during the late summer and early autumn months from the vegetable marrow we ate.

The tender and savoury texture of zucchini and vegetable marrow, flavoured with spices and herbs, are a vegetarian's gourmet dream.

To those not acquainted with zucchini or vegetable marrow, these few vegetarian dishes will give an insight into their world. Remember that the zucchini called for in all the dishes can be replaced by vegetable marrow—there is no difference. ⌗

ZUCCHINI DIP

2	zucchini, 6 to 7 inches (15 to 18 cm) long	2
4	boiled eggs	4
4 tbsps	finely chopped fresh cilantro	60 ml
1 tsp	oregano	5 ml
½ tsp	salt	2 ml
½ tsp	black pepper	2 ml
⅛ tsp	cayenne	½ ml
4 tbsps	lemon juice	60 ml
4 tbsps	olive oil	60 ml
1	small tomato, finely chopped	1

1. Peel and chop zucchini. Place in a food processor and process for a moment. Add remaining ingredients, except 2 tablespoons (30 ml) of the olive oil and tomato, then process into soft paste. Place on a flat serving platter, then sprinkle with remaining oil. Decorate with tomato pieces just before serving.

Trust in God but tie your camel.

ZUCCHINI APPETIZER

4	zucchini, about 7 to 8 inches (18 to 20 cm) long	4
½ tsp	salt	2 ml
	oil for frying	
4	cloves garlic, crushed	4
1	small hot pepper, seeded and finely chopped	1
4 tbsps	lemon juice	60 ml
½ tsp	black pepper	2 ml
2 tbsps	chopped parsley	30 ml

1. Peel zucchini and slice into ½-inch (1 cm) thick slices. Sprinkle with salt, then place in a strainer with a weight on top. Allow to drain for 1 hour.

2. Pour oil in a saucepan to ½ inch (1 cm) deep, then heat to medium-high. Fry zucchini, a few pieces at a time, until they turn limp, turning them over once. Drain on paper towels, then chop into small pieces and place in a mixing bowl. Add garlic, hot pepper, lemon juice, and black pepper, then mix. Place on a flat serving platter, then decorate with parsley. Serve warm or cold, scooped up with crackers or Arab (pita) bread.

While the word is yet unspoken, you are the master of it; when once it is spoken, it is master of you.

FRIED ZUCCHINI WITH SESAME SEED SAUCE

4	zucchini, about 7 to 8 inches (18 to 20 cm) long	4
1 tsp	salt	5 ml
⅓ cup	flour	75 ml
½ cup	water	125 ml
2	eggs, beaten	2
½ tsp	black pepper	2 ml
⅛ tsp	cayenne	½ ml
	oil for frying	
4	cloves garlic, crushed	4
4 tbsps	tahini * (sesame seed paste)	60 ml
4 tbsps	lemon juice	60 ml

1. Peel zucchini, slice lengthwise into ¼-inch (6 mm) thick slices. Sprinkle with salt, then place in a strainer with a weight on top. Allow to drain for 1 hour.

2. In the meantime, make a batter by thoroughly combining flour, ¼ cup (60 ml) of the water, eggs, pepper, and cayenne, adding a little more water if necessary, then set aside.

3. Pour oil in a saucepan to ½ inch (1 cm) deep, then heat to medium.

4. Gently place zucchini slices, a few at a time, in the batter, then fry until golden, turning them over once. Drain on paper towels, then place on serving platter.

5. While zucchini are frying, place remaining ingredients in a food processor, including remaining ¼ cup (60 ml) water, then process for a few seconds to make a smooth sauce.

6. Serve hot with each person, spooning sauce on zucchini slices to taste.

Tahini can be purchased from Middle Eastern grocery or health food stores.

Middle Eastern and North African vegetarian soups are one of the staples of the peasants and working classes in the Arab countries. These succulent broths made from readily available vegetables are simple to prepare, inexpensive, and filling, and they do not require exotic ingredients. Herbs and spices give them their zest and tang. One does not need meat to produce a rich and full-bodied stock. Any vegetable that is slow-simmered with condiments produces a tasty, delectable soup.

—adapted from Habeeb Salloum's article on vegetarian soups, published in Vegetarian Journal 14:5.

ZUCCHINI AND MINT SOUP / SHAWRABAT KOOSA WA NA'NA'

SERVES ABOUT 10

Mother was able to make zucchini interesting with almost every dish she made. One of my favourites was and is still Zucchini and Mint Soup, a hearty meal unto itself.

2	zucchini, each 6 to 7 inches long (15 to 18 cm)	2
2 tbsps	olive oil	30 ml
2	medium onions, finely chopped	2
1	hot pepper, seeded and finely chopped	1
4	cloves garlic, crushed	4
4	medium tomatoes, chopped	4
1½ cups	cooked chickpeas	375 ml
¼ cup	rice, rinsed	60 ml
½ tsp	salt	2 ml
½ tsp	ground coriander	2 ml
½ tsp	black pepper	2 ml
½ tsp	cinnamon	2 ml
7 cups	water	1750 ml
3 tbsps	lemon juice	45 ml
4 tbsps	finely chopped fresh mint or 2 tsps (10 ml) dried mint	60 ml

1. Peel zucchini and dice into ½-inch (1 cm) cubes.

2. Heat oil in a saucepan, then sauté onions and hot pepper over medium heat for 10 minutes. Stir in garlic and tomatoes, then sauté for a further 10 minutes. Add zucchini and remaining ingredients, except the lemon juice and mint, then bring to a boil, cover and cook over medium heat for 30 minutes. Remove from heat, then stir in lemon juice and mint. Serve hot.

TOMATO AND ZUCCHINI SALAD

SERVES ABOUT 6

A refreshing salad on a hot summer's day.

4	zucchini, each 4 to 6 inches (10 to 15 cm) long	4
½ tsp	salt	2 ml
4	medium tomatoes	4
2 tbsps	finely chopped fresh cilantro	30 ml
4 tbsps	olive oil	60 ml
3 tbsps	lemon juice	45 ml
1 tsp	dried mint	5 ml
¼ tsp	black pepper	1 ml

1. Peel zucchini, then dice into ½-inch (1 cm) cubes. Sprinkle with salt, then place in a strainer with a weight on top. Allow to drain for 1 hour.

2. Dice tomatoes into ½-inch (1 cm) cubes.

3. Combine zucchini and tomatoes in a salad bowl, then make dressing with remaining ingredients. Pour over vegetables in salad bowl, then toss and serve immediately.

NOTE: *If salad is allowed to stand for a long period of time, it becomes too watery.*

A known mistake is better than an unknown truth.

WARM ZUCCHINI SALAD

SERVES 4 TO 6

2	zucchini, each 7 to 8 inches (18 to 20 cm) long	2
4 tbsps	olive oil	60 ml
2	cloves garlic, crushed	2
½ tsp	salt	2 ml
½ tsp	black pepper	2 ml
½ tsp	ground fennel	2 ml
2 tbsps	finely chopped fresh cilantro	30 ml
2 tbsps	lemon juice	30 ml
1	medium tomato, finely chopped	1

1. Peel zucchini, then dice into ½-inch (1 cm) cubes.

2. Heat oil in a frying pan, then stir-fry zucchini over medium-high heat for 3 minutes. Transfer to a mixing bowl, then sprinkle remaining ingredients, except tomato, over top. Toss, then place on a flat serving platter. Decorate with tomato pieces, then serve warm.

A beggar and he bargains!

BAKED ZUCCHINI AND TOMATOES

SERVES ABOUT 8

With the amount of zucchini and tomatoes our garden produced, there were plenty of ways Mother could blend the two together to make a tasty casserole. Today, I use Parmesan in place of the kishk she would use.

1	zucchini, about 12 inches (30 cm) long	1
½ tsp	salt	2 ml
3	medium tomatoes	3
½ cup	Parmesan cheese	125 ml
2 tbsps	olive oil	30 ml
½ cup	finely chopped green onions	125 ml
4 tbsps	finely chopped parsley	60 ml
2	cloves garlic, crushed	2
½ tsp	black pepper	2 ml
⅛ tsp	cayenne	½ ml

1. Peel zucchini, then slice into ½-inch (1 cm) thick slices. Sprinkle with salt, then place in a strainer with a weight on top. Allow to drain for 1 hour.

2. Slice tomatoes in ½-inch (1 cm) thick slices. Set aside.

3. Thoroughly combine remaining ingredients to make a paste, then set aside.

4. Place half of the zucchini slices and half of the tomato slices, intermixed, in a greased casserole, then spread half of paste over top. Repeat for a second layer, then cover and bake in a 350°F (180°C) preheated oven for 40 minutes or until zucchini is well cooked. Serve hot.

CHICKPEA AND ZUCCHINI STEW

SERVES ABOUT 8

It may well have been one of our Syrian visitors who gave Dad some zucchini seeds to get our first batch started. Our supply was bountiful from late summer to early fall. We had to grow it to enjoy it, unlike today when it can be purchased all year-round.

2	zucchini, each 8 to 10 inches (20 to 25 cm) long	2
1 ¼ tsps	salt	6 ml
4 tbsps	olive oil	60 ml
2	medium onions, finely chopped	2
4	cloves garlic, crushed	4
2 tbsps	finely chopped fresh cilantro	30 ml
1	hot pepper, seeded and finely chopped	1
2 cups	cooked chickpeas	500 ml
2 cups	stewed tomatoes	500 ml
½ tsp	cumin	2 ml
½ tsp	black pepper	2 ml
¼ tsp	cinnamon	1 ml
2 cups	water	500 ml

1. Peel zucchini, then dice into 1-inch (2.5 cm) cubes. Sprinkle with ¼ teaspoon of the salt, then place in a strainer with a weight on top. Allow to drain for 1 hour.

2. Heat oil in a saucepan, then sauté onions, garlic, cilantro, and hot pepper over medium heat for 10 minutes. Stir in zucchini and remaining ingredients, then bring to boil. Cover and cook over medium heat for 30 minutes or until zucchini is cooked, adding more water if necessary. Serve hot or cold.

When the stomach gets full, it tells the head to sing.

POTATO AND ZUCCHINI STEW

SERVES ABOUT *8*

One of our 'fun' chores was digging out potatoes from our garden when they were ready to be picked. The 'fun' was not the chore itself, but rather digging one out, wiping off the dirt, and biting into it.

2	zucchini, each 6 to 7 inches (15 to 18 cm) long	2
1¼ tsps	salt, divided	6 ml
4	medium potatoes	4
2 tbsps	olive oil	30 ml
2	medium onions, finely chopped	2
4	cloves garlic, crushed	4
4 tbsps	finely chopped fresh cilantro	60 ml
1	hot pepper, seeded and finely chopped	1
2 cups	stewed tomatoes	500 ml
2 cups	water	500 ml
1 tsp	oregano	5 ml
½ tsp	black pepper	2 ml
¼ tsp	allspice	1 ml

1. Peel zucchini, then dice into 1-inch (2.5 cm) cubes. Sprinkle with ¼ teaspoon (1 ml) of the salt, then place in a strainer with a weight on top. Allow to drain for 1 hour.

2. Peel potatoes, then dice into ½-inch (1 cm) cubes.

3. Heat oil in a saucepan, then sauté onions, garlic, cilantro, and hot pepper over medium-low heat for 10 minutes. Add potatoes and remaining ingredients, except zucchini, then bring to boil. Cover and cook over medium heat for 20 minutes, adding more water if necessary. Stir in zucchini, then cook for further 20 minutes or until zucchini and potatoes are well cooked, adding more water if necessary. Serve hot.

ZUCCHINI STUFFED WITH RICE AND PINE NUTS / KOOSA MAHSHEE MA'A RUZ WA SNOBAR

SERVES 6

One of the most important kitchen utensils for the Syrian homemaker is a vegetable corer. This was not available where we lived so Dad cleverly created, from a piece of metal and a piece of wood, a corer that Mother would come to use for years and years.

A corer can be purchased in any Middle Eastern grocery outlet and can be used to core most vegetables. When coring, one must be careful not to puncture the skin. Called in Arabic manqara, *it is one of the most used kitchen utensils in the eastern Arab world.*

12	zucchini, about 6 inches (15 cm) long	12
	Stuffing	
5 tbsps	butter	75 ml
1	large onion, finely chopped	1
1	hot pepper, seeded and finely chopped	1
3	cloves garlic, crushed	3 cloves
½ cup	pine nuts	125 ml
2 tbsps	tomato paste	30 ml
½ cup	rice, rinsed	125 ml
½ cup	finely chopped parsley	125 ml
4 tbsps	finely chopped fresh mint or 2 tsps (10 ml) dried mint	60 ml
½ tsp	each of salt, black pepper, and ground coriander seed	2 ml
¼ tsp	each of allspice and cinnamon	1 ml
	Sauce	
3 tbsps	tomato paste	45 ml
2 cups	water	500 ml
½ tsp	each of salt and black pepper	2 ml

1. Trim the stem end of zucchini, then core with a corer. Reserve tops and set aside.

2. Melt butter in a frying pan, then sauté onion and hot pepper over medium heat for 10 minutes. Stir in garlic and pine nuts, then sauté for a few minutes more. Place frying pan contents in a mixing bowl, then add remaining stuffing ingredients and thoroughly combine.

3. Stuff zucchini about ¾ full, then seal with reserved tops. Place, tightly fitting, in a large saucepan. Cover with inverted flat plate. Mix together sauce ingredients and pour over zucchini, adding more water to barely cover the plate. Bring to a boil, then cover and cook over medium heat for 40 minutes. Serve hot with a portion of the sauce according to taste.

ONIONS

A staple ingredient in cooking, the onion (*allium cepa*) has been available as a food for thousands of years by all strata of society—from peasant to royalty. It is one of the most adaptable vegetables known to humankind and a great creator of flavours in our daily meals. It is said that even though we talk about its offensive smell and cry when we peel this common garden food, we would be much more unhappy if this noble bulb was not to be found on our daily menus.

Onions are thought to have been grown in the Middle East since pre-historic times. To the ancient Egyptians they were divine vegetables which represented eternity. In many of the early civilizations, it was believed that onions increased the production of sperm and gave men strength. They were a staple of the labourers who built the pyramids, and it is thought that Alexander the Great fed his troops this versatile vegetable to imbue them with courage. From the Middle East, the cultivation of onions spread westward throughout the Greek and Roman lands, but, eastward, the inhabitants of ancient India did not develop a liking for them; in fact, they abhorred their very taste and smell.

Nonetheless, in all parts of the world, people have, throughout the centuries, believed onions to be a strong aphrodisiac. Celsus, the Epicurean philosopher; Martial, the Roman poet; and Shaykh Nefzawi, in his erotic work, *The Perfumed Garden*, all mention onions as sexual stimulants. ❖

—*Habeeb Salloum, "When You Chop an Onion…You Know that the Meal will be Good,"* Vitality: Toronto's Monthly Wellness Journal, *December 2004/January 2005: 24–28.*

CHAPTER 17

TOMATOES: OUR FRUIT DURING THE HOMESTEADING YEARS

As a child, for me, the beauty of late summer and early autumn were tomato plants heavy with their ripened red fruit. I enjoyed the colour they gave our garden and, even more, their delicious taste, especially when I picked them fiery-red off the plant. During all our homesteading years, they were the substitute for the fruits that we rarely had the opportunity to taste. A few times a year our father would splurge and bring back from town some fruit, usually apples but, at harvest time, it was almost always tomatoes that we enjoyed as a fill-in for fruit.

Tomatoes were the crowning jewels of our hand-watered garden. Every year we had a bountiful crop that would last us until next year's harvest. For over a month we ate them fresh off the plant, then Mother would can the remainder—perhaps a hundred jars. The green ones that did not ripen, we picked and stored in our dirt cellar, then ate them as they turned red.

I am sure my parents did not know the healthful qualities of tomatoes, but they were plentiful, could be stored or preserved for year-round use, and were free. Without doubt, their saturation with vitamin c kept away many of the usual childhood diseases, and their fine taste, along with the flavour they imbued to the other vegetables and meats, ensured that we needed no urging to eat our meals. They were truly one of our favoured foods.

However, through the ages, the healthful qualities and versatility of tomatoes have not always been appreciated. Even though they are now much sought-after, they were once the most reviled fruit in the vegetable world. Today, among the vegetables grown in North America, they rank second to potatoes in popularity. This once-despised pulpy red or yellow fruit, eaten as a vegetable, is one of the top three garden crops consumed by humankind. No other fruit or vegetable is cultivated more widely or has its mass appeal. Yet, for centuries in Europe and the United States, the tomato was believed to be a poisonous plant.

Tomatoes originated in the highlands of Peru where they still grow wild. From there they spread, before the time of Christopher Columbus, to all of South and Central America. Called by the Indigenous peoples of Mexico *tomatl*, from which we derive the name tomato, they were one of the first plants brought back to Europe after first contact with the Americas. However, it was not until the mid-nineteenth century that they were widely accepted as a food.

For some three hundred years, most Europeans and North Americans believed that tomatoes were poisonous; therefore, for hundreds of years they were only cultivated as floral ornaments. In the United States, it took until about the middle of the 1800s before they were eaten as a food. Reputedly, the first person to consume a tomato was Robert Gibbson Johnson, who ate it in public on the steps of the courthouse in Salem, New Jersey, dumbfounding the thousands who were waiting to see him drop dead. Since that episode, Americans have become the world's largest consumers of tomatoes.

Before tomatoes were accepted as a food in Europe, they went by a number of different names. The Spaniards, known in the sixteenth century to a good number of Europeans as 'Moros' (Moors), first introduced them into the neighbouring countries. According to one story, this led the Italians to label tomatoes *pomi dei Moro* (apple of the Moors). Another version of this anecdote is that the first tomatoes seen in Italy were probably yellow—the original colour of tomatoes the Spanish found in the

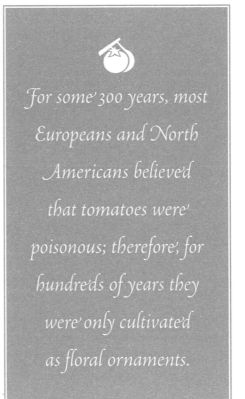

For some 300 years, most Europeans and North Americans believed that tomatoes were poisonous; therefore, for hundreds of years they were only cultivated as floral ornaments.

Americas—and were called by the Italian *pomo d'oro* (apples of gold). Later, Italian traders introduced them to the Greater Syria area, where today they carry a corrupted form of the Italian name, *banadoora* —the name I knew them by as a young boy. The tale goes on to relate that, to the French, both names—*pomi dei Moro* and *pomo d'oro*— sounded like *pomo d'amore* (apples of love), leading to their reputation as having aphrodisiac qualities.

Known for decades as "scarlet love apples" or "golden love apples," they became the favourite of sweethearts and a symbol of passion. Their reputation as a wicked, sensuous, and powerful sexual stimulant made them feared by virtuous maidens. The expression "hot tomato" to describe a willing woman is common in many languages.

Botanically a fruit but in reality a vegetable, tomatoes belong to the nightshade family of plants, which include some deadly types—no doubt the root of the belief, held for centuries, that they were poisonous. A rapid-growing, short-lived, sun-loving annual, they come in hundreds of varieties. It is said that every year a new type of tomato is developed. Very prolific, they are easy to grow in fields, gardens, patios, or pots on window sills.

When allowed to mature on the vine, they are the epitome of taste and colour. The sun develops the choicest flavour and texture. Nothing can match the sweet lusciousness of sun-ripened tomatoes. However, for market, most are harvested green or partially ripe and then matured by ethylene gas before being retailed. This deprives them of much of their vitamin content and delectable taste. Millions of North Americans who buy their tomatoes in supermarkets do not know what the vine-ripened ones taste like.

On the other hand, householders, like ourselves during our homesteading days, who grow their own tomatoes can enjoy this brilliantly coloured delicious vegetable during the summer months, then pick the last firm green ones just before frost and store them in dry cellars. They last for weeks and can be eaten as they ripen.

Fresh tomatoes are available year-round, but May to September is their peak season. At this period of the year, when purchased firm and red, they can be stored at room temperature for about a week without losing their vitamin C content or taste. When they become totally ripe they should be used immediately or they will quickly spoil.

Tomatoes provide North Americans with a greater percentage of their nutrition than any other vegetable. This is not to say that they contain more nourishment than other garden produce, but they are more widely consumed. The dieter's delight—a medium tomato has about 30 calories—they contain no cholesterol and are low in carbohydrates. When sun-ripened, tomatoes are rich in vitamins A and C and minerals, especially potassium. In addition, they contain some calcium, fibre, iron, magnesium, phosphorous, as well as traces of fat, protein, sodium, and vitamins B, E, and G.

Unlike green vegetables, they lose few of their vitamins in cooking. Canned tomatoes, as nutritious as fresh fruit, are the most widely used of all canned garden products. The whole fruit is edible—skin, flesh, and seed. More versatile than any other vegetable, tomatoes can be canned, dried, frozen, pickled, pureed, or made into paste. They can be eaten raw, baked, broiled, fried, and stewed; or used as the main component in ketchup, relish, sauces, soups, and as garnish for all types of dishes.

The following few examples, a number of which we ate often during our homesteading days, point to the wide-ranging use of tomatoes as a tasty ingredient in foods. ✂

TOMATO AND EGGPLANT APPETIZER / MUSAQAʻA

SERVES ABOUT 6

Some historians have suggested that the eggplant originated in China about four thousand years ago and has been grown and eaten as a vegetable in Iran and India since 1500 BCE. When, in the seventh century CE, the Arab armies entered Persia and India, they were fascinated with this vegetable and brought it back home under the name badhinjan, *an Arabized form of the Persian* badnjan. *In the next century, after the Islamic conquest of the Iberian Peninsula, the Arabs introduced this vegetable into Europe.*

1 lb	whole eggplant	454 g
2	medium, firm, ripe tomatoes, finely chopped	2
1 tbsp	finely chopped fresh cilantro	15 ml
3 tbsps	olive oil	45 ml
2 tbsps	lemon juice	30 ml
1	clove garlic, crushed	1
½ tsp	salt	2 ml
½ tsp	black pepper	2 ml
⅛ tsp	cayenne	½ ml

1. Preheat oven to 350°F (180°C). Pierce eggplant with fork on all sides, then place in oven and bake for about 1 hour, until skin turns dark and crisp. Remove and allow to cool.

2. Peel, then place in a food processor. Process for a minute, then transfer to a mixing bowl and stir in remaining ingredients.

3. Transfer to a serving platter, then serve.

May the coffee of hospitality be always in your house.

GARLIC, LENTIL, AND TOMATO SOUP / SHAWRABAT 'ADAS WA BANADOORA

SERVES ABOUT 8

Soups such as this were carried with my parents from their native homeland. When times were tough, wholesome and hearty soups did their job of nourishing a growing family. We never went hungry.

4 tbsps	olive or cooking oil	60 ml
1	head of garlic, peeled and crushed	1
1	small hot pepper, seeded and finely chopped	1
4 tbsps	finely chopped fresh cilantro	60 ml
5	medium tomatoes, chopped	5
2 tsps	salt	10 ml
1 tsp	black pepper	5 ml
1 tsp	cumin	5 ml
¾ cup	lentils, rinsed	175 ml
6 cups	water	1500 ml

1. Heat oil in a saucepan, then sauté garlic, hot pepper, and cilantro over medium heat for 5 minutes. Add tomatoes, then sauté for a further 10 minutes. Stir in remaining ingredients, then bring to boil. Cover, then cook over medium heat for 40 minutes. Serve hot.

NOTE: *A 28-ounce (796 ml) can of stewed tomatoes can be substituted for the fresh tomatoes in this recipe.*

O departing one, leave behind good deeds.

TOMATO SALAD / SALATAT BANADOORA

SERVES 8

6	large firm tomatoes	6
1	medium Spanish onion	1
½ cup	finely chopped green onions	125 ml
3	cloves garlic, crushed	3
¼ tsp	thyme	1 ml
1 tsp	dried mint	5 ml
¼ cup	lemon juice	60 ml
¼ cup	olive oil	60 ml
½ tsp	salt	2 ml
¼ tsp	black pepper	1 ml

1. Slice tomatoes into thin slices, then place in a salad bowl. Slice onion very thin, then add to tomatoes and set aside.

2. Combine remaining ingredients, then add to tomatoes and onion. Gently mix, then chill. Toss lightly, then serve.

Salt is as necessary in food as grammar is in speech.

BAKED TOMATO AND SWEET PEPPER SALAD

SERVES ABOUT 6

Baked or grilled ingredients are often used for salads in North Africa. This makes these salads quite different from those in the Middle East. I do not remember my mother ever making salads based upon this method of vegetable preparation. However, after my many trips to North Africa, I have come to appreciate these types of salads.

3	large, firm, ripe tomatoes	3
3	large sweet peppers	3
1	medium onion, finely chopped	1
2	cloves garlic, crushed	2
2 tbsps	finely chopped parsley	30 ml
3 tbsps	olive oil	45 ml
3 tbsps	lemon juice	45 ml
1 tsp	oregano	5 ml
½ tsp	salt	2 ml
½ tsp	black pepper	2 ml
⅛ tsp	cayenne	½ ml

1. Place tomatoes and sweet peppers in oven, then bake at 350°F (180°C) until skins darken. Tomatoes take less time to bake than peppers. Remove as they darken, then plunge into cold water and peel. (The process can take up to 1 hour.) Chop into small pieces, then place in a mixing bowl. Stir in remaining ingredients and thoroughly mix. Transfer to a serving platter, then let stand for about 30 minutes before serving.

TOMATO AND CUCUMBER SALAD / SALATAT BANADOORA WA KHIYAAR

SERVES 6 TO 8

Tomatoes and cucumbers are the most common combination of ingredients for salad in the Middle East. In my version, I prefer to add olives.

5	medium tomatoes	5
1	medium cucumber, peeled, about 8 inches (20 cm) long	1
1 cup	finely chopped green onions	250 ml
4 tsps	finely chopped fresh mint	20 ml
1	clove garlic, crushed	1
4 tsps	olive oil	20 ml
3 tbsps	vinegar	45 ml
½ tsp	salt	2 ml
½ tsp	black pepper	2 ml
½ cup	black olives, pitted and halved	125 ml

1. Dice tomatoes and cucumber into ½-inch (1 cm) cubes.

2. Place tomatoes, cucumber, onions, and mint in a salad bowl, then set aside.

3. In a small bowl, combine garlic, olive oil, vinegar, salt, and black pepper, then pour over vegetables and toss. Decorate with olives, then serve immediately.

Believe what you see and lay aside what you hear.

EGGS WITH TOMATOES / BANADOORA WA BAYD

SERVES 4

From our early homesteading years, we were never without eggs and tomatoes. One of our favourites for breakfast was this very appetizing dish.

2 tbsps	butter	30 ml
1	medium onion, finely chopped	1
2	medium tomatoes, finely chopped	2
4	large eggs	4
¼ tsp	salt	1 ml
¼ tsp	black pepper	1 ml

1. Melt butter in a frying pan, then sauté onion over medium heat for about 10 minutes or until golden. Stir in tomatoes, then sauté for a further 5 minutes.

2. In the meantime, beat together eggs, salt, and pepper, then pour over onion and tomatoes. Stir-fry for about 3 minutes or until eggs are cooked. Serve immediately.

NOTE: *1 cup (250 ml) of mashed potatoes may be substituted for the 4 eggs.*

Dawn does not come twice to awaken a man.

RICE AND TOMATOES / RUZ WA BANADOORA

SERVES 4

½ lb	beef or lamb	227 g
4 tbsps	olive oil	60 ml
2	medium onions, finely chopped	2
2	cloves garlic, crushed	2
4	medium tomatoes, finely chopped	4
1 tsp	oregano	5 ml
¼ tsp	salt	1 ml
¼ tsp	black pepper	1 ml
¼ tsp	allspice	1 ml
1 cup	rice, rinsed	250 ml
1¾ cups	water	425 ml

1. Cut beef or lamb into ¼-inch (6 mm) cubes.

2. Heat oil in a frying pan, then sauté meat over medium heat for 10 minutes. Add onions and garlic, then stir-fry for a further 5 minutes. Add tomatoes, then sauté for another 10 minutes. Stir in remaining ingredients, then bring to boil. Cover, then cook over medium-low heat for 20 minutes. Turn off heat, stir, then allow rice to cook in own steam for 30 minutes. Serve hot.

Only the tent pitched by your own hands will stand.

STUFFED TOMATOES WITH CHEESE / MAHSHEE BANADOORA MA'A JIBN

SERVES 4

8	medium, firm, ripe tomatoes	8
1	medium onion, finely chopped	1
1	small avocado, peeled, pitted and finely chopped	1
2	cloves garlic, crushed	2
1 tbsp	finely chopped fresh cilantro	15 ml
½ cup	crumbled feta cheese	125 ml
½ tsp	salt	2 ml
½ tsp	black pepper	2 ml
¼ tsp	cayenne	1 ml
2 tbsps	olive oil	30 ml
2 tbsps	lemon juice	30 ml
1 tsp	oregano	5 ml
½ cup	water	125 ml

Alternate recipes for stuffed tomatoes are on pages 95 and 271.

1. Cut off stem ends of tomatoes and reserve, then scoop out pulp, leaving flesh on walls and bottom. Reserve pulp.

2. Make stuffing by combining remaining ingredients, except olive oil, lemon juice, oregano, and water, then arrange tomato shells packed side by side in a casserole. Fill tomatoes with stuffing, then replace stem ends.

3. Purée tomato pulp, then stir in olive oil, lemon juice, oregano, and water. Pour over the tomatoes. Cover and bake in a 350°F (180°C) preheated oven for 50 minutes, then serve tomatoes with their sauce.

    NOTE: *¼ cup (60 ml) raisins, soaked overnight and drained, may be substituted for the feta cheese.*

VEGETARIAN CASSEROLE

SERVES 8 TO 10

1 cup	dried chickpeas	250 ml
1 lb	eggplant	454 g
1 lb	potatoes (about 4 medium)	454 g
2 tsps	salt, divided	10 ml
4 tbsps	cooking oil	60 ml
3	medium onions, finely chopped	3
4	cloves garlic, crushed	4
4 tbsps	finely chopped parsley	60 ml
1	small hot pepper, seeded and finely chopped	1
28 oz	stewed tomatoes	796 ml
1 tsp	oregano	5 ml
1 tsp	black pepper	5 ml
1 tsp	ginger	5 ml

1. Soak chickpeas overnight in 4 cups water (1 L) into which ¼ teaspoon (1 ml) of baking soda has been stirred.

2. Place chickpeas with their water in a pot and bring to a boil, then cover and cook over medium heat for 1 hour, adding more water if necessary. Peel eggplant, then dice into ½-inch (1 cm) cubes. Place in a strainer, then sprinkle with ½ teaspoon (2 ml) of the salt. Place a heavy object on top and allow to drain for 1 hour. Peel potatoes, then dice into ½-inch (1 cm) cubes. Set aside.

3. In the meantime, heat oil in a frying pan, then sauté onions over medium heat for 8 minutes. Add garlic, parsley, and hot pepper, then stir-fry for 5 minutes. Add eggplant cubes, then stir-fry for further 5 minutes, adding more oil if necessary. Transfer frying pan contents into a casserole, then stir in chickpeas with their water, potatoes, and remaining ingredients, including remaining 1½ teaspoons (7 ml) salt. Bake uncovered in a 350°F (180°C) preheated oven for 1 hour, then serve hot or cold.

For this recipe, you will need to get the chickpeas ready the night before.

It seems that Mother must have always been soaking chickpeas, because whenever either Dad or we children unexpectedly requested a certain dish that included chickpeas, there was never a "wait until tomorrow!"

A CULINARY ODYSSEY

One day, as we walked around the Zócalo in the heart of Acapulco—Mexico's top resort—my daughter and I were surprised to find a small café with an Arab owner. Seemingly overjoyed at meeting us, he invited us to come join him for breakfast a few days later.

During that morning's repast, I discussed with him Mexican food for an article I was in the process of writing. When I asked him about the original dishes of Mexico, he thought for a while, then said, "Oh! I don't know! All their foods came from the Arabs. One of their most favoured dishes is *paella*—a true Arab invention."

Although the old man—who had spent forty years in Mexico, most of them cooking its food—might have been exaggerating, his words had a ring of truth. In addition to Mexico, Latin America owes much of its culinary traditions to the Arabs. The nine hundred years they were in the Iberian Peninsula and their nearly four hundred years in Sicily and southern France, first as conquerors then as conquered, have left a lasting influence in the form of Arab foods and seasonings. The restaurant owner, without knowing the sophisticated history of Arab foods, had nonetheless grasped the essence of the greatness of the Arab culinary odyssey. ✳

—adapted from an article by Habeeb Salloum published in Silver Kris, May 1990, *and in* Gulf Weekly, 1993.

CHAPTER 18

POTATOES: MOTHER'S DISHES STILL MAKE MY MOUTH WATER

It was potato-picking time, and our whole family was at work in our garden. As my father spaded out the potatoes, my siblings and I brushed the soil off of them, then placed them in pails. Every once in a while I would stop to eat one that caught my fancy, dirt and all. Even today, I remember vividly the delicious taste of that freshly picked potato. The potato harvest I always enjoyed, thinking of the many potato dishes my mother would prepare in the coming weeks.

Our garden's potato yield, which we placed in our dirt cellar covered with soil, would last us for almost the whole year. The dishes my mother prepared were never-ending. In soups, salads, as the main course, and for snacks, she seemed always to come up with new creations. During the bitter cold winter evenings as we sat around a red-hot stove, many a time she would barbecue sliced potatoes on top of the stove for an evening snack. The cooking aroma which filled the room whetted my appetite night after night.

I wonder if my mother knew when she cooked her numerous potato dishes that this vegetable was a storehouse of nutrients. Potatoes grew easily in our garden and kept for a long period of time in our dirt cellar. In the Depression years these attributes, when very little else grew, were heaven-sent. Yet, even though in those harsh years we did not know the healthful benefits of the potato, this vegetable, what some call a "near perfect food," has been valued as a nutritious edible for untold centuries.

The potato (*Solanum tuberosum*) was a staple for the Indigenous peoples living in the South American Andes, its region of origin, since at least 750 BCE. They developed some two hundred varieties from the original peanut-size wild potato and these became the basis of their diet. Potatoes became so important in their society that they used them to measure time. Units of time correlated to how long it took for the potato to cook.

When the Spanish conquistadors went rampaging through the land of the Incas looking for gold and silver, they were not aware that the potato would be the true treasure of the Andes—the most important of all their discoveries in the Americas. This realization would come later.

A half-century after arriving in Peru in 1532, the Spanish introduced this culinary treasure into Europe. They called it *patata*—derived from the word *batata* that was used by the Indigenous peoples of the Andes region—the word from which we get our name "potato." At first, potatoes were not readily accepted as a food for humans. The Scots, at one time, refused to eat them because they were not mentioned in the Bible. Many in Europe associated potatoes with diseases, such as leprosy and rickets; others blamed them for encouraging lust. Indeed, potatoes were fed to livestock long before they became an important popular staple food for Europeans.

However, all this was to change. Potatoes adapted well to Europe's climate and soon became a mainstay food in most countries on that continent. By the end of the seventeenth century, they had become a vital part of the basic food supply in Ireland, where people took to them with great enthusiasm. This gave birth to a saying: "there are only two things too serious to joke about—potatoes and marriage." When the potato crop in that country was destroyed by blight in the mid-nineteenth century, over a million people died during what became known as the "Irish Potato Famine."

The potato, called now by some the "noblest of vegetables," is one of the healthiest foods in the human larder. Potatoes are jam-packed with fibre, minerals (chiefly potassium), proteins, all the vitamins, and complex carbohydrates—the body's

> *At first, potatoes were not readily accepted as a food for humans. The Scots, at one time, refused to eat them because they were not mentioned in the Bible.*

main source of fuel. A medium 6-ounce potato has about 120 calories, is virtually fat free, and contains no cholesterol and only a small amount of sodium. Potatoes provide more protein and calories than any other food crop—five times more than corn, soy beans, and wheat.

The Incas cherished the potato's medicinal qualities. They believed that potatoes made childbirth easier and used them to treat all types of injuries. The large amount of vitamin c that potatoes contain (which is mostly lost if cooked for over 15 minutes) made them ideal to be eaten aboard ships to prevent scurvy. Also, potatoes can allegedly help in weight-loss diets, since they quickly make one feel full.

However, many of the nutrients are just under the skin, and to preserve them, potatoes should be cooked unpeeled. Cooked in this way, they do not lose any of their food value. They are a superb food: tasty, inexpensive, healthy, and versatile.

In our times, almost every country in the world grows and consumes potatoes—and in many, it is on a large scale. The chief food of the Incas has become the most popular garden produce in the world. Today, China leads the world in potato production. There are hundreds of species grown throughout the globe, but only a fraction of that number is commercially cultivated.

The best potatoes, no matter which type, are fairly clean, smooth, firm, and regular in shape—producing little waste in peeling. Those that are wrinkled, have shrivelled skins, soft dark areas, or gashed surfaces should be avoided. During our farming years, we ate the best potatoes after harvest time, but, as the weeks slipped by, the potatoes preserved by the covering soil became more and more shrivelled. We did not have the luxury of supermarkets as we have today.

Nevertheless, smooth and firm or wrinkled and dark, Mother was able to produce gourmet meals from this delicious gift of the earth, based upon the dishes of her mother country, Syria. The following recipes include a number of her dishes, some with added spices. The others are my own creations—a few of which are variations on common dishes we ate on the homestead. Yet, all have their roots in the traditional dishes of the Arab world. ✄

Derived from the Arabic word summâq, *sumac (also spelled sumach or sumak) may be the last of the great condiments still to be introduced into the West. Middle Eastern cooks have used it for thousands of years when they wanted to add a tart, sharp flavour to a dish, much as Western cooks have used lemon juice or vinegar. Mother used lemon juice in the Syrian dishes that required sumac simply because it was not available where we lived. This sour seasoning obtained from the Rhus coriaria, a species of the sumac tree, is still as indispensable to*

(continued on next page...)

POTATO AND SUMAC APPETIZER

SERVES 4

We enjoy this dish for breakfast but also as a late-evening snack.

4	large potatoes	4
	oil for frying	
2 tbsps	sumac *	30 ml
3	cloves garlic, crushed	3
½ tsp	salt	2 ml
¼ tsp	black pepper	1 ml
¼ tsp	cumin	1 ml
½ cup	warm water	125 ml
1	large onion, thinly sliced	1

1. Peel potatoes, then dice into ½-inch (1 cm) cubes.

2. Pour oil in a frying pan to 2 inches (5 cm) deep, then heat to medium. Deep fry potato cubes until golden. Remove with a slotted spoon, then set aside to drain on paper towels. Also, retain about 4 tbsps (60 ml) of oil in frying pan, then set aside.

3. Combine remaining ingredients, except onion, then set aside.

4. Heat reserved oil in frying pan, then sauté onion until golden. Set aside.

5. Place potato cubes on a platter, then spoon sumac mixture evenly over potato cubes. Spread onions evenly over top, then allow to stand for at least 30 minutes before serving.

* Sumac can be found in Middle Eastern stores.

EGGS AND POTATO OMELET
/ BAYD MA‘A BATAATA

SERVES 4 TO 6

5	medium potatoes	5
4 tbsps	cooking oil	60 ml
1 cup	water	250 ml
1 tsp	salt	5 ml
½ tsp	black pepper	2 ml
⅛ tsp	cayenne	½ ml
5	eggs, beaten	5

1. Peel potatoes and dice into very small pieces.

2. Heat oil in a frying pan, then add potatoes, water, salt, pepper, and cayenne. Cook over medium heat until water has been absorbed by potatoes, stirring occasionally. They should be tender, but still intact.

3. Pour eggs over potatoes, then turn heat down to low. Cover and cook without stirring for about 5 minutes, or until eggs are done. Serve immediately.

(…continued)

Middle Eastern cuisine as it was in the kitchens of the Sumerians and ancient Egyptians. Today, in the spice stalls of the historic cities of Aleppo, Baghdad, Cairo, Damascus, and Jerusalem, one still sees displays of this unique spice. Its tart flavour lends an inviting sharp taste to barbecues, chicken, curries, fish, salads, sauces, stews, stuffings, and vegetables. In the eastern Arab countries and adjoining lands, it is also used extensively with onions and salt as a savoury spice for roasts.

POTATO SALAD / BATAATA MUTABBALA

SERVES ABOUT 6

This Arab version of potato salad, which Mother often prepared, makes a refreshing change from the usual mayonnaise type and is perfect for picnics and barbecues.

4	large potatoes	4
2	hard-boiled eggs	2
4 tbsps	finely chopped green onions	60 ml
4 tbsps	finely chopped parsley	60 ml
2 tbsps	finely chopped fresh mint	30 ml
	Dressing	
4 tbsps	olive oil	60 ml
4 tbsps	lemon juice	60 ml
2	cloves garlic, crushed	2
¾ tsp	salt	3 ml
½ tsp	black pepper	2 ml

1. Boil potatoes with their skin until tender but still intact, then peel and dice into ½-inch (1 cm) cubes. Allow to cool.

2. Peel and chop hard-boiled eggs.

3. Place all but dressing ingredients in a salad bowl.

4. Combine dressing ingredients, then stir into salad bowl ingredients. Toss gently, making sure potatoes and eggs do not crumble too much. Chill for at least one hour before serving.

POTATO AND YOGURT SALAD / SALATAT BATAATA WA LABAN

SERVES ABOUT 6

1 lb	potatoes (about 4 medium)	454 g
2 tbsps	olive oil	30 ml
1	large onion, finely chopped	1
4	cloves garlic, crushed	4
2 tbsps	finely chopped cilantro	30 ml
½	small hot pepper, seeded and finely chopped	½
¾ tsp	salt	3 ml
½ tsp	black pepper	2 ml
1 cup	plain yogurt	250 ml

1. Peel potatoes, then dice into ½-inch (1 cm) cubes.

2. Heat oil in a saucepan, then sauté onion over medium heat for 8 minutes. Add garlic, cilantro, and hot pepper, then stir-fry for a further few minutes. Add remaining ingredients, except yogurt, then barely cover with water. Bring to boil, then cover and cook over medium-low heat for 20 minutes or until potatoes are done. Place in a serving bowl, then stir in yogurt and serve.

Ask the experienced rather than the learned.

POTATO CROQUETTES / 'IJJA

SERVES ABOUT 8

6	medium potatoes	6
6	eggs	6
1	large onion, finely chopped	1
1	small bunch parsley, stemmed and finely chopped	1
6	green onions, finely chopped	6
1 tbsp	finely chopped mint leaves	15 ml
1 tsp	salt	5 ml
1 tsp	cinnamon	5 ml
½ tsp	black pepper	2 ml
½ tsp	nutmeg	2 ml
⅛ tsp	cayenne	½ ml
¼ tsp	dried sage	1 ml
1 cup	flour	250 ml
	oil for frying	

Mother often made this dish but did not use all the included spices because they were unavailable during our early farming days.

1. Wash and boil potatoes, then peel and mash. Allow to cool.

2. To cooled mashed potatoes, add two eggs, onion, parsley, green onions, mint, salt, cinnamon, pepper, nutmeg, cayenne and sage, then thoroughly combine.

3. In a shallow bowl, beat remaining 4 eggs, then set aside.

4. Place flour on a flat plate, then set aside.

5. Form potato mixture into golf ball-sized balls, then dip into beaten eggs. Roll in flour, then flatten into patties and place on a floured tray.

6. Pour oil in a saucepan to 2 inches (5 cm) deep, then heat to medium. Fry patties until golden brown, then remove with a slotted spoon. Allow to drain on paper towels, then place on a platter and serve hot.

FRIED GARLIC-POTATOES / BATAATA MAQLEEYA MA'A THOOM

SERVES 4 TO 6

The English eat their fried potatoes or chips with vinegar and North Americans consume them with ketchup and vinegar, but the Arabs relish their fried potatoes with garlic and lemon.

2 lbs	potatoes (about 6 large)	907 g
	oil for frying	
½	head of garlic, peeled and crushed	½
4 tbsps	finely chopped cilantro	60 ml
1 tsp	salt	5 ml
½ tsp	black pepper	2 ml
⅛ tsp	cayenne	½ ml
2 tbsps	butter	30 ml
1	lemon, cut into wedges	1

1. Peel and dice potatoes into ½-inch (1 cm) cubes, then set aside.

2. Place oil in saucepan up to a 2-inch (5 cm) depth, then heat to medium. Fry potato cubes until they barely begin to brown, then remove with slotted spoon and drain on paper towels.

3. Combine remaining ingredients, except butter and lemon wedges, in a bowl, then stir in potato cubes and set aside.

4. Melt butter in a frying pan, then stir-fry potato mixture over medium heat for about 2 to 3 minutes. Place on a serving platter, then garnish with lemon wedges. Serve hot with each diner squeezing lemon to taste.

Go and wake up your cook.

Used extensively in North Africa and the Middle East, cumin is also a vital flavouring in the cuisines of many nations. Tantalizing and seductive, this ancient spice is today widely used throughout most of the Asian, Mediterranean, and Latin American worlds. Its sharp, pungent aroma seems to go well with the robust and hearty foods of these lands.

It is believed that cumin was first used as a flavouring in the Nile Valley from where its use spread to the neighbouring countries. It became an important spice in the Middle East, being mentioned in both the Old and New Testaments. Later, Arab traders carried its seeds to the Indian subcontinent and the Far East where it became a favoured spice.

STUFFED POTATO PATTIES / QARAAS BATAATA

MAKES 24 PATTIES

This dish, served with a salad, makes a tasty meal.

4 heaping cups	mashed potatoes	1 L (generous)
3 tbsps	flour	45 ml
1 tsp	salt	5 ml
2 tbsps	butter	30 ml
2	medium onions, finely chopped	2
4	cloves garlic, crushed	4
½ cup	pulverized almonds	125 ml
4 tbsps	raisins	60 ml
1 tsp	cumin	5 ml
½ tsp	black pepper	2 ml
⅛ tsp	cayenne	½ ml
½ cup	finely chopped cilantro	125 ml
2	eggs, beaten	2
1 cup	fine bread crumbs	250 ml
	oil for frying	

1. Place potatoes, flour, and salt in a mixing bowl, then thoroughly combine into a dough, adding a little milk if necessary. Form into 24 balls, then set aside.

2. Melt butter in a frying pan, then sauté onions over medium heat for 10 minutes. Add garlic, almonds, raisins, cumin, pepper, cayenne, and cilantro, then stir-fry for 3 minutes. Set aside as a filling, allowing it to cool.

3. Place eggs on a plate and bread crumbs on another plate, then set aside.

4. Make a deep and wide well in each potato ball. Place 1 heaping tablespoon (15 ml) of filling in well, then seal and flatten to about ¾ inch (2 cm) thick. Continue until all balls are done.

5. Pour oil in a saucepan to about 1½ inches (4 cm) deep, then heat to medium. Turn patties over in eggs; then in bread crumbs. Fry until golden brown, then drain on paper towels and serve warm.

An army of sheep led by a lion would defeat an army of lions led by a sheep.

POTATO PIE / SANEEYAT BATAATA

SERVES ABOUT 6

As in Europe, when the potato was introduced into the Arab world, it quickly became a common food. This dish is one of the many Arab foods prepared with this vegetable.

3 cups	mashed potatoes	750 ml
2	medium onions, finely chopped	2
3	cloves garlic, crushed	3
4 tbsps	butter	60 ml
3 tbsps	flour	45 ml
1 tbsp	finely chopped cilantro	15 ml
¾ tsp	salt	3 ml
¾ tsp	cumin	3 ml
½ tsp	black pepper	2 ml
½ tsp	ground ginger	2 ml
⅛ tsp	cayenne	½ ml
2 tbsps	olive oil	30 ml

1. Place all ingredients, except olive oil, in a mixing bowl, then thoroughly combine. Spread in a well-greased pan, then score top into diamond shapes.

2. Drizzle olive oil on top, then bake uncovered in a 350°F (180°C) preheated oven for 35 minutes or until top turns light brown. Serve hot as the main course or as a side dish.

POTATOES AND PINE NUTS
/ BATAATA MA'A SNOBAR

SERVES 6

For this dish, slivered almonds may be substituted for the pine nuts. Those Syrian dishes that required pine nuts were still prepared by my mother despite the unavailability of the nut in southern Saskatchewan. They were only a distant nostalgic memory for my parents.

3 cups	mashed potatoes	750 ml
½ cup	finely chopped green onions	125 ml
¾ tsp	salt	3 ml
½ tsp	black pepper	2 ml
¼ tsp	nutmeg	1 ml
6 tbsps	olive oil	90 ml
1	medium onion, finely chopped	1
2	cloves garlic, crushed	2
½ cup	pine nuts	125 ml

1. Thoroughly combine potatoes, green onions, salt, pepper, nutmeg, and 3 tbsps (45 ml) of the olive oil, then spread on a platter and set aside.

2. Heat remaining oil in a frying pan, then sauté onion and garlic over medium heat for 5 minutes. Add pine nuts, then stir-fry for another 5 minutes or until nuts begin to brown. Spread frying pan contents evenly over potatoes and serve.

POTATO STEW / YAKHNIT BATAATA

SERVES ABOUT 6

2 lbs	potatoes (about 6 large)	907 g
4 tbsps	olive oil	60 ml
1	small sweet pepper, seeded and finely chopped	1
1	medium onion, finely chopped	1
⅛ tsp	cayenne	½ ml
1 tbsp	cumin	15 ml
½ cup	finely chopped cilantro	125 ml
8	cloves garlic, crushed	8
3 cups	water	750 ml
1 tsp	salt	5 ml
	rind of 1 lemon, finely chopped	

1. Peel potatoes and dice into ¾-inch (2 cm) cubes.

2. Heat oil in a saucepan, then add sweet pepper and sauté for 5 minutes. Add potatoes and remaining ingredients and bring to boil. Cover and cook over medium-low heat for 40 minutes or until potatoes are well done, adding more water if necessary. Serve hot.

Choose the neighbour before the house.

CHAPTER 19

ARAB STEWS: I LOVED THEM ON THE FARM

I was always hungry when I returned home after helping my father working in the fields. As I opened the front door, almost always the aroma from the kitchen would overwhelm my senses. Usually this would stream out of a simmering pot atop our wood and coal stove. In summer, it was chicken or rabbit stew with fresh vegetables from the garden; in winter, the goulashes were beef or mutton with dried beans, chickpeas, or lentils. During the cold winter days after finishing our barn chores, I always looked forward to the delectable stew that our mother had prepared. The cold would fade into memory as my body would warm up, supping on that piping-hot people's food.

In the ensuing years when I roamed the Middle East and North Africa, I discovered that the stews of our farming days were only a part of the world of Arab goulashes. From Morocco to the Arabian Gulf, I came to know a whole series of new stew dishes—a good number of which are now included in my repertoire of foods. Yet, I remember most my mother's recipes and their appeal after a hard day's work. Intoxicating in their flavour and fragrant with their tantalizing aromas, these stews would always satisfy my hunger pangs. With a history as old as time, they had not lost their appeal.

Known to the eastern Arabs as *yakhni* and to the North Africans as *tajine*, these zesty dishes are perhaps the most delectable stews in the world, yet they are simple to prepare and require scant attention. Evolving for unnumbered centuries in the lands of antiquity, they have been perfected by thousands of years of civilized living.

The peoples of the ancient civilizations and later their heirs, the Arabs, all had a hand in perfecting today's Middle Eastern and North African stews. Arab authors who wrote about food over a thousand years ago have left us written records about these historic dishes. In the Abbasid era (750 to 1258 CE), when the Arabs were the pathfinders of world civilization, cookbooks were written which praised the succulent *yakhnis* of Baghdad and the eastern Islamic world. During the same centuries, when the Iberian Peninsula and Sicily were both Arab lands, Arab writers ecstatically described their racy, delicious cuisine.

In this same period, many new fruits and vegetables were introduced into western Europe through these countries. In the irrigated gardens developed by the Arabs in the Iberian Peninsula and Sicily, these foods flourished and later became a part of the food supply for all of Europe. The Arabic names of many fruits and vegetables in the European languages attest to this fact.

The Arabs considered the enjoyment of savoury foods to be one of the topmost pleasures in life, and with the newly introduced fruits and vegetables, they began to develop their *tajines*. Today, in parts of Europe, especially the Iberian Peninsula, many stews that grace the tables of these lands originated in the Arab East, which itself was influenced by the foods of Persia and the Indian subcontinent over millennia. Without doubt, the eggplant, chickpea, and lentil stews that one finds in Spain and Portugal owe their origins to dishes developed in the Middle East.

To eat Arabian goulashes is a delightful experience, surprising those who have never tasted these delectable stews. The meats and simple vegetables are transformed to create a taste that is smooth and intoxicating. Sautéeing the meats with the onions and garlic, then adding the other well-proportioned ingredients, produces a harmony of flavours and aromas, reflecting the richness and tastes of old civilizations. Like my mother's stews, these sumptuous and hearty *yakhnis* are prepared with meat and all types of vegetables, or they can be simply meatless, and then the ingredients simmer away in spices and herbs in order to generate a delicate texture and sapidity most Western stews fail to produce.

Two essential ingredients in almost all of the enormous repertoire of Arab stews are garlic and onions. They are always sautéed to golden brown. However, the numerous exotic herbs and spices, many of which the Arabs first introduced into Europe, are the ingredients which produce the subtle sauces, stimulating the taste buds.

Some of these condiments still carry their Arabic names. Caraway is the Arabic *karāwiyā*; cumin, *kammūn*; ginger, *zanjabīl*; saffron, *zaʿfarān*; sesame, *simsim*; sumac,

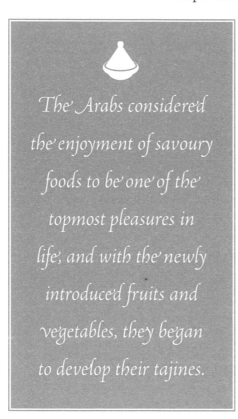

The Arabs considered the enjoyment of savoury foods to be one of the topmost pleasures in life, and with the newly introduced fruits and vegetables, they began to develop their tajines.

summāq; and tarragon, ṭarkhūn. Combined with other ingredients, such as allspice, basil, cayenne, cinnamon, coriander, mint, nutmeg, oregano, paprika, sage, and thyme, they work to sharpen the zest of the stews and create the waves of enticing aromas. The taste resulting from these seasonings seems to transform the meats and vegetables.

In Arab yakhnis and tajines, all types of inexpensive cuts of meat and fresh or dried vegetables can be used interchangeably. For centuries, the Arab peasants have dined on these simple dishes and in the process have learned the art of blending and balancing textures and aromas.

To appreciate these superb foods, one must eat at a villager's home where there is always a pot of stew simmering on the fire. With large families and limited incomes, like our family on the farm, stews are, in almost all cases, the core of the household's menu. The farmers consider them the ideal food for their way of life.

Renowned for their hospitality, the Arab peasants are always ready for unexpected guests. When a guest arrives, they exercise their inventiveness by adding a little more water and perhaps a few more vegetables to the simmering pot of yakhni or tajine. With rice or burghul, which are generally served as side dishes, the cook of the house is always ready. No Arab host will be embarrassed by running out of food as he or she reminds each guest: "The more you eat, the more we know how much you love us."

At one time, in the cities of the Arab East, the wealthy looked down upon appetizing yakhnis as peasant food, and for this reason they were rarely served in the fine restaurants or on the tables of the opulent. Time has brought reason, however. Eating healthy and nutritiously has overcome pompousness and, instead, almost everyone recognizes the nutritious benefits of these stews. Yet, to the toiling masses, it is another story, especially when all the family works. Arab stews do not become tasteless or stale and will still be good for two to three days after they have been cooked—in many cases, they even improve when reheated. Hence, the cook of the house need only cook once or twice a week, yet the family and their guests will dine on what really are gourmet meals.

The tajines of North Africa differ somewhat from the yakhnis of the Middle East. In these lands, the stews are, in many cases, sweetened with honey and fruits and decorated with nuts. Also, the North Africans, more so than their counterparts in the Middle East, make much more use of the herbs and spices that Arab traders carried from the East through their countries to the Iberian Peninsula and Sicily. Every dish cooked in North Africa entices not only with its subtle aroma, but by appealing to the eye in its method of decoration. In Morocco and Algeria, the dishes are generally not hotly spiced. On the other hand, the stews in Tunisia and Libya are fiery with their ginger and hot peppers.

No matter what yakhni or tajine one cooks, the taste of garlic, coriander, and other herbs or spices mixed with the juices of the meat and vegetables make every morsel an exquisite delight. These recipes that follow, a good number of which were prepared by my mother during our homesteading days, reflect all the glory of these Arab stews. ✖

NOTE: *In all the Arab stews, including the ones we have listed, other meats, vegetables, herbs and spices can be substituted. Should the cooks in North America continue to experiment as their counterparts in the Middle East and North Africa have been doing for centuries, who knows—perhaps, one day, the Arab stews, evolving since time immemorial, will reach their apex here on this continent!*

COOKED RICE / RUZ MUFALFAL

SERVES 4 TO 6

With every stew, cooked rice, burghul, or couscous (in North Africa) is usually served. This recipe of cooked rice is a simple dish to prepare.

5 tbsps	butter	75 ml
1 cup	long grain white rice, rinsed	250 ml
2 cups	boiling water	500 ml
½ tsp	salt	2 ml

1. Melt butter in a frying pan, then stir-fry rice over medium heat for two minutes. Add water and salt, then bring to boil. Turn heat to low, then cover and cook for 12 minutes. Turn off heat, stir rice, re-cover, and allow to cook in own steam for 20 minutes.

RICE DREAMS

In the countries of the Arabian Peninsula and the Greater Syria area, no greater honour can be bestowed upon a guest than a steaming dish of lamb and rice. An Arab mark of hospitality, it has been on the menu of Arab hosts since rice was first introduced into the Middle East some 2,000 years ago.

(continued on next page...)

PEAS WITH MEAT / BIZILLA MA'A LAHAM

SERVES 4 TO 6

1 lb	lamb or beef, cut into ½-inch (1 cm) cubes	454 g
4	tablespoons olive oil	60 ml
1	large onion, finely chopped	1
4	cloves garlic, crushed	4
3 cups	water	750 ml
2 cups	stewed tomatoes mixed with 1 cup (250 ml) water	500 ml
2 cups	shelled fresh peas (frozen peas may be substituted)	500 ml
1 ½ tsps	salt	7 ml
1 tsp	dried oregano	5 ml
¾ tsp	black pepper	3 ml
¾ tsp	allspice	3 ml
½ tsp	cumin	2 ml
⅛ tsp	cayenne	½ ml

1. Heat oil in a saucepan, then add the meat and sauté over medium heat until it begins to brown. Stir in onion and garlic, then sauté for a further 10 minutes, stirring a number of times.

2. Add water, then cover and simmer over low heat for 40 minutes, stirring occasionally and adding more water to ensure that there is just enough during the process to cover the meat.

3. Stir in remaining ingredients, cover and cook over medium-low heat for a further 20 minutes. Serve hot with Cooked Rice (page 244).

(...continued)

The members of the Canadian-Arab Middle Eastern community in Toronto have brought this love for rice dishes with them, and today, numerous restaurants, Eastern markets, and stores cater to their needs. The taste for these foods has now spread to wide sections outside this community, making a delectable mark on other Canadians.

—Habeeb Salloum, *"Arabian Rice Dreams,"* The Toronto Star, *June 2, 2004, D1 & D3.*

Once treasured as a delicacy in Moorish Spain, this small, attractively shaped vegetable had its origin in Ethiopia. From that ancient land, it travelled north to the Mediterranean shores and east to India. The African Arabs who called it uehka, from which the word "okra" could have derived, carried it to West Africa and the Iberian Peninsula. In Spain, after the Christian conquest, it fell out of favour, but in much of Africa and the eastern Mediterranean, okra thrived and became a popular food.

OKRA STEW / BAAMIYA WA LAHAM

SERVES 4 TO 6

1 lb	fresh or frozen okra	454 g
1 lb	beef or lamb	454 g
5 tbsps	butter	75 ml
1	large onion, finely chopped	1
3	cloves garlic, crushed	3
2 tbsps	lemon juice	30 ml
3	medium tomatoes, chopped	3
1 tsp	salt	5 ml
½ tsp	black pepper	2 ml
½ tsp	ground coriander	2 ml
¼ tsp	allspice	1 ml
1½ cups	water	375 ml

1. If okra is fresh, cut off stems; if frozen, allow to thaw, then set aside.

2. Cut beef or lamb into ½-inch (1 cm) cubes.

3. Melt butter in a saucepan, then add meat and sauté over medium heat until browned. Add onion and garlic, then sauté further for 10 minutes. Cover, then simmer on low heat until meat is almost cooked. Stir in okra, then stir-fry gently until it begins to brown. Add lemon juice, tomatoes, salt, pepper, coriander, allspice, and water, then stir and bring to boil. Cover, then simmer over medium-low heat for 45 minutes or until meat and okra are tender, stirring occasionally and adding more water if necessary to increase sauce to desired consistency.

4. Taste and adjust seasoning, then serve hot with rice.

BEAN STEW / YAKHNIT FASOOLIYA

SERVES ABOUT 8

1 cup	dried white navy beans	250 ml
6 cups	water	1.5 L
1 lb	beef	454 g
1	medium carrot	1
1	medium potato	1
4 tbsps	olive oil	60 ml
2	medium onions, finely chopped	2
4	cloves garlic, crushed	4
2 cups	stewed tomatoes	500 ml
4 tbsps	finely chopped fresh cilantro	60 ml
2 tsps	salt	10 ml
1 tsp	cumin	5 ml
½ tsp	black pepper	2 ml
½ tsp	tarragon	2 ml
⅛ tsp	cayenne	½ ml

1. Soak navy beans overnight and drain.

2. Place beans and water in a saucepan, then cook for 1½ hours or until beans are tender. Set aside with their water.

3. In the meantime, cut beef into ½-inch (1 cm) cubes. Peel carrot and slice into thin rounds. Peel potato and chop into medium-size pieces.

4. Heat oil in another saucepan, then sauté meat over medium heat until it begins to brown. Add onions and garlic, then sauté for a further 10 minutes. Stir in remaining ingredients, including beans with their water, then cover and simmer over medium heat for 40 minutes or until meat and vegetables are tender, adding more water if necessary to increase sauce to desired consistency. Serve hot with rice.

A loving eye to all your faults is blind, while hating eyes will every weakness find.

POTATO AND TOMATO STEW / YAKHNIT BANADOORA

SERVES ABOUT 8

1 lb	beef	454 g
5	medium potatoes	5
4 tbsps	olive oil	60 ml
3	medium onions, finely chopped	3
4	cloves garlic, crushed	4
1	small hot pepper, seeded and finely chopped	1
1½ tsps	salt	7½ ml
1 tsp	black pepper	5 ml
1 tsp	dried basil	5 ml
½ tsp	nutmeg	2 ml
5	medium tomatoes, chopped	5
5 cups	water	1.25 L

1. Cut beef into 1-inch (2.5 cm) cubes. Peel potatoes and dice into 1-inch (2.5 cm) cubes.

2. Heat oil in a saucepan, add meat, onions, garlic, and hot pepper, then sauté over medium heat for 10 minutes. Add remaining ingredients, except potatoes, then cover and cook over medium-low heat for 40 minutes. Add potatoes, re-cover then cook for an additional 30 minutes or until meat and potatoes are well-cooked, stirring occasionally and adding more water if necessary to increase sauce to desired consistency. Serve hot with rice.

FISH STEW WITH RICE / YAKHNIT SAMAK MA'A RUZ

SERVES 6 TO 8

2 tsps	salt, divided	10 ml
6 tbsps	lemon juice, divided	90 ml
2 lbs	fish fillet, any kind, cut into large pieces	907 g
5 tbsps	olive oil	75 ml
1	medium onion, chopped	1
3 tbsps	finely chopped fresh cilantro	45 ml
3	cloves garlic, crushed	3
1 tsp	black pepper	5 ml
½ tsp	thyme	2 ml
4 tbsps	tomato paste	60 ml
1½ cups	water	375 ml
2 cups	cooked rice	500 ml
½	lemon, sliced	½
1	small tomato, sliced	1
	sprigs of parsley	

1. Sprinkle 1 teaspoon (5 ml) of salt and 3 tbsps (45 ml) of lemon juice on fish fillet, then refrigerate for about 4 hours.

2. Heat oil in a frying pan, then add onion, coriander, garlic, pepper, thyme, and the remaining 1 teaspoon (5 ml) of salt, then stir-fry over medium heat until onions begin to brown. Stir in tomato paste, water, and the remaining 3 tbsps (45 ml) of lemon juice, then stir and simmer over low heat for 5 minutes.

3. Place fish in another frying pan. Pour the contents of the first frying pan over fish. Cover and allow to simmer over low heat for 25 minutes or until fish is cooked.

4. Place cooked rice on a serving platter, then carefully arrange fillet pieces over top of rice. Pour stew over fish and rice, then decorate with lemon and tomato slices and sprigs of parsley. Serve hot.

SERVES 6 TO 8

CARDAMOM

Today, throughout the world, cardamom seeds are utilized in a wide range of foods. In India and the Arab countries, they are used to flavour coffee, tea, soups, meat and vegetable dishes, sherbets, and sweets. In addition, they form an important ingredient in curries and, in Morocco, ras el hanout—a mixture of spices.

3 to 4 lbs	chicken	1.5 to 2 kg
½ cup	olive oil	125 ml
2	medium onions, chopped	2
2 cups	stewed tomatoes	500 ml
5	cloves garlic, crushed	5
4 cups	hot water	1 L
5	cardamom pods	5
2 tsps	salt	10 ml
1 tsp	ground coriander	5 ml
½ tsp	cinnamon	2 ml
½ tsp	black pepper	2 ml
1	large carrot, grated	1
1½ cups	rice, rinsed	375 ml
3 tbsps	raisins	45 ml
3 tbsps	slivered almonds	45 ml

1. Cut chicken into large pieces.

2. Heat oil in a saucepan, then sauté onions over medium heat until they begin to brown, about 8 minutes. Add chicken, tomatoes, and garlic, then stir-fry for another 8 minutes. Stir in water, cardamom, salt, coriander, cinnamon, pepper, and carrot, then cover and cook over for 40 minutes or until chicken is tender. Remove chicken pieces from sauce, but keep pieces warm. Discard cardamom pods.

3. Measure sauce. If necessary, add water to make 3 cups (750 ml), then stir in rice. Cover, then simmer over low heat for 25 minutes. Turn off heat, then allow rice to cook in own steam for 30 minutes, stirring occasionally to ensure rice does not stick to the bottom.

4. Place rice on a serving platter, then arrange pieces of chicken over top. Decorate with raisins and almonds, then serve hot.

MEAT AND NOODLE STEW / YAKHNIT SHI'REEYA

SERVES 4 TO 6

1½ lbs	beef or lamb	680 g
4 tbsps	butter	60 ml
2	large onions, finely chopped	2
2	large tomatoes, chopped	2
¼ cup	finely chopped fresh mint	60 ml
4	cloves garlic, crushed	4
2 tsps	salt	10 ml
1 tsp	black pepper	5 ml
½ tsp	tarragon	2 ml
4 cups	water	1 L
2 oz	wide noodles	57 g

1. Cut beef or lamb into ½-inch (1 cm) cubes.

2. Melt butter in a saucepan, then sauté onions over medium heat until they begin to brown, about 8 minutes. Add meat and remainder of ingredients, except noodles, then bring to boil. Cover, then simmer over low heat for 1 hour or until meat is tender, adding more water if necessary. Stir in noodles, then simmer for a further 20 minutes, adding more water if necessary to increase sauce to desired consistency. Serve hot.

Those who buy cheap meat will regret it when they taste its broth..

CHICKEN-POTATO STEW / YAKHNIT DAJAAJ WA BATAATA

SERVES ABOUT 6

3 to 4 lbs	chicken	1.5 to 2 kg
2 tsps	salt	10 ml
½ tsp	black pepper	2 ml
½ tsp	nutmeg	2 ml
½ tsp	cinnamon	2 ml
⅛ tsp	cayenne	½ ml
2	large potatoes	2
4 tbsps	butter	60 ml
4	cloves garlic, crushed	4
3	medium onions, thinly sliced	3
2 cups	stewed tomatoes	500 ml
2 cups	water	500 ml

1. Cut chicken into medium-size pieces.

2. Mix salt, pepper, nutmeg, cinnamon, and cayenne together then sprinkle all over chicken pieces. Allow to stand for 1 hour.

3. Dice potatoes into ½-inch (1 cm) cubes.

4. Melt butter in a saucepan, then add chicken pieces, garlic, and onions. Sauté until golden brown. Stir in remaining ingredients, including potatoes, then bring to boil. Cover, then cook over medium-low heat for 40 minutes or until the chicken and potatoes are well cooked, adding more water if necessary to increase sauce to desired consistency. Serve hot.

Better to die with honour than to live with humiliation.

MEAT STEW / YAKHNIT L'AHAM

SERVES 4 TO 6

1 ½ cups	grapefruit juice	375 ml
1 tbsp	orange blossom water	15 ml
½ tsp	nutmeg	2 ml
½ tsp	ginger	2 ml
2 lbs	sirloin	907 g
2 tsps	salt	10 ml
½ tsp	black pepper	2 ml
¼ tsp	cayenne	1 ml
1 cup	finely chopped parsley	250 ml
1 tbsp	flour or cornstarch, mixed with 2 tbsps water	5 ml
2 cups	water	500 ml
½ cup	raisins	125 ml

1. Combine grapefruit juice, orange blossom water, nutmeg, and ginger, then set aside.

2. Cut meat into 2-inch (5 cm) cubes. Place meat pieces in a casserole, then pour grapefruit mixture over meat. Let stand for 1 hour, turning a few times, then remove meat. Add salt, pepper, cayenne, and parsley to grapefruit mixture in the casserole, then thoroughly mix. Return meat to mixture, then cover and place in a 350°F (180°C) preheated oven. Bake for 1 hour and 15 minutes or until meat is cooked, then remove meat and place in a serving platter, reserving the sauce in the casserole.

3. Stir flour or cornstarch into sauce in casserole, then add water and raisins. Stir, then cover and return to oven for about 10 minutes, adding more water if too thick. Pour over meat, then serve with rice or mashed potatoes.

GINGER

Ginger in all its forms can be employed as a seasoning in a great number of foods and beverages. A tasty, aromatic rootstock, it adds a spicy touch and zest to appetizers, bakery products, curries, jams, marinades, pickles, preserves, puddings, sauces, soups, stews, drinks, and all types of fruits, meats and vegetables. Imbuing foods with a mouth-watering tang, this spice of the ages has become an essential ingredient in the kitchens of the world.

MEAT AND CARROT STEW / SHTATHA ZRUDIYA

SERVES 4 TO 6

I vividly remember my first experience being served a stew cooked with fresh cilantro. The dish was prepared by a family friend who had recently arrived from the Middle East. Since that first taste of this savoury herb over half a century ago, I have become a fanatical advocate of this exquisite, parsley-like plant.

1 lb	beef or lamb	454 g
4 tbsps	olive oil	60 ml
1	head of garlic, finely chopped	1
1 tsp	paprika	5 ml
1 tsp	ground caraway	5 ml
1 tsp	salt	5 ml
½ tsp	black pepper	2 ml
½ cup	finely chopped fresh cilantro	125 ml
2 cups	thinly sliced carrots	500 ml
3½ cups	boiling water	875 ml
4 tbsps	tomato paste	60 ml

1. Cut beef or lamb into ½-inch (1 cm) cubes. In a saucepan, sauté meat in olive oil over medium heat until it begins to brown, then add garlic and sauté further until garlic is golden. Add remainder of the ingredients, except tomato paste, then bring to boil. Cover and simmer over medium-low heat for 1 hour or until meat and carrots are cooked, adding more water if necessary to increase sauce to desired consistency. Stir in tomato paste, then simmer for a further 10 minutes. Serve hot.

ALMOND STEW / AL-QIDRA BI LAWZ

SERVES 4 TO 6

During our homestead era, Mother would often talk of almonds and their delicious taste. However, they were unavailable in the nearby towns where we shopped. It was to be in my later years that she first used almonds in her cooking and then only sparingly. I became a true fan of almonds, and also fruit and sweets in stews—never ingredients used by my mother—when I encountered the stews of North Africa.

This and the following three recipes were inspired by my many trips to North Africa.

2 lbs	beef or lamb	907 g
4 tbsps	butter	60 ml
4	medium onions, finely chopped	4
4	cloves garlic, crushed	4
1 ½ tsps	salt	7 ½ ml
1 tsp	black pepper	5 ml
½ tsp	ginger	2 ml
½ tsp	cinnamon	2 ml
⅛ tsp	saffron	½ ml
½ cup	slivered almonds	125 ml
2 cups	water	500 ml
½ cup	finely chopped fresh cilantro	125 ml
½ cup	finely chopped parsley	125 ml

1. Cut beef or lamb into 1-inch (2.5 cm) cubes.

2. Melt butter in a saucepan, then add meat, onions, garlic, salt, pepper, ginger, cinnamon, and saffron, then stir-fry over medium heat for 10 minutes. Add almonds and water, then cover and cook over medium heat until meat is almost done, about 30 minutes, adding more water if necessary. Stir in coriander and parsley, then simmer over low heat until meat is well done. Serve hot with rice or plain couscous.

LAMB STEW WITH PRUNES AND HONEY / TAJINE FAS

SERVES 4 TO 6

Unlike in Moroccan cuisine, Mother never used fruits in her Syrian meat dishes. It was only later in North Africa that I was introduced to the combination of the two and I learned of what I refer to as heavenly stews. This dish is a specialty of the city of Fez in Morocco.

2 lbs	lamb	907 g
4 tbsps	olive oil	60 ml
1	medium onion, finely chopped	1
½ cup	finely chopped fresh cilantro	125 ml
2	cloves garlic, crushed	2
2 tsps	salt	10 ml
½ tsp	ginger	2 ml
½ tsp	black pepper	2 ml
½ tsp	tarragon	2 ml
½ tsp	cinnamon	2 ml
2 cups	water	500 ml
2 cups	small prunes, pitted	500 ml
3 tbsps	honey	45 ml
1 tsp	orange blossom water	5 ml
2 tbsps	toasted sesame seeds	30 ml

1. Cut lamb into 1-inch (2.5 cm) cubes.

2. Heat oil in a saucepan, then add lamb, onion, cilantro, garlic, salt, ginger, pepper, tarragon, cinnamon, and water. Cover, then bring to a boil. Turn heat to low, then simmer for 1 hour or until lamb is well cooked, adding more water if necessary. Stir in prunes and honey, then simmer over low heat for 15 minutes, stirring frequently. If more sauce is desired, add more water. Stir in orange blossom water, then bring to a boil. Place on a serving platter, then sprinkle with toasted sesame seeds. Serve immediately with rice or couscous.

EGG AND ALMOND STEW / TAJINE TUFAAYA

SERVES 4 TO 6

1½ lbs	beef	680 g
3 tbsps	butter	45 ml
2	medium onions, finely chopped	2
1½ tsps	salt	12 ml
½ tsp	black pepper	2 ml
½ tsp	paprika	2 ml
⅛ tsp	cayenne	½ ml
1 pinch	saffron	1 pinch
2 cups	water	500 ml
4 tbsps	finely chopped fresh cilantro	60 ml
4 tbsps	olive oil	60 ml
½ cup	slivered almonds	125 ml
4	hard-boiled eggs, shelled and quartered	4

1. Cut beef into 1-inch (2.5 cm) cubes.

2. Melt butter in a saucepan, then add onions, salt, pepper, paprika, cayenne, saffron, and meat. Stir-fry over medium heat until meat begins to brown, then add water and cilantro. Cover, then cook over medium heat about an hour or until meat is well cooked, adding more water if necessary. Turn off heat and set aside.

3. Heat oil in a frying pan, then add almonds and sauté until golden. Remove from oil and set aside.

4. Place meat with its sauce in a serving platter, then garnish with almonds. Place egg quarters evenly spaced on top, then serve hot.

TUNISIAN LAMB AND POTATO STEW

SERVES 4 TO 6

1½ lbs	lamb	680 g
3	medium potatoes	3
4 tbsps	butter	60 ml
3	medium onions, finely chopped	3
4	cloves garlic, crushed	4
2 tsps	salt	10 ml
1 tsp	black pepper	5 ml
1 tsp	sage	5 ml
½ tsp	ground caraway seeds	2 ml
½ tsp	allspice	2 ml
⅛ tsp	cayenne	½ ml
2 cups	water	500 ml
3	medium tomatoes, sliced in half	3
½ cup	finely chopped parsley	125 ml
½ cup	toasted slivered almonds	125 ml

1. Cut lamb into 1-inch (2.5 cm) cubes. Peel and dice potatoes into 1-inch (2.5 cm) cubes.

2. Melt butter in a frying pan, then add meat, onions, and garlic, and sauté over medium heat until meat begins to brown. Stir in potatoes, salt, pepper, sage, caraway, allspice, cayenne, and water, then bring to boil. Cover, and cook over medium-low heat for about 10 minutes.

3. Transfer frying pan contents into a casserole, then arrange tomato pieces, cut-side down on top of stew. Cover, then bake in a 350°F (180°C) preheated oven for 1 hour or until meat is well cooked.

4. Garnish with parsley and slivered almonds, then serve hot from casserole with rice.

Our lamb and potato stew that Mother made was less spicy but nonetheless just as delicious as what Tunisia offers.

CHAPTER 20

STUFFED VEGETABLES: THE FOOD OF SULTANS

Our garden flourished during autumn in 1935, and, as a result, we enjoyed fabulous meals, mostly of stuffed vegetables. It was harvest time, and our garden was heavy with vegetable marrow, cabbage, tomatoes, potatoes, peppers, and other types of vegetables. In this time of bounty, my mother made us gourmet meals of stuffed vegetables day after day, and yet she still could barely keep up with the ripening garden produce.

I remember vividly these succulent repasts. In later years I would replicate them, often adding condiments that were beyond my mother's reach in our lean farming years. Relatively unknown to many in the Western world, these dishes have a long and distinguished history in the Middle East and other eastern lands.

Known to the Greeks as *dolmath*, the Turks as *dolma*, the Persians as *dolmeh*, and the Arabs as *mahshī*, stuffed vegetables have been a favoured food in the Middle East and the Balkans for centuries. It is believed that their origins go back to the ancient Middle East and Greece, where stuffed leaves of fig, hazelnut, or mulberry trees—combined with a number of vegetables—became part of the daily meal.

However, the Turkish upper classes were the ones who refined these dishes and evolved them into the cuisine of sultans. The elaborate preparation needed to ready them for the pot made stuffed vegetables the specialty of the affluent. They became known as "the food of aristocrats," and were, for centuries, the top culinary delicacies in the grand banquets of the Turkish court.

The most widely known of these are meat-filled cabbage leaves—known, of course, as cabbage rolls. Besides their traditional home in the Middle East and eastern Europe, they are now well-known in western Europe and North America. Carried to the Western Hemisphere by the millions of immigrants from the lands surrounding the eastern Mediterranean and the Balkans, today they appear on many restaurant menus in North American urban centres, as well as in homes across the prairies.

More exotic, yet akin to cabbage rolls, are the stuffed tender leaves of the grape—known more commonly in North America as *dolma* or stuffed grape leaves. Very common in the eastern Mediterranean countries, they are a delicacy still to be discovered by some in the West. The epitome of stuffed foods to their great number of culinary fans, *dolmas* are a very delicious gourmet treat.

These two traditional and commonly used leaves—the cabbage and the grape leaf—and, in fact, almost any other leaf and many edible vegetables, can be stuffed with meat or meatless ingredients. The subtle flavour produced from the fusion of the leaves and vegetables with their fillings give these dishes an irresistible appeal. An expert or an ordinary cook can create tantalizing dishes which will titillate the palate from what are the everyday consumed vegetables so readily available.

There is, however, one drawback in the preparation of these foods: the work can be considerable. Nevertheless, if cooks exert a little effort and time, they can prepare dishes that are truly mouth-watering. Indeed, a meal prepared with a combination of these stuffed vegetables makes the repast a feast fit for a sultan's table—a fantastic feast we ourselves often enjoyed in our farming years.

> *These two traditional and commonly used leaves—the cabbage and the grape leaf—and, in fact, almost any other leaf and many edible vegetables, can be stuffed with meat or meatless ingredients.*

STUFFED GRAPE LEAVES / MAHSHEE WARAQ 'INAB

SERVES ABOUT 8

1 lb jar	grape leaves*	454 g jar
1 cup	lentils, soaked overnight and drained	250 ml
1 cup	rice, rinsed	250 ml
2	medium onions, finely chopped	2
2	medium tomatoes, finely chopped	2
4	cloves garlic, crushed	4
½ cup	finely chopped fresh mint	125 ml
4 tbsps	olive oil	60 ml
1 tsp	black pepper	5 ml
1 tsp	cumin	5 ml
½ tsp	allspice	2 ml
½ tsp	salt	2 ml
2 cups	tomato juice, mixed with ½ tsp salt and 1 tsp (5 ml) oregano	500 ml

1. Thoroughly wash out salt from grape leaves. Pour boiling water over leaves and let sit in water for 10 minutes, then drain well in a strainer to eliminate excess water. Set aside.

2. Prepare stuffing by combining all remaining ingredients, except the tomato juice mixture. Place approximately 1 heaping tablespoon (15-20 ml) stuffing (depending on size of leaf) on wide end of each grape leaf, then roll tightly, making sure to tuck in ends when rolling. Continue until all leaves are rolled.

3. Place any extra leaves on bottom of a saucepan, then tightly arrange rolls side by side in alternating layers. Sprinkle salt over top, then pour tomato juice over rolls. Cover with inverted plate, then add enough water to barely cover plate. Bring to boil, then cover. Cook over medium-low heat for 1 hour or until rice is done. Serve hot or cold as main course or for snacking.

* *If using fresh grape leaves, increase the salt in the stuffing to 1 teaspoon.*

Grape leaves were not available where we homesteaded in Saskatchewan. It was only when Dad and Mom moved to Neville that they were able to have grape leaves shipped in bulk from Montreal.

Swiss chard, kohlrabi leaves, or other vegetable leaves may be substituted for the grape leaves. Be sure to pour boiling water over them to soften them before use. Also, the same stuffing that is used for cabbage rolls may be substituted.

CABBAGE ROLLS / MALFOOF MAHSHEE

SERVES ABOUT 8

Cabbage grew well in our garden, weather permitting. Mother would boil cabbage when she made Safoof and Tabboula so that we could scoop up each mouthful. However, it was Mother's cabbage rolls that we loved the best. Meat-filled cabbage rolls are the most widely eaten of all the stuffed vegetables.

3 lbs	cabbage (about 1 medium head)	1.3 kg
	Stuffing	
2 tsps	salt, divided	10 ml
1 lb	lamb or beef, ground or cut into very small pieces	454 g
1 cup	rice, rinsed	250 ml
2 cups	stewed tomatoes	500 ml
3 tbsps	melted butter	45 ml
4 tbsps	finely chopped fresh mint	60 ml
2 tbsps	finely chopped fresh cilantro	30 ml
1 tsp	black pepper	5 ml
1 tsp	allspice	5 ml
½ tsp	cinnamon	2 ml
½ tsp	cumin	2 ml
⅛ tsp	cayenne	½ ml

❧

8	cloves garlic, chopped into large pieces	8
½ cup	lemon juice	125 ml

1. Place cabbage in a pot of boiling water, then boil for a few minutes to soften leaves. Loosen leaves with a knife from bottom. Trim thick ribs, then cut large leaves in half. (If inner leaves are not soft, boil again for a few minutes.) Set leaves aside and reserve ribs.

2. To make the stuffing, in a bowl, mix together 1 teaspoon of the salt and the remaining ingredients, except the garlic and lemon juice.

3. Place some stuffing (depending on size of leaf) on wide end of cabbage leaf and roll, tucking in ends while rolling. Continue until all leaves are stuffed.

4. Cover bottom of a saucepan with trimmed ribs. Arrange rolls side by side in alternating layers, placing garlic pieces between rolls. Sprinkle remaining 1 teaspoon salt over top. Cover with inverted plate, then add enough water to barely cover plate.

5. Bring to boil, then cover and cook over medium-low heat for 1 hour or until meat and rice are done. Remove plate and drizzle lemon juice on top of cabbage, re-cover and cook a further 5 minutes. Serve hot.

A table without vegetables is like an old man without wisdom.

STUFFED ZUCCHINI / MAHSHEE KOOSA

SERVES 8

This was one of my favourite dishes while growing up in southern Saskatchewan. I still do not know how my mother had the patience to core, then stuff, these small zucchini, and at the same time rear eight children. Of course, my father, working in the field all day, would look forward to coming home and feasting on this tasty dish.

16	small zucchini, about 5 inches (12 cm) long	16
1 lb	ground lamb or beef	454 g
1 cup	rice, rinsed	250 ml
4 tbsps	melted butter	60 ml
1	large onion, finely chopped	1
4	cloves garlic, crushed	4
4 tbsps	finely chopped parsley	60 ml
2 tbsps	finely chopped fresh cilantro	30 ml
1 tsp	black pepper	5 ml
1 tsp	oregano	5 ml
1 tsp	salt	5 ml
½ tsp	allspice	2 ml
⅛ tsp	cayenne	½ ml
2 cups	tomato juice mixed with 1 tsp (5 ml) nutmeg	500 ml

1. Cut off stem ends of zucchini and reserve, then core zucchini. (Corer can be purchased from Middle Eastern stores.) Set aside.

2. To make the stuffing, combine remaining ingredients, except the tomato juice.

3. Stuff zucchini, then close with inverted stem ends. Arrange tightly in a saucepan, then place inverted plate on top. Add tomato juice and enough water to cover plate, then bring to boil. Cover saucepan, then cook over medium heat for 1 hour. Serve hot.

STUFFED SWEET PEPPERS / MAHSHEE FLAYFLA

SERVES 6

A mixture of red and green peppers make a colourful dish.

6	large sweet peppers	6
1 lb	ground beef or lamb	454 g
½ cup	rice, rinsed	125 ml
2	medium tomatoes, finely chopped	2
1	medium onion, finely chopped	1
4 tbsps	finely chopped fresh cilantro	60 ml
2 tbsps	olive oil	30 ml
1 tsp	salt	7 ml
½ tsp	black pepper	2 ml
½ tsp	cumin	2 ml
½ tsp	allspice	2 ml
⅛ tsp	cayenne	½ ml
2 cups	tomato juice mixed with	500 ml
	1 tsp (5 ml) garlic powder	

1. Cut out stem ends of peppers and reserve. Remove seeds and fibres from peppers, then set aside.

2. Combine remaining ingredients, except tomato juice, to make stuffing.

3. Stuff peppers, then close with stem ends. Arrange in a saucepan with opening to top, cover with inverted plate then add tomato juice and enough water to top of peppers. Bring to boil, then cover and cook over medium heat for 50 minutes or until peppers are done. Serve hot with their sauce.

PEPPERS

Unknown in the "Old World" before Columbus, capsicums (known also as bell or sweet peppers) were brought back to Europe by the Spaniards, and in the ensuing centuries, their cultivation spread across the globe. Notwithstanding the fact that many believe they are native to India, it was the Portuguese who introduced them into the subcontinent in the seventeenth century. They caught on like wildfire nonetheless in India, and thereafter became a favourite in that land of countless spices.

STUFFED POTATOES / MAHSHEE BATAATA

SERVES 6

6	large baking potatoes	6
4 tbsps	olive oil	60 ml
1	medium onion, finely chopped	1
2	cloves garlic, crushed	2
2 tbsps	finely chopped fresh cilantro	30 ml
½	small hot pepper, seeded and finely chopped	½
1 cup	ground beef or lamb	250 ml
1 tsp	cumin	5 ml
1 tsp	salt	5 ml
¾ tsp	black pepper	3 ml
1½ cups	water	375 ml
4 tbsps	tomato paste	60 ml

1. Bake potatoes in skins, until tender but still firm.

2. Cut off top of potatoes, then core or scoop out pulp, leaving from ¼- to ½-inch (½ to 1 cm) shells. Set aside. Reserve pulp.

3. To make the stuffing, heat oil in frying pan, then sauté onion, garlic, cilantro, hot pepper, and meat over medium heat for 10 to 15 minutes or until meat is browned. Allow to cool, then stir in two-thirds of pulp and remaining ingredients, except water and tomato paste. (Discard the other one-third of the pulp.)

4. Stuff potato shells, then place in a greased casserole.

5. Combine water and tomato paste. Pour mixture over potatoes, then cover. Bake in a 300°F (150°C) preheated oven for 30 minutes, then serve hot.

STUFFED TURNIPS / MAHSHEE LIFT

SERVES 8

Kohlrabi may be substituted for the turnips.

4 lbs	medium white turnips (about 8), trimmed and washed	1.8 kg

Stuffing

1 cup	pulverized almonds	250 ml
2	medium onions, finely chopped	2
4 tbsps	butter, melted	60 ml
1 tsp	salt	5 ml
1 tsp	black pepper	5 ml
½ tsp	ground ginger	2 ml
⅛ tsp	cayenne	½ ml

Cooking Mixture

1½ cups	water	375 ml
2 tbsps	finely chopped cilantro	30 ml
½ tsp	each of salt, black pepper, and garlic powder	2 ml

1. Place turnips in a saucepan, then cover with water. Bring to boil, then cook over medium heat for 15 minutes or until turnips are half-cooked. Remove from heat, then discard water and allow turnips to cool. Cut off tops and scoop out to form the thickness of about ¼-inch (6 mm) shells. Reserve tops.

2. Combine stuffing ingredients. Stuff turnips, then secure tops with toothpicks. Place in a greased casserole with cut tops up, then pour in cooking mixture. Cover, then bake in a 350°F (180°C) preheated oven for 1 hour or until turnips are well done. Serve hot directly from the casserole.

    NOTE: *For a side dish, the turnip pulp can be further cooked, then mashed. Butter and spices can be added to taste.*

Turnips seemed to be part of our meals year-round. This does not mean that Stuffed Turnips were daily fare, but rather pickled turnips that Mother made at harvest time, during the autumn. Pickled they were multi-purpose: condiment, side dish, and vegetable serving.

STUFFED CARROTS / MAHSHEE JAZAR

SERVES ABOUT 6

A similar dish called zanahorias rellenas *is prepared in the Latin-American countries.*

12	large carrots, scraped and washed	12
4 tbsps	olive oil	60 ml
½ lb	ground beef or lamb	227 g
2	medium onions, finely chopped	2
1	small sweet pepper, seeded and finely chopped	1
1	small hot pepper, seeded and finely chopped	1
4	cloves garlic, crushed	4
1½ tsps	salt, divided	10 ml
1 tsp	ground coriander seeds	5 ml
½ tsp	black pepper	2 ml
4 tbsps	tomato paste	60 ml
1 tsp	dried basil	5 ml
1 tsp	oregano	5 ml

1. Place carrots in a saucepan, then cover with water. Cook until carrots are somewhat tender, then remove from heat and allow to cool. Remove carrots, but reserve broth.

2. Cut each carrot lengthwise, then scoop out heart and set aside. Chop carrot hearts and reserve.

3. To make the stuffing, heat oil in frying pan, then sauté meat, onions, sweet pepper, hot pepper, and garlic over medium heat for 10 minutes. Stir in 1 teaspoon of the salt, coriander, and black pepper.

4. Stuff carrots, then firmly attach pieces together with toothpicks. Place carefully in a greased casserole, then set aside.

5. Stir into the reserved carrot broth the tomato paste, basil, oregano, the chopped carrot hearts, and the remaining ½ teaspoon of salt, then add water to make 3 cups (750 ml). Pour over carrots in the casserole, cover, then bake in a 350°F (180°C) preheated oven for 40 minutes or until carrots are cooked and very tender. Serve hot with sauce.

A dog remains a dog even if you dress it in gold.

STUFFED PEPPER SQUASH / MAHSHEE QAR'

SERVES 10 TO 12

Small pumpkins may be substituted for the pepper squash.

3	pepper squash, from 1 to 2 lbs (.5 to 1 kg) each	3
1½ cups	roasted pulverized raw cashews	375 ml
1 cup	mashed potatoes	250 ml
2	medium onions, finely chopped	2
2	cloves garlic, crushed	2
4 tbsps	olive oil	60 ml
1 tsp	salt	5 ml
1 tsp	black pepper	5 ml
1 tsp	ground coriander	5 ml
⅛ tsp	cayenne	½ ml

1. Cut out stem ends of squash and reserve. Scoop out seeds and fibres and discard.

2. Combine remaining ingredients to make stuffing. Stuff squash, then replace stem ends.

3. Place in a greased baking pan, then bake in a 350°F (180°C) preheated oven for 1 hour or until squash is well done. Allow to cool, then peel and slice each squash into serving pieces before serving.

STUFFED TOMATOES WITH MEAT / MAHSHEE BANADOORA MA'A LAHAM

SERVES 8

The stuffing for this recipe can be used to stuff a mixture of tomatoes and peppers.

8	medium, firm tomatoes	8
4 tbsps	olive oil	60 ml
½ lb	ground beef or lamb	227 g
1	medium onion, finely chopped	1
½	hot pepper, seeded and finely chopped	½
2	cloves garlic, crushed	2
1½ tsps	salt, divided	7 ml
½ tsp	black pepper	2 ml
¾ cup	rice, rinsed	175 ml
2½ cups	water, divided	625 ml
1 tsp	basil	5 ml
1 tsp	thyme	5 ml

Alternate recipes for stuffed tomatoes are on pages 95 and 224.

1. Cut out stem ends of tomatoes and reserve. Scoop out pulp and reserve. Set both aside.

2. To make the stuffing, heat oil in a frying pan, then sauté meat, onion, hot pepper, and garlic over medium heat for 10 minutes. Stir in ½ teaspoon (2 ml) of the salt, black pepper, rice, and 1 cup (250 ml) of water, then cover and cook over low heat for 20 minutes to make stuffing.

3. Stuff tomato shells, then replace stem ends. Arrange side by side in a greased casserole, tops up.

4. Combine remainder of salt and water, basil, thyme, and tomato pulp, then pour over tomatoes. Cover and bake in 350°F (180°C) preheated oven for 1 hour. Serve hot with their sauce.

MOROCCAN FOOD

Even more so than in Spain, food in Morocco is the mirror of the nation. During my first visit to that country in the early 1960s, as we sat down to dine in a Moroccan friend's home in the beautiful capital of Rabat, I was astonished at the eating ritual. Living all my life in North America, I was ignorant of the cultures of other people.

I had become acquainted with my Moroccan friend, Idriss, during his student years in Canada. He had dined in our home many times, and now I was enjoying his hospitality.

In a Moorish-style dining room, made stunning by exquisitely tiled walls, we sat down on low stools around a huge copper platter on which course after course of different dishes were served. With the exception of the soup, everyone scooped up the food with their right hand from common dishes. It was a scene as old as time.

Idriss was a member of one of the aristocrat families in Morocco, and his family followed the traditions of his ancestors in dining and food. His roots went back to medieval Arab Spain—to the time when Morocco and Spain were one nation. Proud of what the Arabs had accomplished in the Iberian Peninsula, he carried on the traditions of his ancestors.

That evening as we feasted with Idriss and his family, he talked about Andalusia and of how many of his relatives and friends still eat the same food and live as their ancestors had done in that once-Arab land. Eating with his hand from a common dish and dining in the atmosphere of Moorish arches and seductive tiles was a way of keeping the pride and traditions of his ancestors alive. There is little doubt that these embellishments and the food once eaten in Moorish Spain, along with its traditions, gave him pride and kept his connections with the past alive.

—Habeeb Salloum, "Do Nations Express Themselves in Their Foods?" Contemporary Review, *278.1621 (2001): 107–11.*

CHAPTER 21

STUFFED STOMACH: THE EPITOME OF ALL THE SULTAN'S FOODS

Even though, year after year, our family enjoyed a bounty of stuffed vegetables during late summer and early autumn, the time that I always looked forward to was when the frost came and my father butchered a few sheep or a steer for our winter meat. An outside shed was our food freezer; from these animals, we had meat all winter long. Yet, it was not the meat dishes that I so anticipated but rather the thought of our yearly feast of stuffed tripe and intestines. For it was these two dishes that tempered my loathing of the bitter cold and frost that winter would bring.

My mother would spend hours scrubbing and cleaning the stomach and intestines of the sheep and/or steer, preparing them for stuffing. First, she would scrub them on the outside with soap, then turn them inside out and repeat the procedure. This she would do a number of times until the stomach and intestines were very clean. The cleansed stomach and intestines were then soaked in salt and vinegar and placed in the cool shed ready to be stuffed the next day.

As was usual in doing most farm chores, we children would also lend a hand. We would bring the hot water that my mother had boiling on the stove and carry the remains from the stomach and intestines to the manure pile behind the nearby barn. It was a task I did not detest for I knew that soon we would be feasting on stuffed stomach and intestines.

In the evening, my mother would soak the chickpeas, readying them for the stuffing. In the morning, she would drain, then split, the chickpeas by placing them on one half of a towel. Next, she would fold the other half of the towel over the chickpeas, then roll with a rolling pin. This would loosen the skin and split each chickpea into two. Finally, she would discard the skins and place the split chickpeas into a bowl, ready to mix with the other ingredients to make a stuffing.

That morning, as the stuffed stomach and intestines were cooking, their aroma would make my hunger pangs increase by the minute. By the time the dish was ready, I was in a dream world, mesmerized by my thoughts of the mouth-watering meal. I will always remember this particular meal, which happened every year, with great fondness.

In the subsequent years, I have often prepared this dish, sans the work of cleaning the stomach and intestines. For today, in the many Greek and Middle Eastern meat markets found in the larger cities throughout the world, one can find cleaned lamb stomachs, ready for stuffing. No longer does a cook have the arduous task of cleaning. As a friend of mine remarked, "Thank goodness for our modern meat markets!" ✿

STUFFED SHEEP STOMACH / MAHSHEE QIRSH

During the Second World War, while I was stationed in Great Britain, I once dined on haggis, the Scottish version of stuffed intestines. I ate it but was not impressed with the stuffing made with the animal's heart, lungs, and liver, all mixed together with oatmeal. It was probably because the stuffing that Mother made was much richer and tastier.

1	sheep stomach, scraped, then scrubbed with soap and very thoroughly washed	1
5½ tsps	salt, divided	27 ml
4 tbsps	vinegar	60 ml
1 tsp	allspice	5 ml
1 tsp	garlic powder	5 ml
½ lb	lamb or beef with a little fat	227 g
4 tbsps	butter	60 ml
4	large onions, finely chopped	4
2 cups	split chickpeas or cooked chickpeas	500 ml
1½ cups	rice, rinsed	375 ml
1 tsp	black pepper	5 ml
½ tsp	nutmeg	2 ml
½ tsp	cinnamon	2 ml
4 tbsps	toasted pine nuts	60 ml

1. Cut stomach into 4 pieces, then rub with 4 teaspoons (20 ml) of the salt. Place in a bowl, then add vinegar and cover with water. Allow to stand overnight, then drain. Thoroughly wash, then dry. Mix allspice and garlic powder, then rub both inside and outside of the stomach pieces. Using a needle and strong thread (preferably nylon), sew into bags with an opening, then set aside.

2. Cut lamb or beef into ½-inch (1 cm) cubes. Melt butter in a frying pan, then sauté meat over medium heat until it begins to brown. Stir in the remaining 1½ teaspoons (7 ml) of salt, ¾ of the onions, and remaining ingredients, then set aside as a stuffing.

3. Stuff stomach bags, then sew openings to close. Place in a large saucepan along with the remaining ¼ of the onions, then cover with water to about three inches above the stomach bags and bring to boil. Cover and cook for 1 hour over medium heat or until the stomach is well cooked, adding more water, if necessary, to keep the stomach covered.

4. Serve hot along with the "stomach water" as a soup, after adding spices to taste.

NOTE: *If one can find cleaned intestines in the meat markets, the same stuffing that is used for the stomach may be used. The intestine should be twisted, sausage size, and cooked with the stomach.*

A TRADITIONAL TALE OF GOHA

Watered-down Friendship

Usually pictured as an old man with a white beard, a floppy hat, and black robes, Goha is a character out of Arab folklore, a "wise fool" who is lovable, eccentric, simple, optimistic, and generous. Goha stories have been passed down through the generations in the Arab world; here is one of them.

An Egyptian acquaintance from Helwan presented Goha with a fine lamb and stayed on for dinner to help eat it. The next day two men came to Goha's home, saying, "We are friends of the man who gave you the lamb." Goha invited them for dinner.

Two days later, six men came to Goha's door, saying, "We are friends of the friends of the man who gave you the lamb." So Goha invited them to stay for dinner. After waiting more than two hours, the hungry guests were served from a kettle which contained only hot water with a few grease spots floating on top. "What kind of hospitality is this?" they asked. Goha replied, "This water is the friend of the friend of the water in which the lamb was boiled."

CHAPTER 22

IT WAS THE BOLOGNA SANDWICHES, NOT ROASTED RABBITS, FOR WHICH I YEARNED AT HARVEST TIME

Perhaps threshing time was the most memorable time in our lives during those years of homesteading, providing us with drawbacks as well as cherished memories. Thanks to the various primitive threshing methods we used, along with getting to eat some of the finest food of my life, that time of the year will always be firmly imprinted on my mind, especially the first harvests of our early homesteading years. Indeed, I can recall those days as if they were yesterday.

What I remember with little fondness is my young body sitting on a stoneboat as the old mare pulled me around in circles for hours. Again and again, as I sat on that wooden drag atop the ripe-dry wheat stalks spread on the hard clay soil (which had not felt a drop of rain for many months), the horse moved about in a dizzying fashion. Sitting on this stoneboat so that my body could give extra weight to it, I would guide the plodding mare by slightly pulling the bridle, steering her to move in what felt like a never-ending circuit. It was a method of threshing grain as old as time, which my father brought with him from the Middle East.

All that summer we watched helplessly as, day after day, the searing sun slowly burned the tender wheat shoots while the winds played havoc with the soil. Like churning ocean waves, the hot wind with its whirling clouds of dust battered in endless forays our southern Saskatchewan home. It seemed that every day, in Saharan fashion, the fine grains of sand and dust rose skyward, blocking out the noonday sun. A darkness that was more all-encompassing than a starless night sky blotted out the day. Often, in what would take fewer than five minutes, the hot, shining sun was lost behind a blanket of dusty darkness.

By late July, due to the lack of rain, the wheat had ripened much too early, producing shrivelled, sickly-looking grain—grain that, in better times, would have been used to feed the farm animals. It was only in the sloughs that enough moisture was retained to nourish the tender wheat shoots. By early August, the few dried-up sloughs were the only places where there was anything left from our wheat fields that we could harvest.

The dry wheat kernels were so withered that our neighbours had not even thought of harvesting their sloughs. We, on the other hand, with no money and few other means of keeping ourselves alive, were in dire need of anything we might salvage from the almost desert fields. The

shrivelled slough wheat was, to my father, one of the few ways of helping to feed our family.

So, as had his Syrian ancestors in centuries past done, my father, in our makeshift blacksmith shop, fashioned a crude scythe. With this simple reaper, used long ago in the Biblical lands, he harvested the slough wheat by hand, turning, as he moved along, the grain with its stem to my mother for her to tie into sheaves.

Cement threshing stone used on our farm in the early 1930s.

These were then loaded on a wagon and brought to our yard where they were spread to be threshed by horse and stoneboat. After the kernels were loosened, we threw them, with their straw, up in the air to allow the wind to divide the grain from the straw. It was an inefficient, tedious process of threshing in order to produce the few bushels of wheat. Yet, if we were to make our yearly burghul supply, the basic ingredient of our diet in that era, we had to find the needed grain.

The next year (it would have been either 1932 or 1933), the drought continued; again, only the sloughs showed signs of life. However, this time there was something new for threshing the puny wheat—advanced technology compared to our primitive method of farming.

During the previous year, one of our Ukrainian neighbours who had pioneered in Saskatchewan long before my parents arrived, had come for a visit and had seen us using the stoneboat for threshing. He told my father that during his early years of homesteading, he had used a cement threshing stone which was pulled by a horse over the spread-out grain. It had lain in his yard for many years and, if we wanted it, it was ours to use.

When my father realized that again we had to make use of our usual primitive method for producing the needed burghul-grain, he picked up the cement thresher. In the same manner as threshing by stoneboat, it was pulled by a horse atop the spread-out grain. Yet, it was much more efficient than the stoneboat. As it was pulled along, it turned on an axle, quickly breaking up the dry stems and loosening the kernels at a much faster rate.

Now, instead of riding the stoneboat, I walked in front of the plodding mare, leading her with the reins in an endless circle. It was not as restful as riding, but it

seemed that in no time at all the job was completed. Technology, even primitive style, had its advantages.

In 1935, the rains returned, and the fields became heavy with wheat; thereafter, it became worthwhile to custom thresh our grain. In just a few years, the stoneboat and the cement thresher became only a memory of the past.

To pay for the cost of the custom thresh, my father worked as a member on the threshing crew. When it came time to thresh our grain, I, as a lad of twelve, had to help him fill the hayrack with the sheaves of the stacked wheat. The work was so strenuous that I actually yearned for the time when I rode the stoneboat or pulled the cement thresher over the spread-out grain.

In the following years, after I left home, seeking the exciting and comfortable life of the city, I would return once or twice a year to visit my family. Always, the cement thresher, in a far corner of our farmyard in the midst of worn-out machinery, would catch my eye. Almost covered with weeds, it was to me a reminder of the hours I had spent leading a horse in circles in order to produce a few bushels of wheat that would feed us.

When our family eventually moved to the city of Swift Current, for some unknown reason, my

parents took the cement thresher with them. For years, it lay in their backyard—a reminder of our homesteading years. And when my parents passed away, my sister Rose then inherited this relic from our past. Subsequently, when our family members gathered in that south Saskatchewan city, we would discuss what to do with the thresher. Eventually, we decided to donate it to the city's museum. But, alas! They turned down our offer!

Today, as it has for over half a century, the cement thresher remains in the possession of our family, my niece Lisa being the custodian of it in Brooks, Alberta.

Even more vividly than the cement thresher and my endless circles atop the grain or helping my father load the hayrack with sheaves of wheat, I remember my mother's daily feasts for the threshing crew, in which she incorporated store-bought foods that we rarely dined on. I recall my mother exclaiming to herself, "I don't know what I'm going to do with all this bologna!" as she tried to find room for two huge bologna rolls in our kitchen cupboards. Watching her storing the bologna, I was elated. For me, it would be fine-dining time after the threshing crew had moved to the next farm. I could hardly wait. My taste buds came alive as I thought of the leftover bologna we children would enjoy in the days to come. For us, it truly was a joyful time of year. There was always some bologna—to me like the Biblical manna—falling from the sky. Strange as it is when I think of it now, in those youthful years, this processed meat was to me the epitome of foods.

Yes, indeed, it was the time of the year I loved best. Every late summer, just before threshing time, my father would drive with horse and buggy into town to buy food for the hard-working crew. Of course, with little money, he had to buy affordable meats, and this meant, in the main, bologna—enough to make sandwiches for two days to feed a threshing crew of eight to ten.

And then, for a few days, our usual wholesome Middle Eastern dishes disappeared from the daily menu. My mother would never think of preparing chickpea and lentil stews or our scrumptious Middle Eastern salads, or even *kubba*—that tasty burghul and meat dish (see pages 36–44). Like most other new immigrants, she believed that our food was not good enough for the palate of non-Syrians. For meals, she served the crew fried or roast chicken, along with boiled or fried garden vegetables; lunch was bologna sandwiches. The hard-working crew never had an inkling that this was not our usual fare.

One particular year, during the first day of threshing, one of the men shot three jackrabbits and asked my mother if she would cook them for the next day's din-

ner. An excellent cook who could quickly improvise a meal, she agreed. To her, a new dish was a challenge she relished. Apparently, he had heard from our neighbours that she prepared exceptionally delicious exotic meals.

That evening, she skinned and cleaned the rabbits, then rubbed them with vinegar mixed with herbs and spices, leaving them to marinate

Enjoying a roasted rabbit dinner with all the side dishes.

overnight. The next morning, after washing, drying, then stuffing them with a rice-nut stuffing, she slowly roasted them in the oven, basting them often with a basting juice enhanced by more herbs and spices.

My mother had never had so much praise for her cooking as she did at dinner that evening. I remember vividly every member of the threshing crew lauding her culinary ability, insisting that they had never feasted on such a delectable meal. Later, they asked her to make sandwiches from the leftover meat for the next day's lunch. Listening to them, I became excited thinking of the extra leftover bologna.

As for myself, even though I enjoyed the delicious rabbit meat and the savoury stuffing, I still yearned for bologna sandwiches. In the days to come, we children were to glory in the leftover bologna—made possible by the succulent roasted rabbits. It was bologna gourmet time which lasted for over a week. And yet, as the years have passed by, my love for bologna has faded away; today, I can hardly stand its taste. The taste of the rabbits my mother prepared for the threshing crew, on the other hand, has remained with me through the years. More than once, I have replicated my mother's roasted rabbits, with what I believe to be some success. Nevertheless, it still seems to me that these attempts cannot truly match her meal for the threshing crew that day. The work crew were quite correct when they had come to their consensus that her roasted rabbits were unmatched in the field of cooking. ✥

> *The taste of the rabbits my mother prepared …has remained with me through the years. More than once, I have replicated my mother's roasted rabbits, with what I believe to be some success. Nevertheless, it still seems to me that these attempts cannot truly match hers.*

ROASTED RABBIT

WITH SIDE DISHES, SERVES 6 TO 8

Walnuts were less expensive and more available than almonds, and thus our rice and nut dishes would include walnuts more often. Even though not an exact replica of my mother's handiwork, this recipe for roasted rabbits is delectable.

1	farm-raised rabbit, about 4 lbs (1.8 kg), cleaned, washed, and dried	1
3 tbsps	lemon juice	45 ml
1 tsp	each of ground fennel seeds, sage, and salt	5 ml
½ tsp	black pepper	2 ml

Stuffing

¼ lb	beef or lamb	113 g
3 tbsps	butter	45 ml
½ cup	rice, rinsed	125 ml
1 cup	boiling water	250 ml
½ tsp	each of salt and rosemary	2 ml
¼ tsp	black pepper	1 ml
⅛ tsp	each of nutmeg, allspice, and ground cardamom	½ ml
½ cup	toasted blanched almonds	125 ml
1	medium onion, finely chopped	1

Basting Juice

½ cup	water	125 ml
¼ cup	cooking oil	60 ml
1 tsp	thyme	5 ml
½ tsp	each of salt, garlic powder, black pepper, and cumin	2 ml
⅛ tsp	cayenne	½ ml

1. Rub the rabbit inside and out with a mixture of the lemon juice, fennel, sage, salt, and pepper, then set aside for at least two hours.

2. Stuffing: Cut beef or lamb into ½-inch (1 cm) cubes. Melt butter in a saucepan, then sauté meat over medium heat until it begins to brown. Add rice, then stir-fry for a minute. Stir in water, salt, rosemary, pepper, nutmeg, allspice, and cardamom. Cover and bring to boil, then allow to simmer over medium-low heat for 10 minutes. Stir in almonds and onion, then set aside for stuffing.

3. Combine the ingredients for the basting juice. Set aside.

4. Stuff rabbit, then sew closed, using a needle and strong thread (preferably nylon). Place in a roasting pan with 1 cup water, then baste generously with prepared basting. Cover, then place in a 350°F (180°C) preheated oven. Roast for 1 hour, basting generously every 20 minutes. Remove pan cover, then cook and continue basting, using pan juices if basting juice has finished, for another hour or until meat turns tender. If rabbit is not brown, broil for a few minutes. Serve piping hot.

NOTE: *Wild rabbits, since not raised on a farm, may carry bacteria or some disease from the wild. To avoid contact with wild bacteria or germs, clean and wash the rabbit wearing gloves. Roasting will kill any bacteria, making the rabbit safe to eat. Also, to eliminate the gamey taste, soak the cleaned animal for at least 2 hours in 1 cup (250 ml) vinegar mixed with enough water to cover the rabbit.*

CHAPTER 23

OUR FAMILY RARELY ENJOYED THE "MEAT OF THE SEA" DURING OUR FARMING YEARS

It was the spring of 1931 and everything around me was green and smelled fresh as I hurried through our pasture carrying my father's lunch, which overflowed with a tempting aroma. He was seeding a part of our land, a mile away from our home, and every day, as a child of seven, I had the task of taking to him his hot lunch, prepared daily by my mother. At that time, I did not know that a child of my age should be in school. In any case, there was no school near our homestead. We had to wait until the following year for the first public school to open.

As I hurried through the unspoiled prairie land beautified by newly blooming flowers, I was not thinking of the scenery. My thoughts were overpowered by the tempting aroma streaming from the basket I was carrying. Lifting the towel covering the *Sayyadeeya*, a fish and rice dish, I broke a small piece of the fish off with my fingers, then quickly returned the cover. The fish was divine. Again and again, I munched morsel after morsel of the fish until it triggered a guilty feeling and, at the same time, I began to think of my father's impending wrath when he would discover that I had eaten half his lunch.

"Is this all the food your mother sent?" My father looked at me with a frown and signs of disappointment. Seeking to neutralize what I believed was his gathering anger, I blushed, mumbling, "I just tasted a little of the fish. The smell coming out of the basket made me so hungry." I felt relieved, as my father did not seem angry. Instead, he patted me on the head, saying, "Next time tell your mother to feed you before you bring me my lunch."

Over the years, I never forgot the taste of the fish that I stole from the basket that day. In those days, it was rare indeed to have fish for a meal. Only when a neighbour returned from visiting a friend or relative in northern Saskatchewan and brought back with him a few fish to sell did we enjoy a meal of that "meat of the sea." Unlike southern Saskatchewan, where I rarely saw even a pond, the northern part of the province teemed with countless lakes filled with fish.

Perhaps because I rarely enjoyed a meal of fish in my youth, I have always yearned for it. In later years when I travelled to the four corners of the world, I always searched for new fish dishes and, after returning home, recreated them to suit my taste. From the Canadian salmon to the sharks of the Caribbean, my fish world expanded, and I came to enjoy more and more this earliest of foods.

Hunted by Stone Age people about forty thousand years ago, fish is believed to be the first of the world's creatures consumed by humans. From the lordly caviar to the lowly smelt, these animals of the sea have always been a major contributor to the human diet. However, today, more so than in the past, they are becoming more important as a nourishing food. With the increase of the world's population and the shortage of fertile land for agriculture, humans are looking more and more to the waters that cover three-quarters of the earth's surface as a source of human subsistence.

On the other hand, in many countries of the world, the natural harvest of these sea creatures does not satisfy the demand. Hence, sea farming, an old industry which once almost died out, is becoming more and more popular. The human cultivation of the ocean was first established by the Romans, who ate more seafood than meat. However, after their demise, this industry lay dormant until modern times.

Besides being an important food, fish has, since the dawn of civilization, been associated with religion. In the early cultures, a number of sea animals were held sacred and holy, only fit for the gods. The Babylonians, Assyrians, Aramaeans, Phoenicians, and ancient Egyptians worshipped a fish god called Nun. In India, the Buddhists have for centuries venerated the "Lord of Fishes," Matsyendranatha.

Some of the beliefs of these early cultures and religions passed into the Greek, Roman, and later the Christian traditions. The early Christians used the fish as a symbol for Christ. Later, the Christians' abstinence from meat on Fridays and Lent, and the church enjoining its members to eat the creatures of the sea, gave fish consumption a great impetus.

Many of the ancients believed fish to be an aphrodisiac. A fair number of ancient religions forbade eating of fish among their priests. It was believed that consuming sea animals made one ardent in love. The Greek physician Asclepiades advocated a meal of fish for anyone planning to spend an evening with a willing woman. In Roman times, a fish sauce was made to arouse sexual feelings. The eighteenth-century Madame de Pompadour, the greatest of French mistresses, often dined on seafood as a prelude to l'amour. Casanova, who usually ate fifty oysters for breakfast, firmly believed that fish would increase his sexual powers.

This association of fish with sex has some scientific basis. In *Lewd Food*, Robert Henderickson points out that fish contain an amount of phosphorous which has a limited but direct reaction to the genitourinary tract. Others have asserted that the phosphorous and iodine content of sea creatures effects a direct reaction upon males and females alike.

Even if the claims of fish being a love potion are somewhat exaggerated, fish have excellent nutritive properties. Fish contains about 20 percent protein and small amounts of calcium, iodine, iron, magnesium, phosphorous, potassium, and sodium. In addition, fish is a good source for vitamins A, B, D, and E, and is nearly carbohydrate and fat free—making it popular as a low-fat fare. And unlike a good number of foods, the animals of the sea rarely cause food poisoning since, in the majority of cases, they are cooked immediately before eating. It has generally been accepted that most of the so-called poisonings by shellfish are due to allergies.

Besides making use of the flesh as a food, fish by-products are also of great value. Fish oils, such as cod-liver oil, are used as medicines and vitamins such as Omega 3 as well as for industrial purposes. Very nourishing animal food is made from the discarded parts and fish skins are worked into the production of gelatin, glue, and leather. In addition, scales from a number of types of fish are used for making novelties and jewellery.

Fish come in two types: fin-fish and shellfish. The most common of the fin-fish are bass, cod, haddock, herring, kingfish, mackerel, perch, pickerel, pike, salmon, sardine, smelt, sole, trout, tuna, and whitefish; of the shellfish, clam, crab, lobster, oyster, scallop, and shrimp. There are some 240 varieties of fish in North America alone.

All types of fish are at their height of taste when eaten fresh, spoiling quickly when not cooked at once. If not used immediately, they should be frozen. The modern method of blast freezing preserves the flesh so well that decomposition is barely detectable. Other methods of preservation are canning, drying, salting, smoking, or marinating.

A cook can always tell if a fish is fresh or frozen soon after capture by the brightness of the eyes

Many of the ancients believed fish to be an aphrodisiac. A fair number of ancient religions forbade the eating of fish among their priests. It was believed that the consuming of sea animals made one ardent in love.

and the firmness of the flesh. To preserve its fresh taste if it has been frozen, the chef should thaw the fish slowly in cold water, then cook soon thereafter.

For preparation, the fish should first be scaled, then the organs removed and the fins and tail clipped. After being thoroughly washed, it can be cooked whole, filleted, or cut into steaks. The beauty of our modern supermarkets is that all this work has been done and the fish is ready for the cook.

Fish can be eaten raw (if extremely fresh, otherwise Salmonella and Vibrio infections from undercooked fish are a danger), baked, grilled, boiled, broiled, fried, pickled, smoked, or steamed. It is excellent prepared alone, stuffed, or as an ingredient in soups or stews. All fish are tender and cook quickly. When the flesh can easily be flaked with a fork, the fish is done. If overdone, it becomes dry, tough, and rubbery.

By whatever method fish is cooked, especially when fresh, it has a delectable taste. Yet I believe that the very best flavour is reached if grilled. But a person must be very careful cooking in this manner since, if turned frequently on a grill, it tends to fall apart. Halibut, snapper, and salmon have a fairly solid flesh and are the best types of fish to barbecue.

Even though in taste and nutritional value fish has few equals, this meat of the sea has a number of drawbacks. It is not as economical as other meat, since 70 percent of the total weight, including bones, fins, guts, head, and skin, is waste. In addition, bones are a problem in enjoying most types of fish. If a diner is not careful, bones may lodge in the mouth or throat, and, at times, can be very painful. The problem can only be eliminated if the fish is filleted or a person picks out the bones while eating. In very small fish, such as sardines and smelts, this does not constitute a problem. The bones can be eaten with the meat, especially if one wishes to increase the calcium intake.

In spite of these drawbacks, fish is a very important food. In the past, in parts of the world where nearby oceans teemed with fish, cities and states rose and fell with the rise and fall in their fishing fields. In the future, it may be that fish could be the deciding factor between starvation and plenty. A truly versatile fare which, at times, decided the destiny of empires, this ancient food, I hope, still has a bright future.

My mother's fish dishes were not only superb, but, as fish was so seldom available during our farming years, any such dish was considered heavenly by the whole family. In later years while travelling, I became acquainted with countless fish dishes, some of which I have prepared according to my taste and have included among the following recipes.

Tasty in whatever way it is prepared, fish adds colour, flavour, and attractiveness to any meal. The few recipes which follow—which I have cooked for many years—will give one an idea of the culinary richness derived from the meat of the sea. ✄

FISH SOUP / SHAWRABAT SAMAK

SERVES 8 TO 10

1 lb	fish fillet (any type)	454 g
6 tbsps	olive or vegetable oil	90 ml
2	medium onions, finely chopped	2
4	cloves garlic, crushed	4
½	small hot pepper, seeded and finely chopped	½
1 tsp	oregano	5 ml
1 tsp	tarragon	5 ml
1 tsp	salt	5 ml
1 tsp	black pepper	5 ml
1 tsp	cumin	5 ml
4 tbsps	tomato paste	60 ml
8 cups	water	2 L
½ cup	rice, rinsed	125 ml
4 tbsps	finely chopped fresh cilantro	60 ml

1. Cut fish fillets into 1-inch (2.5 cm) cubes. Heat oil in a saucepan, then sauté fish over medium heat for 8 minutes, turning them over once. Remove fish with a slotted spoon, then set aside.

2. In the same oil, sauté onions, garlic, and hot pepper over medium heat for 10 minutes, adding more oil if necessary. Stir in remaining ingredients, except cilantro and fish, then bring to boil. Cover, then cook over medium heat for 20 minutes. Add fish, then cook for a further 15 minutes. Remove from heat, then stir in cilantro just before serving.

SHRIMP SALAD

SERVES 4

1 lb	fresh or frozen shrimp, medium-size	454 g
1 cup	finely chopped green onions	250 ml
4 tbsps	finely chopped parsley	60 ml
2 tbsps	finely chopped fresh cilantro	30 ml
2 tbsps	olive oil	30 ml
3 tbsps	lemon juice	45 ml
1	clove garlic, crushed	1
1 tsp	oregano	5 ml
½ tsp	salt	2 ml
½ tsp	black pepper	2 ml
pinch	cayenne	pinch

1. In a saucepan, bring water to boil, add shrimp, and cook over medium heat for 4 to 5 minutes or until they turn pink, then drain and allow to cool. Shell, then place in a mixing bowl.

2. Combine the remaining ingredients, then add to shrimp and toss. Place on a serving platter, then chill for 1 hour and serve.

The wound of words is worse than the wound of swords.

FISH AND RICE / SAYYADEEYA

SERVES 4 TO 6

This dish was my first introduction to the fish world. It is a simple-to-prepare food, popular in the Greater Syria area—and beyond. Versions of this recipe are prepared from the Arabian Gulf countries to North Africa. Simple to make and delicious, it has remained my favourite through the years.

1 lb	fish fillet, any kind, cut into large pieces	454 g
½ tsp	black pepper	2 ml
½ tsp	cumin	2 ml
4 tbsps	butter	60 ml
1	large onion, finely chopped	1
2	cloves garlic, crushed	2
½ cup	pine nuts	125 ml
1 cup	rice, rinsed	250 ml
1 tsp	salt	5 ml
⅛ tsp	cayenne	½ ml
2 cups	water	500 ml

1. Sprinkle fish on both sides with pepper and cumin, then set aside.

2. Melt butter in a frying pan, then sauté fish over medium heat until light brown, turning over once. Remove fish with a slotted spoon, then set aside.

3. In the same butter, adding more if necessary, sauté onion, garlic, and pine nuts over medium heat for 10 minutes. Add the rice, then stir-fry for 2 minutes. Stir in remaining ingredients. Transfer frying pan contents into a greased casserole, then arrange fish evenly over the top. Cover, then bake in a 350°F (180°C) preheated oven for 1 hour or until rice is cooked. Remove cover for the last 5 to 10 minutes of baking. Serve hot from casserole.

FISH SCRAMBLED WITH EGGS

SERVES 4

This makes a hearty and tasty breakfast dish.

½ lb	fish fillet (any kind)	227 g
4 tbsps	butter	60 ml
1	large onion, finely chopped	1
2	cloves garlic, crushed	2
2 tbsps	finely chopped fresh cilantro	30 ml
5	eggs, beaten	5
½ tsp	black pepper	2 ml
½ tsp	salt	2 ml
¼ tsp	cumin	1 ml
pinch	cayenne	pinch

1. Cut fish fillets into 1-inch (2.5 cm) cubes. Melt the butter in a frying pan, then sauté fish cubes over medium heat for about 10 minutes or until they begin to brown. Remove fish with a slotted spoon, then flake with a fork and set aside.

2. Sauté onion in the same butter for 10 minutes, adding more butter if necessary, then stir in garlic and cilantro and sauté for further 5 minutes.

3. In the meantime, in a bowl, mix together remaining ingredients along with the fish. Add to the frying pan mixture, then stir-fry for a few minutes until eggs are done. Serve immediately.

CLAM CHOWDER

SERVES 6 TO 8

A great combination of Canadian and Syrian culinary tastes, this chowder is enjoyed often by our family.

½ lb	beef or lamb	227 g
2	medium potatoes	2
4 tbsps	butter	60 ml
2	medium onions, finely chopped	2
2	cloves garlic, crushed	2
4 tbsps	finely chopped fresh cilantro	60 ml
½	small hot pepper, seeded and finely chopped	½
2 cups	stewed tomatoes	500 ml
1 tsp	thyme	5 ml
½ tsp	black pepper	2 ml
¼ tsp	allspice	1 ml
¼ tsp	cumin	1 ml
3 cups	water	750 ml
10 oz	canned clams, with their water	284 g

1. Cut beef or lamb into ½-inch (1 cm) cubes. Peel potatoes and dice into ½-inch (1 cm) cubes.

2. Melt butter in a saucepan, then sauté meat cubes over medium heat until light brown. Remove meat with a slotted spoon and set aside, then sauté onions over medium heat in same butter, adding more butter if necessary, until golden. Add garlic, cilantro, and hot pepper, then stir-fry for a few minutes. Stir in remaining ingredients, including meat and potatoes, and bring to boil. Cover, then cook over medium heat for 40 minutes, adding more water if necessary. Serve hot.

GARLIC FRIED FISH STEAKS

SERVES 4 TO 6

6	cloves garlic, crushed	6
4 tbsps	olive oil	60 ml
2 tbsps	lemon juice	30 ml
1 tsp	tarragon	5 ml
½ tsp	salt	2 ml
½ tsp	black pepper	2 ml
½ tsp	ground coriander	2 ml
pinch	cayenne	pinch
2 lbs	fish steaks (any kind of firm flesh, such as salmon)	907 g
	flour	
	cooking oil for frying	

1. Make paste by thoroughly mixing all ingredients, except fish steaks, flour, and cooking oil. Rub steaks with paste, then refrigerate for 2 hours.

2. Dredge steaks in flour and set aside.

3. Pour oil in a frying pan to ½ inch (1 cm) deep, then heat to medium. Fry steaks until they turn golden brown, turning over once.

4. Serve hot with Sesame Sauce (page 131) or Garlic Sauce (page 130).

FISH PATTIES / KUBBAT SAMAK

MAKES ABOUT 48 SMALL PATTIES

When Mother had extra fish, she made these tasty patties. This was a dish that I cherished as a child because fish was such a novelty for our family on our Saskatchewan homestead.

1 cup	burghul	250 ml
1 lb	cod or similar fish fillet, cut into pieces	454 g
1	medium onion, finely chopped	1
3	cloves garlic, crushed	3
3 tbsps	flour	45 ml
1½ tsps	salt	7 ml
1 tsp	black pepper	5 ml
½ tsp	allspice	2 ml
½ tsp	cinnamon	2 ml
¼ tsp	nutmeg	1 ml
⅛ tsp	cayenne	½ ml
	oil for frying	

1. Soak burghul in warm water for 10 minutes, then thoroughly drain by pressing out the water through a fine strainer.

2. Place burghul and the rest of the ingredients, except the oil, in a food processor, then process into firm paste. Form into small patties about 1½ inches (4 cm) in diameter, then set aside.

3. Pour oil in a frying pan to ½ inch (1 cm) deep, then heat to medium. Fry patties, turning them over once, until they turn golden brown.

4. Serve hot with Sesame Sauce (page 131) or Garlic Sauce (page 130).

FISH STEW / YAKHNIT SAMAK

SERVES 8 TO 10

2 lbs	fish fillet (any kind)	907 g
3	medium potatoes	3
½ cup	cooking oil	125 ml
2	medium onions, finely chopped	2
4	cloves garlic, crushed	4
4 tbsps	finely chopped fresh cilantro	60 ml
2 cups	stewed tomatoes	500 ml
2 cups	water	500 ml
2 tsps	salt	10 ml
1 tsp	black pepper	5 ml
1 tsp	cumin	5 ml
¼ tsp	allspice	1 ml
⅛ tsp	cayenne	½ ml

1. Cut fish fillet into 1-inch (2.5 cm) cubes.

2. Peel potatoes and dice into ½-inch (1 cm) cubes.

3. Heat oil in a saucepan, then sauté fish cubes over medium-high heat for 4 minutes, turning them over once. Remove fish cubes with a slotted spoon, then set aside. Sauté onions, garlic, and cilantro in the same oil, adding more oil if necessary, over medium heat for 10 minutes. Add potatoes and remaining ingredients, except fish cubes, then bring to boil. Cover, then cook over medium heat for 20 minutes, adding more water if necessary. Add fish cubes, then cook for a further 15 minutes. Serve hot.

FISH FILLET BAKED IN TAHINI / SAMAK BI TAHEENA

SERVES 6 TO 8

2 lbs	fish fillet (any kind)	907 g
4	medium potatoes	4
½ cup	cooking oil	125 ml
5 tbsps	tahini (sesame seed paste)	75 ml
4 tbsps	lemon juice	60 ml
½	small hot pepper, seeded and finely chopped	½
4 tbsps	finely chopped fresh cilantro	60 ml
2	cloves garlic, crushed	2
1 cup	water	250 ml
1 tsp	sage	5 ml
1 tsp	salt	5 ml
½ tsp	black pepper	2 ml

1. Cut fish fillets into 2-inch (5 cm) cubes. Peel and slice potatoes.

2. Heat oil in a frying pan, then fry fish over medium heat for 4 minutes, turning them over once. Remove fish and place in a casserole, then set aside.

3. In the same oil, fry potato slices until they begin to brown, turning them over once and adding more oil if necessary. Remove potato slices and place evenly over fish in the casserole, then set aside.

4. Place all remaining ingredients in a food processor, then process for a few moments. Pour over potatoes and fish in casserole. Cover, then bake in a 400°F (200°C) preheated oven for 15 minutes. Serve piping hot.

TAHINI

In Canada, during the years of my youth, tahini was an unknown ingredient, but Mother would talk constantly about this healthy sesame seed paste. It was only when we moved off the homestead to our farm near the city of Swift Current that she was able to purchase this oily sesame paste, now sold in Middle Eastern markets, supermarkets, and in health stores. She was never able to go back to Syria but she could "taste" Syria in the tahini.

PICKLED FISH STEAKS

SERVES 6 TO 8

Once prepared by the Moors in Spain, this dish, called Escabeche de Pescados in Spanish, derives its name from the Arabic al-sikbāj (the pickles). Of course, this dish was unknown to my mother, but I learned to appreciate it during my travels in Spain. It makes an excellent appetizer.

½ cup	cooking oil	125 ml
2½ lbs	salmon or similar type steaks	1135 g
2	medium onions, thinly sliced	2
4	cloves garlic, crushed	4
1 cup	water	250 ml
¾ cup	olive oil	175 ml
½ cup	vinegar	125 ml
4 tbsps	finely chopped green onions	60 ml
4 tbsps	finely chopped fresh cilantro	60 ml
1 tsp	salt	5 ml
1 tsp	oregano	5 ml
1 tsp	ground ginger	5 ml
½ tsp	paprika	2 ml
½ tsp	black pepper	2 ml
½ tsp	cumin	2 ml

1. Heat cooking oil to medium in a frying pan, then fry fish steaks for about 10 minutes or until they turn golden brown, turning them over once. Remove steaks, then place in a casserole and set aside.

2. In the same oil, sauté onions over medium heat for 10 minutes, adding more oil if necessary, then remove with a slotted spoon and spread over the fish steaks. Combine remaining ingredients, then pour over onions and fish steaks.

3. Refrigerate, then allow to marinate for one day before serving. Serve cold.

FISH KABAB / KABAAB SAMAK

SERVES 4 TO 6

2 lbs	halibut fillet	907 g
2	medium, green sweet peppers	2
2	medium, firm tomatoes	2
1	small onion, finely chopped	1
4 tbsps	finely chopped fresh cilantro	60 ml
4	cloves garlic, crushed	4
4 tbsps	olive oil	60 ml
4 tbsps	lemon juice	60 ml
1 tsp	oregano	5 ml
1 tsp	salt	5 ml
½ tsp	black pepper	2 ml
½ tsp	cumin	2 ml
⅛ tsp	cayenne	½ ml

1. Cut halibut fillets into 1½-inch (4 cm) cubes. Cut green peppers into 1-inch (2.5 cm) squares. Quarter tomatoes. Set aside.

2. Thoroughly combine all ingredients, except fish, green peppers, and tomatoes, in a large bowl, then add fish, peppers, and tomatoes and gently toss. Allow to marinate for 4 hours, tossing every 30 minutes, then thread the fish, green peppers, and tomatoes intermingled on skewers.

3. Grill over charcoal for about 10 minutes or until fish is done, basting with the marinade every few minutes. Serve immediately with Garlic Sauce (page 130).

BAKED HERB-STUFFED FISH

SERVES 6 TO 8

4 tbsps	butter	60 ml
2	medium onions, finely chopped	2
1	small bunch parsley, finely chopped	1
1	small bunch fresh cilantro, finely chopped	1
1	lemon with rind, very finely chopped	1
6	cloves garlic, crushed	6
1 tsp	finely chopped hot pepper	5 ml
1 tsp	paprika	5 ml
1 tsp	salt	5 ml
½ tsp	black pepper	2 ml
½ tsp	cumin	2 ml
4 to 5 lb	salmon or similar type fish, scaled and washed	1.8 to 2.2 kg
	oil	

1. Melt butter in a frying pan, then sauté onions over medium heat for 8 minutes. Stir in parsley, cilantro, lemon, garlic, and hot pepper, then stir-fry for 4 minutes. Remove from heat, then stir in paprika, salt, pepper, and cumin to make filling.

2. Stuff fish, then sew, using a needle and strong thread (preferably nylon) to close. Rub fish with oil, then wrap in aluminum foil. Bake in a 400°F (200°C) preheated oven for 30 minutes. Remove foil, then place under the broiler for a few minutes to lightly brown. Serve immediately with Sesame Sauce (page 131) or Garlic Sauce (page 130).

CHAPTER 24

OH! THE JOYS OF SASKATOONS DURING OUR FARMING YEARS

The cool Saskatchewan dawn in July 1936 was invigorating as my parents readied the family for the yearly saskatoon berry harvest. We children were barely awake as we were herded into a wagon for the trip to the Coulee of Saint Clair—a few miles north of the town of Cadillac and six miles west of our farm. To us youngsters, it was a true picnic—one of the few enjoyments we looked forward to during our formative years in the harsh Depression era. It was a day when we ate our fill of succulent saskatoons while frolicking with the children of our most cherished neighbour.

The sun was just beginning to move over the horizon when our entire family of ten—father, mother, and children ranging in age from three to fourteen—found our good friend and neighbour Albert Hattum waiting for us in the coulee. With his family of twelve, he had come to join us in gathering our yearly supply of berries.

The shrubby trees were heavy with saskatoons as, carefree and happy, we played while our parents visited. As we romped around, we gorged ourselves on the tasty berries—the only fruit we consumed in abundance during those lean prairie years. However, after an hour or so, our youthful mirth came to an end. It was time to work. Soon everyone was busy filling the tubs we had brought along with the colourful saskatoons.

All day long, with only a stop for lunch, every member of both families, except the toddlers, harvested this prairie fruit. We did not stop until each family had gathered over three heaping tubs-full—our yearly supply. When evening drew nigh, everyone was content. It had been a day full of labour intermixed with pleasure.

Back home, my mother canned about a hundred jars and made enough jam to fill another two dozen. These preserved sweets would last us until the next saskatoon-picking season. During the long winter months, they were virtually the only fruit we ate.

We placed the remainder of the berries in pails and dangled them with a rope above the water level in our well. In the 1920s and 1930s, this was the only form of summer refrigeration we could afford for our fruits, vegetables, and meats. For two weeks, we feasted on fresh saskatoons in a seemingly endless variety of ways. To me, in my younger years, they were the epitome of sweets. Even today, I still vividly remember the many times we enjoyed these luscious berries. They made our lives in the semi-desert of southwestern Saskatchewan a little more gratifying and delightful. For us children, saskatoons were synonymous with dessert, and we were always ecstatic when they were served.

Like us, the western First Nations and the early pioneers always looked forward to the saskatoon berry season. In the centuries before contact occurred, these berries were a welcome addition to the diets of the Indigenous peoples of the plains. They utilized them—and many continue to do so—both as a food and as a condiment. For example, the famous pemmican is prepared using dried buffalo meat made toothsome with saskatoons.

To the early settlers, no less than to the Indigenous peoples of the region, these berries were of prime importance. They sustained many voyageurs through their rigorous journeys, supplying them with some of the essential vitamins, especially vitamin C. Before the age of railroads, they were the principal fruit consumed by the peoples of the Great Plains.

Not surprising, saskatoons derive their appellation from the Cree word *misâskwatômin*. Also called service berry, shad-berry, juneberry, and sometimes saskatoon blueberry, they grow wild and are one of thirteen species found in Canada, of the genus *amelanchier*. A favourite food of birds, bears, and other animals, they are commonly found in the

> *...we feasted on fresh saskatoons in a seemingly endless variety of ways. To me, in my younger years, they were the epitome of sweets.*

bluffs, coulees, and open woodlands throughout North America. However, they grow in abundance and are best known in western Canada. Saskatoon—Saskatchewan's largest metropolis—received its name from the profusion of this fruit found in the vicinity of the city.

The plant itself, *amelanchier canadensis*, or saskatoon, is a bushy tree which averages six to twelve feet in height but, at times, reaches up to thirty feet. It has oblong, toothed leaves up to three inches (7.62 cm) in length and produces clusters of white blossoms. During April and May, these flowers turn the bluffs and coulees of western Canada into a breathtaking vision.

The fruit, which ripens during the latter part of July and early August, is purplish-black and about ¼ inch (6 mm) in diameter. Its fleshy pulp surrounding about ten large seeds is sweet; when cooked, it has an almond-like flavour.

As yet, saskatoons have never been truly domesticated. Yet, the future for the cultivation of these berries looks bright. Plant breeders are developing a number of varieties for commercial purposes.

Appealing in colour and delicious in taste, saskatoons are versatile and appetizing. They can be eaten raw by themselves; served with cream and sugar; used as an ingredient in salads and bakery products; made into fruit cups, jellies, pies, and wines; and used as a topping for ice cream. They are also excellent when preserved and served as a dessert—the homesteaders' treat in western Canada.

Besides canning, the berries can be preserved by having them dried or frozen. Indigenous peoples and early farmers always dried their winter supply. However, today they are usually frozen. Only a few farm families still can or dry their annual harvest.

Saskatoons should be frozen unwashed when they are fresh and firm. By freezing them when they are newly picked, their natural colour, flavour, and nutrient value are preserved for a lengthy period of time. When ready for use, they should be washed quickly with cold water. If they are allowed to remain in the water for any length of time, they lose much of their natural colour and food value.

Although not as sought-after as in the past, saskatoons are still, to many, an important fruit. A good number look forward to the few weeks when these blueberries of western Canada are in season. Year after year, they prepare their own versions of the following recipes which our family enjoyed in the bygone years.

DATES

In the Middle Eastern lands, where the date palm carries an aura of mystery and romance, there is a common belief that it is the oldest cultivated fruit tree in the world. In its native homeland, the Arabian Peninsula, the inhabitants have no doubt that it was first grown in paradise. According to Muslim belief, the Archangel Gabriel told Adam in the Garden of Eden: "Thou art created from the same substance as this palm tree which henceforth shall nourish you."

To the Arabs, the date palm has a definite personality and human qualities. Indeed, they might have a point! Like man, if the tree's head is severed, it will die. In the same fashion as a human limb, a frond cut will not grow again; and the palm's crown is covered with thick foliage, like the hair on a human head.

Historians have theorized that perhaps 7,000 years ago, the date palm was first cultivated in the Arabian Peninsula. From its native Arabia, the cultivation of the date palm spread to the Fertile Crescent. Description of this historic tree and its fruit can be found in writings on clay tablets by the Sumerians, Assyrians, and Babylonians. Murals depicting palms from the days of these civilizations have been uncovered, proving beyond doubt that dates were well-known in the days of antiquity.

Perhaps at the beginning of the Pharaonic era, the cultivation of date palms spread to the Valley of the Nile. Paintings found in the tombs of the Pharaohs indicate that they were known in that ancient land, at least since the time that the hieroglyphics were invented.

In later centuries, Phoenician traders carried the date palm from the Fertile Crescent and Egypt to North Africa and Spain. However, in Spain, the date palm was not cultivated on a large scale until 712 CE after the Arabs occupied the Iberian Peninsula. In the Alicante province of the eastern coast of Spain, palm orchards, first established by the Arabs, are today still flourishing.

From Spain, the conquistadors brought along with them the date palm to the Americas. However, as a food crop in both North and South America, it did not thrive until this century and, even then, it grows only in a few locations.

In the United States, at the beginning of the 1900s, the date palm was introduced from North Africa to be planted on a commercial basis. ▨
—*Habeeb Salloum, "The Fruit of Paradise: Dates,"* A La Carte, 2.8 (1985): 62-7.

SASKATOON PUDDING

SERVES 6 TO 8

This is a delightful baked pudding which is good to serve on Thanksgiving or Christmas—or, better still, whenever one craves pudding!

4 cups	saskatoons, fresh or frozen	1 L
½ cup	brown sugar	125 ml
4 tbsps	lemon juice	60 ml
1 cup	quick-cooking oats	250 ml
1 cup	milk	250 ml
½ cup	sugar	125 ml
6 tbsps	butter, melted	90 ml
2	eggs, beaten	2
4 tbsps	flour	60 ml
2 tsps	baking powder	10 ml
1 tsp	vanilla	5 ml

1. In a mixing bowl, combine saskatoons, brown sugar, and lemon juice, then transfer to a greased casserole and set aside.

2. Thoroughly combine remaining ingredients in a mixing bowl, then spread evenly over the saskatoons. Cover, then bake in a 350°F (200°C) preheated oven for 40 minutes. Uncover, then bake for another 15 minutes or until the top turns golden.

3. Allow to cool slightly, then serve with whipped cream.

SASKATOON MUFFINS

MAKES 16 MEDIUM MUFFINS

Saskatoon muffins can compete easily with any muffins found in the popular coffeehouses and bakeries across North America.

2	eggs, beaten	2
½ cup	butter, melted	125 ml
1¼ cups	milk	310 ml
1 tsp	vanilla	5 ml
1¾ cups	flour	425 ml
¾ cup	sugar	175 ml
3 tsps	baking powder	15 ml
½ tsp	salt	2 ml
1 cup	saskatoons, fresh or frozen	250 ml

1. In a small mixing bowl, thoroughly combine eggs, butter, milk, and vanilla, then set aside.

2. In a larger mixing bowl, combine flour, sugar, baking powder, and salt, then add contents of the small mixing bowl and thoroughly mix into soft batter, adding more milk if necessary.

3. Gently stir in saskatoons, then fill well-greased muffin pans three-quarters full.

4. Bake in a 400°F (200°C) preheated oven for 25 minutes or until tops turn golden-brown, then remove and allow to cool for a few minutes.

5. Remove from muffin pans, then serve hot.

UPSIDE-DOWN SASKATOON CAKE

*If you enjoy pineapple upside-down cake, you may have met
its match once you have tried it with saskatoons.*

4 tbsps	butter	60 ml
½ cup	brown sugar	125 ml
2 cups	saskatoons, fresh or frozen	500 ml
1 cup	milk	250 ml
½ cup	cooking oil	125 ml
2	eggs, beaten	2
1 tsp	vanilla	5 ml
1¾ cups	flour	425 ml
¾ cup	sugar	175 ml
3 tsps	baking powder	15 ml
½ tsp	salt	2 ml

1. Preheat oven to 350°F (180°C).

2. In the oven, melt butter in a 9-inch (23 cm) square baking pan,
   remove then stir in brown sugar, mixing well. Top evenly with
   saskatoons, then set aside.

3. In a mixing bowl, thoroughly combine milk, oil, eggs, and vanilla,
   then set aside.

4. In another mixing bowl, combine flour, sugar, baking powder,
   and salt, then stir in contents of the first bowl to make batter.

5. Spoon batter evenly over berries, then bake for 40 minutes or
   until cake turns golden brown. Remove and let sit for 5 minutes,
   then invert onto a serving plate. Cut just before serving.

SASKATOON BERRY PIE

MAKES ONE 9-INCH PIE

Pie Dough

2 tbsps	cold water	30 ml
1	egg, beaten	1
1½ tsps	vinegar	7 ml
½ tsp	salt	2 ml
1¾ cups	flour	425 ml
½ lb	butter	227 g

Filling

4 heaping cups	saskatoons, fresh or frozen	1 L (generous)
1 cup	sugar	250 ml
2 tbsps	lemon juice	30 ml
¼ cup	flour	60 ml

Topping

1 tbsp	butter	15 ml

1. To make the pie dough, in a bowl, thoroughly combine water, egg, and vinegar, then set aside.

2. In another mixing bowl, combine salt and 1¾ cups (425 ml) flour, then cut butter into the dry ingredients. Slowly pour in contents of other bowl and work into a dough, adding more flour or water if necessary. Form into a ball, cover with plastic wrap, and refrigerate for 30 minutes.

3. To make the filling, in another mixing bowl, gently mix together the saskatoons, sugar, lemon juice, and ¼ cup (60 ml) flour, then set aside.

4. Take two-thirds of dough, then roll out to about ⅛ inch (3 mm) thickness. Fit into 9-inch (22 cm) pie plate, then trim edges. If dough sticks, add a little more flour. Pour filling evenly over crust. Roll out remaining dough to about ⅛ inch (3 mm) thickness, then place over filling. Pinch top and bottom crusts together, then flute. Puncture top in a few places with a fork, then dot with the 1 tablespoon of butter. Cover fluted edge with strip of aluminum foil, then bake in a 425°F (220°C) preheated oven for 40 minutes or until crust becomes golden.

5. Allow to cool before serving.

COFFEE

Records indicate that coffee was first cultivated around 600 CE in South Arabia. A number of historians indicate that long before utilized to make a beverage, the beans were crushed and mixed with fat to produce a simple food.

The first mention of coffee as a drink was made around 900 CE, in the writings of the Arab medieval scholar Al-Razi, known in the West as Rhazes. Avicenna, an Arab physician/philosopher in about 1000 CE, introduced coffee as a medicinal tonic. From the writings of this scholar and others, it is believed that in the period between 800 and 900 CE, the Arabs learned to crush and boil the coffee beans to make a hot drink. ✶

—Habeeb Salloum, "Coffee: Arabia's Gift to the World," Khaleej Times, *August 6, 1985, 3.*

SASKATOON TARTS

MAKES ABOUT 16 MEDIUM TARTS

Saskatoon time was also tart time. Freshly baked with their aroma flowing out of the kitchen, Mother's tarts were always a welcome event.

Pie dough (page 306)

Filling

3½ cups	saskatoons, fresh or frozen	825 ml
1½ cups	brown sugar	375 ml
4 tbsps	melted butter	60 ml
¼ cup	flour	60 ml
¼ cup	water	60 ml

1. Follow instructions for pie dough on page 306. Divide dough into 16 balls, then roll out balls into rounds about ⅛ inch (3 mm) thick.

2. Place each circle snugly in well-greased muffin tray, then flute in same fashion as a pie. Trim excess dough, then puncture tart shells in the bottom a few times with a fork. Bake in a 400°F (200°C) preheated oven for 10 minutes, then remove pan from oven and set aside.

3. In the meantime, to make the filling, place all remaining ingredients in a saucepan and, stirring continually, bring to a boil. Cook and continue stirring over medium heat for 3 minutes.

4. Fill partially baked tart shells, then bake in a 350°F (180°C) preheated oven for 15 minutes or until crust becomes golden. Remove from oven and allow to cool, then gently remove tarts from tray and serve.

CHAPTER 25

ARAB PASTRIES: OUR CHRISTMAS SWEETS

Even though we always enjoyed our saskatoon-berry sweets, we children always looked forward to Christmas when Mother prepared her mouth-watering *baklawa*—to me, then and now, my favourite of all sweets. Dripping with syrup and loaded with butter, this king of sweets in the Middle East was, for me, more precious than the mythical pot of gold at the end of the rainbow. I can still remember, as if it were yesterday, how I begged my mother to let me munch on the *baklawa* crumbs left in the pan.

For my mother, it was a whole day's work preparing two pans of this tasty sweet. Unlike today, when one can find the *baklawa* dough in Mediterranean and Middle Eastern stores and in many supermarkets (filo dough), in our homesteading days, my mother prepared the dough by hand from scratch. In the village where she was born, like in all other villages of the Middle East at that time, every girl was taught by her mother how to prepare *baklawa*. My wife did the same.

All through the Arab East, it was said that no young lady would make a good wife unless she knew how to make *baklawa* dough. Fortunately, today, not only in the Arab countries but also throughout the Western world, this dough is prepared commercially, and young girls and women are spared the ordeal of proving their suitability for marriage. Watching my mother stretching by hand for hours sheets of dough to paper thinness, I can well see how Arab women had to suffer to prove that they would make good wives.

Of course, *baklawa* was only one of the Arab sweets my mother prepared. My favourite after *baklawa* was *ghurayba*—a buttery Arab-type of shortbread. I remember many times sneaking into the pantry where Mother stored the *ghurayba* and stealing a piece of that tasty sweet.

In the following years as I roamed the Arab countries, I came to know many other delicious pastries. Added to those my mother prepared, Arab sweets became for me a never-ending world of delectable delights with a rich and long history. Indeed, the delicious foods of the Middle East and North Africa are not the invention of today or yesterday. Their roots can be traced to the many civilizations which flowed, then ebbed, in that part of the globe.

From this ancient world, the West inherited numerous dishes which it now calls its own. Case in point, the Spanish turrone, Europe's marzipan, Sicily's cannoli, and the English mawmenny all go back to an Arab origin. However, it is in the Arab world that a great number of these dishes evolved through the centuries into today's delectable Middle Eastern and North African dishes. Not least among the many foods whose bases go back to the bygone ages are the exotic pastries and other sweets which are found from Morocco on the Atlantic to the countries of the Arabian Gulf. In these lands, located at the crossroads of the world, sweets prepared to tantalize the taste and please the eye reflect this rich past.

Arab sweets are very different from the cakes and pies of the Western world. In the majority of cases, they are paper-thin layered pastries filled with nuts, spices, cheese, and butter, then soaked in *qatr*, a syrup of sugar or honey. Their tempting, juicy taste has inspired poets and men of letters through the centuries. Poems have been composed, songs have been sung, and legends born wherever these marvellously delicate pastries have been served.

An Arab poet once said, "With our exquisite and luscious sweets can the beauty of any woman compare?" Another bard asserted,

> To eat the pastries
> of the Arabs is
> to make a person's
> life serene
> and happy and
> keep away evil.

"To eat the pastries of the Arabs is to make a person's life serene and happy and keep away evil."

Golden-coloured when baked and oozing with syrup, they have a tempting and irresistible appeal. Many who have tasted the sweets of the Arab countries have had the taste of these luscious sweets linger for many days or even months. The Arabs themselves quickly forget about diets as they devour these calorie-laden delights.

There is a long history of sweet-making in the Arab world. In the old days, communal ovens located in almost every neighbourhood served as the place to bake the homemade pastries. As time passed, pastry shops emerged, easing for many households the tedious and time-consuming tasks of preparing sweets. Today, these patisseries are located almost everywhere in every city, town, and village. In the homes of the affluent or in those of the middle class, no table of any self-respecting host will be without arrays of trays of Arab pastries while those of lesser means will offer what they can. In the Middle East, sweets are served with tiny cups of piping-hot, strong Arab coffee, while in North Africa they are offered with refreshing mint tea. For the host, the ideal scenario is that guests enjoy every type of sweet that has been served, and for them to take seconds.

A Western writer quoted in *Fodor's Morocco* thus describes a scene where Moroccan sweets were being served:

> The guests were resting on low sofas surrounded by rich colourful cushions in a Moorish-Andalusian style room filled with the aroma of delicate perfume. Sweet mint tea with Moroccan pastries were being served. The tea was poured into silver decorated glasses while the sweets were passed around on shining inlaid silver trays. Making the rounds serving the guests were beautiful maidens in fascinating Arab dress.

His picturesque description of a scene enacted daily in many Arab homes could well have been a page from *One Thousand and One Nights*.

In the eastern Arab lands of bygone ages, Arab sweets reached their height of magnificence. When the rich held their banquets, *baklawa*, the king of Arab pastry, was always there. *Baklawa* is made from a tissue paper–thin dough which is known in the West as strudel or phyllo (also spelled filo); the shredded version is known as *knaafa*. This dough is the basis of the many varieties of syrup-soaked sweets found on the tables of these ancient lands.

With the commercially produced dough, any cook can easily make *baklawa* in its various forms, such as the most common, squares and triangles, or as *Kul wa Ishkur* (Eat and Praise) and *Zunud al-Sitt* (the Lady's Wrists).

My horizons in the world of Arab sweets have greatly expanded since my mother prepared her divine *baklawa* and *ghurayba*. To her repertoire of recipes I have added others from the Middle East and North Africa. Among my favourites are the following few, which I often prepare. ✖

SYRUP / QATR

What gives baklawa *and the majority of other Arab pastries their unique and exquisite taste is a syrup made from this basic recipe. Mazahar (orange blossom water) can be replaced by maa' ward (rose water) as the flavouring agent for this syrup. Both can be purchased from supermarkets specializing in Middle Eastern groceries and in some of the larger supermarkets.*

1½ cups	sugar	375 ml
¾ cup	water	175 ml
2 tbsps	lemon juice	30 ml
2 tbsps	orange blossom water (*mazahar*)	30 ml

1. Place sugar and water in a pot, then cook over medium heat, stirring constantly for 10 minutes or until sugar is thoroughly dissolved. Remove from heat, then stir in lemon juice. Return to heat and bring to boil. Remove from heat and stir in *mazahar*. Allow to cool.

*The whisper of a pretty girl
can be heard further
than the roar of a lion.*

BAKLAWA

MAKES 35 TO 40 PIECES

2 cups	walnuts, coarsely ground	500 ml
1 cup	sugar	250 ml
2 cups	clarified butter, melted	500 ml
2 tsps	cinnamon	10 ml
1 tbsp	orange blossom water (*mazahar*)	15 ml
1 lb	filo dough	454 g
	prepared syrup (*Qatr*) (page 312)	

1. Combine walnuts, sugar, 4 tbsps (60 ml) of the melted butter, cinnamon, and orange blossom water; then set aside. Butter well a 10- × 15-inch (25 × 38 cm) baking pan, then set aside.

2. Remove dough from the package, unroll, and spread out on a towel. Cover with tea towel or plastic wrap to prevent it from drying out as you work. Take one sheet and place in baking pan, then brush with butter. Keep repeating procedure until one-half of package is used. Spread walnut mixture evenly over buttered layers.

3. Take one sheet of dough and spread over walnut mixture and brush with butter, then continue procedure until remainder of dough is used.

4. Re-heat remaining butter, then pour evenly over dough. With a sharp knife, carefully cut into approximately 2-inch (5 cm) square or diamond shapes. Bake in a preheated oven at 400°F (200°C) for 5 minutes, then lower the heat to 300°F (150°C) and bake for 40 minutes or until the sides turn light brown.

5. Place under broiler, then turn pan around until top of *baklawa* becomes golden. Remove from oven, then immediately spoon syrup over each square or diamond. Allow to cool before serving.

If a drier type of baklawa is desired, prepare only half the syrup.

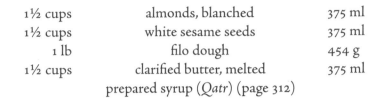

TUNISIAN ALMOND AND SESAME SEED PASTRY / SAMSA

MAKES 35 TO 40 PIECES

1½ cups	almonds, blanched	375 ml
1½ cups	white sesame seeds	375 ml
1 lb	filo dough	454 g
1½ cups	clarified butter, melted	375 ml
	prepared syrup (*Qatr*) (page 312)	

1. Preheat oven to 350°F (180°C).

2. Spread almonds and sesame seeds evenly on a large shallow pan. Bake until light brown, stirring occasionally so that they brown evenly. Remove from oven, let cool, then pulverize and set aside.

3. In a well-buttered 10- × 15-inch (25 by 38 cm) baking pan, place one sheet of filo dough, then brush with butter. Repeat procedure until one-third of sheets are used.

4. Spread half of the almond and sesame seed mixture on buttered filo sheets, then add another one-third of the filo, sheet by sheet, buttering them as before. Spread remaining almond and sesame seed mixture on buttered filo, then cover with remaining one-third of the filo, buttering sheet by sheet as before.

5. Brush top with remaining butter, then with a sharp knife carefully cut into squares or diamond shapes. Bake in preheated oven of 400°F (200°C) for 5 minutes, then lower heat to 300°F (150°C) and bake for approximately 30 minutes, or until sides turn golden.

6. Before removing from oven, place under broiler for a few moments, turning tray around until top is evenly golden. Remove from oven, then pour syrup evenly over top of hot *samsa*. Allow to cool, then serve.

For a drier type of samsa, prepare only half the syrup.

Even though my mother was not familiar with this pastry, she often experimented using different nuts for filling filo dough and she could have easily made a similar sweet.

DEEP-FRIED SWEET BALLS / 'AWAAMEE

MAKES ABOUT 3 DOZEN PIECES

As a child growing up on an isolated prairie farm, I often watched my mother make this simple syrup-drenched fritter.

1 tbsp	dry yeast (one package)	8 g
¼ cup	warm water	60 ml
2 cups	flour	500 ml
4 tbsps	cornstarch	60 ml
½ tsp	salt	2 ml
2 cups	warm water	500 ml
	prepared syrup (*Qatr*) (page 312)	
2 cups	cooking oil	500 ml

1. Dissolve the dry yeast in ¼ cup (60 ml) warm water and allow to sit for 15 minutes.

2. Combine flour, cornstarch, and salt in a mixing bowl, then pour in the yeast and water mixture and mix well. Add 2 cups (500 ml) of warm water, then stir until mixture resembles texture of pancake batter, adding more water if necessary. Cover; then set aside for 1 hour.

3. Heat oil in a saucepan, then drop 1 tablespoon of batter into hot oil. Deep-fry over medium heat until golden on all sides, then remove with a slotted spoon and place on paper towels to drain. Dip *'Awaamee* balls into syrup, then remove with a slotted spoon and arrange on a serving platter. Continue until all batter is used.

    NOTE: *The secret of success with this recipe is working quickly with the batter. Because the batter cooks rapidly, there is the risk of over-frying the balls, so try to work quickly!*

WHEATHEART CAKES / NAMMOORA

MAKES ABOUT 35 PIECES

Also called Hareesat al-Lawz when almonds are used, this sweet is very common throughout the Middle East and was often made by my mother.

2 lbs	cream of wheat	907 g
1½ cups	plain yogurt	375 ml
1½ cups	whipping cream	375 ml
1 cup	shredded coconut	250 ml
4 tsps	baking powder	20 ml
½ cup	sugar	125 ml
1 cup	melted butter	250 ml
	prepared syrup (*Qatr*) (page 312)	

1. Place cream of wheat, yogurt, whipping cream, coconut, baking powder, and sugar in a mixing bowl, then mix thoroughly into a batter. Pour into a 10- × 15-inch (25 by 38 cm) well-greased baking pan, then bake for 30 minutes in a 350°F (180°C) preheated oven.

2. Before removing cake from oven, brown evenly for a few minutes under the broiler. Remove, then cut into 2-inch (5 cm) squares. Spoon melted butter over cake. Pour syrup evenly over the top. Allow to cool before serving.

In seeking honey, expect the sting of bees.

SHREDDED DOUGH CHEESECAKE / KNAAFA BIL-JIBN

SERVES *8 TO 10*

1 lb	Kataifi (*knaafa*) dough	454 g
1 cup	melted butter	250 ml
1 lb	ricotta cheese, broken down with a fork	454 g
1 tsp	orange blossom (*mazahar*) water	5 ml
	prepared syrup (*Qatr*) (page 312)	
¼ cup	crushed pistachios or	60 ml
	ground blanched almonds	

1. Thaw dough according to package instructions. On a large tray, separate threads of dough then mix thoroughly by hand with butter making sure that all threads are coated with butter. Divide dough into two equal portions. Take one portion and flatten by hand into a 9- × 13-inch (23 × 28 cm) well-buttered baking pan that is 2 inches (5 cm) deep.

2. In a mixing bowl, combine cheese and orange blossom water, then spread evenly over dough in pan. Flatten and pat down the other portion of dough evenly over the filling.

3. Bake in a 350°F (180°C) preheated oven for 20-25 minutes or until surface of dough becomes golden.

4. Remove *knaafa* from oven and, while still hot, pour ¾ amount of syrup evenly over top. Garnish with pistachios or almonds and serve while hot. The remaining syrup can be spooned onto individual servings for those who prefer it sweeter.

In the Middle East, knaafa bil-jibn is a traditional breakfast dish. However, it is also an excellent dessert. On the farm, my mother would substitute shredded wheat for the knaafa dough. It was only in her twilight years that she was able to occasionally acquire knaafa dough in Canada. Knaafa dough is sold under the commercial name 'Kataifi' (shredded thin dough) found on the same freezer shelf as filo dough. It is available in Middle Eastern grocery stores and in some of the larger supermarkets.

SESAME COOKIES / BARAAZIK

MAKES ABOUT 40 COOKIES

A specialty of Damascus, these cookies have been peddled in the streets of that city for centuries. I remember the first time I visited Damascus at the beginning of the 1960s, I was ensnared by their taste and I have enjoyed them ever since.

My parents often spoke to us about the sweets of Damascus, especially baraazik, which farmers from their home village would bring back with them when they visited the city. More than once, Mother would say that if she had the ingredients, she would make them. Hence, instead of enjoying the sweets, we could only enjoy their description.

¾ cup	sesame seeds	175 ml
½ cup	honey	125 ml
½ cup	coarsely chopped pistachios	125 ml
2	eggs	2
1½ cups	unsalted butter	375 ml
1½ cups	sugar	375 ml
2½ cups	flour	625 ml
2 cups	wheat hearts or fine semolina	500 ml
2 tsps	baking powder	10 ml
½ tsp	salt	2 ml

1. Place sesame seeds, honey, and pistachios each in separate bowls, then set aside.

2. Place eggs, butter, and sugar in a food processor, then process into paste. Transfer to a mixing bowl, then add flour, wheat hearts or semolina, baking powder, and salt. Work into dough, adding a little water if necessary.

3. Form into golf ball–sized balls, then dip balls, one at a time, on one side only, into the pistachios and flatten with fingers, pistachios side down, on greased baking trays. Continue until all balls are finished, then brush each cookie with honey and sprinkle with sesame seeds.

4. Bake in a 350°F (180°C) preheated oven for 15 minutes or until cookies turn golden brown, then remove and allow to cool before serving.

ARABIAN SHORTBREAD/GHURAYBA

MAKES 40 PIECES

Children in the eastern Arab world look forward to this delicious shortbread often made by their mothers in the family kitchen.

The Spaniards inherited this shortbread-type cookie, which they call Polvorones a la Andaluza, from the Arabs. The ingredients of both versions are still basically the same. Some writers are intrigued with the idea that the shortbread of Scotland had its origin in the Middle East and its recipe was brought back by returning Crusaders.

1½ cups	butter, at room temperature	375 ml
1¾ cups	confectioner's sugar, divided	425 ml
1 tsp	orange blossom water (*mazahar*)	5 ml
1	egg yolk	1
3 cups	flour	750 ml
40	blanched almonds	40

1. Place butter, 1½ cups (375 ml) of the sugar, orange blossom water, and egg yolk in a food processor, then process for 1 minute. Transfer to a mixing bowl, then gradually add flour and, by hand, work quickly into a smooth dough.

2. Form dough into 40 balls, a little smaller than a walnut, then place on an ungreased cookie sheet and flatten slightly to about ½ inch (1 cm) thickness. Press an almond on each piece, then bake in a 300°F (150°C) preheated oven for 20 minutes or until bottoms just begin to brown. Remove from oven and allow to cool completely.

3. Sprinkle with remaining confectioner's sugar, then serve or store in an airtight container.

    NOTE: *The* ghurayba *may feel soft at the end of baking time, but they will harden as they cool.*

As for our family, Christmas on the farm was a time to enjoy food, crowned by the delectable sweets of baklawa and ghurayba—even today my favourites.

BREAD OF THE PALACE / 'AYSH AS-SARAAYA

SERVES 8

The desserts of the Middle East are among the most delicious in the world. Some are still prepared in the same way as when the armies of the famous Syrian Queen Zenobia defeated the legions of Rome in the third century CE. Others have evolved through the many influences that were brought by merchants and conquerors who came to the Greater Syria area throughout the centuries. A number were further developed by the immigrants from that region in North America. One of these is 'Aysh as-saraaya—a dessert once prepared in the homes of the wealthy, as its name implies.

My daughter Leila simplified this recipe to fit into the rushed life of our modern age. Mother made a similar sweet and called it a pudding.

8 slices	white bread, crusts removed and toasted	8 slices
2 cups	half-and-half cream	500 ml
8 slices	white bread, crust removed and cut into tiny pieces	8 slices
2 tbsps	sugar	30 ml
2 tbsps	orange blossom water (*mazahar*)	30 ml
½ recipe	prepared syrup (*Qatr*) (page 312)	½ recipe
4 tbsps	crushed pistachio nuts	60 ml

1. Place toasted bread in a greased 9- × 13-inch (23 × 28 cm) pan, then set aside.

2. Place cream, bread pieces, sugar, and orange blossom water in a saucepan, then, stirring constantly, bring to boil. Continue stirring over medium heat until mixture thickens, then set aside, but keep warm over very low heat.

3. Spoon syrup over toast in pan, then cover evenly with cream mixture. Sprinkle pistachios over top, let cool completely, then cover with plastic wrap. Refrigerate for at least 12 hours. Cut into 8 pieces and serve.

PUDDING / MIHALLABIYYA

SERVES 6

A common pudding throughout the Middle East, mihallabiyya is one of the most popular desserts served in homes and public eating places. Simple to prepare and with a silky and creamy texture, it can be enjoyed anytime of the day.

During our homesteading years, when we had no walnuts Mother made do without them. It was the same with orange blossom water and rose water, key ingredients in Arab sweets which were unavailable, so she substituted the flavourings with vanilla instead. Her mihallabiyya was still delicious.

⅓ cup	cornstarch	75 ml
4 cups	milk, divided	1 L
6 tbsps	raisins	90 ml
⅓ cup	sugar	75 ml
1 tsp	vanilla extract	5 ml
1 tsp	cinnamon	5 ml
2 tbsps	finely chopped walnuts	30 ml

1. In a bowl, dissolve the cornstarch in 1 cup (250 ml) of the milk. Set aside.

2. Place remaining 3 cups (750 ml) of milk, raisins, and sugar in a saucepan, then bring to boil over medium heat, stirring until sugar dissolves. Reduce heat to low, then add dissolved cornstarch and, stirring constantly, simmer for about 10 minutes, or until mixture is thick enough to heavily coat a spoon. Stir in vanilla, then pour mixture into 6 individual dessert bowls. Sprinkle with cinnamon, then scatter walnuts decoratively on top. Let cool completely then cover with plastic wrap. Refrigerate for at least 2 hours before serving.

SWEETS OF ARAB

ANDALUSIA

Many of the mouth-watering desserts of North Africa have their origin in al-Andalus, the Arab-created, earthly paradise in the Iberian Peninsula. One has to only read Ibn Razeen at-Tujeebee's thirteenth-century culinary work, entitled Fadaalat al-Khiwaan fee Tayyibaat at Ta'aam wa al-Alwaan, to know that the sweets North Africans prepare today had a history in Arab Andalusia.

CHAPTER 26

FIGS: DURING OUR HOMESTEADING YEARS, THEY EXISTED ONLY IN MOTHER'S TALES

The cold winds battered our home as we sat in the evening around a red-hot stove. I was perhaps six or seven years old, sitting on the floor at my mother's feet. She was knitting, as she did almost every evening after our supper, and, at the same time, she told us stories about her village life. As usual, when she talked of her early life, she was misty-eyed, relating to us the foods she relished as a young girl.

"When I was your age, I always looked forward to the fig season. Every night my mother or father would pick them, sugary-ripe off the tree, and we would gorge ourselves. There is nothing in the world more tasty than fresh figs plucked off the tree." I listened to her, fascinated. I had no idea what figs were, let alone sugary, fresh figs.

"Why can't we have some of these figs here?" I innocently asked, having no notion of climate or the costs of shipping over such long distances. The only fruit I had ever tasted were the saskatoons we picked in summer, which we ate fresh or subsequently canned.

Years later, when we became a bit more affluent, my father would at times buy dried figs, especially during the autumn season when we sold some grain—that is, if we had grain to sell. While none of our neighbours had even heard of these figs, we would indulge in them, and my mother would make jam with what was left. It was the sweet I most cherished during our farming years.

However, it wouldn't be until decades later, after I had left home, that I would have the opportunity to taste fresh figs right off the tree. And that time came during one of my trips to Syria in the early 1970s. Day after day I stuffed myself on the fruit that Mother raved about during the cold winter days in our south Saskatchewan home. It was then that I came to appreciate her stories about figs and their attributes.

Well, my mother had a point when she would excitedly talk about figs. One of humankind's most ancient foods, figs are the second fruit mentioned in the Bible. They date back to the Garden of Eden where Adam and Eve made garments from its leaves to hide their nakedness and restore their dignity.

One of the most delicious and wholesome fruits in existence, the fig is not only alluded to several times in the Bible, but has been important in all the other major world religions. In the Qur'an, the fig is one of the four sacred symbols; Buddha's revelations came to him under the banyan (a type of fig tree); and the Hindus regard the banyan as sacred.

Figs (*ficus carica*) are believed to have been cultivated in the Middle East since the dawn of history. They were known to the ancient Egyptians as early as 2700 BCE, and from this land their cultivation spread throughout the Mediterranean world, and eastward to India and beyond. In the intervening centuries, to the peoples of the ancient civilizations in the Middle East and the Indian subcontinent, they became a highly esteemed fruit. Historians have found that they were grown in the Hanging Gardens of Babylon and later became a staple in the Greek and Roman diets. The Arabs introduced them into the Iberian Peninsula, and in the sixteenth century they were brought to the Americas by the Spaniards.

Today, there are more than six hundred species of the fig tree, a member of the mulberry family of

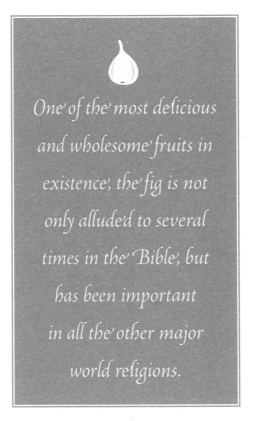

One of the most delicious and wholesome fruits in existence, the fig is not only alluded to several times in the Bible, but has been important in all the other major world religions.

plants which thrive best in areas of low humidity, intense sunshine, and hot summers. The tree, a spread-out shrub with deeply rooted leaves, needs very little pruning. It is said to be the ultimate indoor fruit tree, since inside it will bear two crops a year, tolerate both dry air and alkaline water, and is parthenocarpic—not needing pollination to bear fruit.

Figs, which usually bear fruit from June to October, come in colours ranging from white to red and almost all the hues in between. They are a delicate, sweet, and seedy-pulpy fruit, delicious when harvested at their peak of ripeness. A sure sign that figs are at their height of sweetness and flavour and ready to eat are the droplets of a sweet liquid with a delicious aroma forming at the navel. However, at this stage, they are highly fragile and will easily bruise. Once damaged, fresh figs degenerate very quickly. They must be handled with the utmost care, becoming too perishable to be sold at a great distance from where they are grown.

With a very limited shelf life of seven to ten days, fresh figs are never inexpensive and usually only retail in Middle Eastern and other specialty markets. Only about 5 percent of the California production, which represents over 90 percent of North American grown figs, are sold fresh; nearly all of these are transported by air. Hence, most figs are sold dried.

Besides being cultivated in California, and to a much lesser extent in Texas, figs are grown extensively in the Middle East and the other countries edging the Mediterranean, with Turkey being the top producer of figs in the world. The finest of the dried figs in the world are found near the Turkish city of Izmir (ancient Smyrna).

Fresh figs are nutritionally valuable and have been considered since ancient times as one of the choice foods for the convalescent. They are more alkaline and contain more mineral matter than most fruits. Fresh figs consist of 79 percent water, 18.7 percent carbohydrates, 1.5 percent protein, 0.6 percent mineral matter and 0.2 percent fat. When dried, the sugar content rises dramatically to 74.2 percent, protein to 4.3 percent, fat to 0.3 percent, and the minerals soar to 2.4 percent, but the water content goes down to 18.8 percent.

In general, figs have the largest sugar content of any common fruit. They are rich in calcium, copper, and potassium, and contain some iron, phosphorus, sodium, and traces of vitamins A, B, and C. Figs are among the gentlest natural laxatives in the world. Their unique proteins aid in relieving intestinal disorders, and their juice helps to induce sleep. Some naturalists assert that figs increase the strength of the young and help preserve the elderly—making them look younger and less wrinkled.

However, it is as a food that this "Garden of Eden" fruit reaches its true stature, realizing its ultimate flavour when fully ripe and eaten fresh. In the countries hugging the Mediterranean coast, to eat a fresh fig off a tree in the very early morning is a much anticipated pleasure. An honoured guest in the villages of the Greater Syria area is always taken to the host's orchard to sample the figs.

When the winter months come around, every family has their dried figs to serve visitors and to incorporate into snacks and desserts. Very tasty, nourishing, and usually plentiful, figs continue as a favoured staple in the Mediterranean world.

Today, the dishes enjoyed in these countries for millennia are catching on as far away as the Americas. These few simple recipes, my own versions of traditional Middle Eastern dishes, should give one an insight into the culinary advantages of one of humankind's oldest foods. Even though Mother never tasted fresh figs after she left Syria, she prepared most of these dishes when she was able to purchase dried figs.

FIGS AND CREAM

1. Figs are mouth-watering when served ripe and fresh, but are even tastier when served with cream. Just peel and slice fresh figs in a bowl for each person, then top with whipped cream and serve.

ALMOND-STUFFED FIGS

blanched and toasted whole almonds
dried figs, preferably the Smyrna type

1. Cut a slit in each fig, then insert an almond. Re-cover with the flesh of the fig. Serve as appetizer or as dessert.

FIGS WITH FENNEL

SERVES 4 TO 6

1 lb	fresh figs, peeled	454 g
½ tsp	ground fennel	2 ml
4 tbsps	crushed walnuts	60 ml

1. Halve the figs, then divide evenly on 4 to 6 plates. Sprinkle with the fennel and walnuts, then serve.

FIGS AND POETRY

For a poetic meditation on the sexual symbolism of the fig, you might want to read D.H. Lawrence's poem, simply entitled "Figs." Written in 1921, it was first published in 1923, in Lawrence's Birds, Beasts and Flowers: Poems.

(continued on next page...)

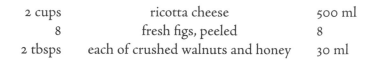

FIG AND HONEY DESSERT

SERVES 4

2 cups	ricotta cheese	500 ml
8	fresh figs, peeled	8
2 tbsps	each of crushed walnuts and honey	30 ml

1. Divide cheese into 4 parts and place on 4 plates. Slice and arrange two figs around ricotta cheese on each plate. Sprinkle walnuts over cheese and figs, then drizzle with honey and serve.

FIG JAM

MAKES ABOUT A QUART

1 lb	dried figs, ground	454 g
1 cup	sugar	250 ml
1 cup	cold water	250 ml
1 tsp	ground fennel seeds	5 ml
6	cloves	6
½ cup	pine nuts	125 ml
1 tbsp	each of sesame seeds and lemon juice	15 ml

1. Place figs, sugar, water, fennel, and cloves in a saucepan; then bring to boil. Cover and cook over medium heat for 20 minutes or until jam consistency is reached, stirring every few minutes during last 15 minutes. Remove from heat and stir in pine nuts, sesame seeds, and lemon juice; then allow to cool before use.

    NOTE: *Store in sterilized containers. Excellent when spread on buttered toast or Arab bread (pita).*

FIGS IN SYRUP

SERVES ABOUT 6

2 tbsps	sugar	30 ml
2 tbsps	lemon juice	30 ml
1	cinnamon stick	1
¼ tsp	aniseed	1 ml
2 cups	water	500 ml
1 lb	dried figs	454 g
2 tbsps	ground almonds	30 ml

1. Place sugar, lemon juice, cinnamon stick, aniseed, and water in a small saucepan, then bring to boil. Drop figs into syrup, then cover and gently cook over low heat for about 40 minutes or until figs plump up. Transfer figs with their syrup to a serving bowl, then sprinkle with almonds and serve.

DATE AND FIG LOAF

MAKES ONE LOAF

½ lb	dates, pitted	227 g
½ lb	figs	227 g
½ lb	ground almonds	227 g
4 tbsps	honey	60 ml
¼ tsp	ground cloves	1 ml
¼ tsp	aniseed	1 ml

1. Place all ingredients in a food processor, then process into a paste. Transfer to a greased 8- × 4-inch (20 × 10 cm) loaf pan, cover with plastic wrap, then refrigerate. Slice and serve as needed, then return remainder to refrigerator.

(...continued)

To the Hindus, figs are a symbol of both the female and male reproductive organs. The Greeks associated them with phallic worship, serving them at Dionysian orgies, and the Romans employed figs in several love potions. Even today, the Berbers of North Africa think of the fig as a fertility symbol.

FIG PIE

SERVES 6 TO 8

Crust

2 cups	flour	500 ml
2 tsps	baking powder	10 ml
½ tsp	salt	2 ml
1 cup	shortening, melted	250 ml
1	egg, beaten	1
1 tbsp	vinegar	15 ml
¼ cup	milk	60 ml

Filling

¾ lb	ground dried figs	340 g
1 cup	brown sugar	250 ml
4 tbsps	butter	60 ml
2 tbsps	lemon juice	30 ml
1 tbsp	cornstarch	15 ml
¼ tsp	each of ground cloves and cinnamon	1 ml
2½ cups	water	625 ml

1. To make crust, combine flour, baking powder, and salt in a mixing bowl. In another small bowl, combine shortening, egg, vinegar, and milk. Pour a little at a time of this mixture into dry ingredients and work into a dough, adding a little water as needed. Divide dough into two balls, one a little larger. Set aside.

2. To make filling, place filling ingredients in a saucepan. Stir constantly and bring to a boil, adding more water if necessary. Cook and stir over medium heat until saucepan contents begin to thicken. Remove from heat and set aside to cool.

3. Roll out the larger ball to about ⅛ inch (3 mm) thick, then use it to line a 9-inch (22 cm) pie plate. Pour in the saucepan's contents, then roll out the remaining ball of dough then top pie plate with it. Trim and flute edges. Bake in a preheated 375°F (190°C) oven for 35 minutes or until pie turns a deep golden colour.

FIG TARTS

MAKES 24 MEDIUM TARTS

¾ lb	dried figs, ground	340 g
1 cup	brown sugar	250 ml
6 tbsps	butter	90 ml
2 tbsps	lemon juice	30 ml
½ tsp	cinnamon	2 ml
¼ tsp	ground cloves	1 ml
1	Fig Pie crust recipe (page 328)	

1. Thoroughly combine all ingredients, except pie crust. Set aside.

2. Roll out pie dough to about ⅛ inch (3 mm) thickness, then cut into 24 rounds. In greased medium-cup muffin trays, carefully place dough rounds. Pat into cups and crimp top edges. Spoon filling evenly into the 24 muffin cups.

3. Bake in a 375°F (190°C) oven for about 20 minutes or until top edges of crust are golden brown. Allow to cool slightly, then serve warm.

After dinner, rest;
after supper, walk a mile.

FIG AND RAISIN CAKE

SERVES 10 TO 12

2 cups	flour	500 ml
3 tsps	baking powder	15 ml
¾ tsp	cinnamon	3 ml
¾ tsp	nutmeg	3 ml
¼ tsp	salt	1 ml
1 cup	raisins, rinsed	250 ml
1 lb	dried figs, ground	454 g
¾ cup	melted butter	175 ml
2 cups	brown sugar	500 ml
¼ tsp	ground cloves	1 ml
4	eggs	4
1 cup	water	250 ml

1. In a bowl, mix together the flour, baking powder, cinnamon, nutmeg, and salt, then add raisins and figs. Thoroughly combine, then set aside.

2. Place remaining ingredients in a food processor and process for a minute.

3. Add the processed ingredients to the dry ingredients, and with a wooden spoon mix into a soft batter, adding more water if necessary. Pour into a well-greased 9-inch (23 cm) square cake pan, then bake in a 300°F (150°C) preheated oven for about 1 hour or until cake is done.

CHAPTER 27

AFTER FOOD, POETRY SOOTHED MY SOUL

Since my youth I have always loved poetry. During my school years, I could never understand why my fellow schoolmates were not interested in literature, especially poetry. When it came to studying Shakespeare, I was in my glory, even though my peers hated attending our Shakespeare classes. I memorized his plays and would recite them to myself as I milked the cows or helped my father in the field. It is a passion that I have never lost.

My favourite bard during my youth was Robert Service. However, as the years slipped by, his lines were replaced somewhat by the verses of Omar Khayyam as translated by Edward Fitzgerald. Khayyam's stanzas became and remain today my ideal in the field of poetry. In the ensuing years, he, along with Service, were the models that I have followed when writing my own poetry—mostly about love, the mysteries of life, and the cruelty of humankind.

From the time when I first read the *Rubaiyat* of Omar Khayyam, I have been enthralled by the poetry of this world-renowned Persian poet and his type of verse. Of course it was not the poet himself but rather Fitzgerald who first translated his stanzas into English, thus making this mathematician-astronomer poet a famous literary figure in the English-speaking world. Although Fitzgerald added to and altered many of Khayyam's lines, he nevertheless brought to this world a taste for the philosophy of the foreign and mysterious lands where Islam held sway.

Since the translation by this English gentleman, who was a poet in his own right, a series of other translations have been made, many of which more accurately relate to the verses of Khayyam. Although these later translations are more accurate, their impact has been far less than the poetic translation of Fitzgerald. If one is to be precise, the *Rubaiyat* is the poetry of Fitzgerald built on the ideas and format of Khayyam.

The *Rubaiyat*, an Arabic word meaning four (quatrains), is a form of verse which follows an Arabic form of poetry. In this type of poetry, each verse is a separate entity and carries its own message. In Khayyam's day, Arabic was the universal language of the Muslim world, which in that era was the height of civilization and scholarship.

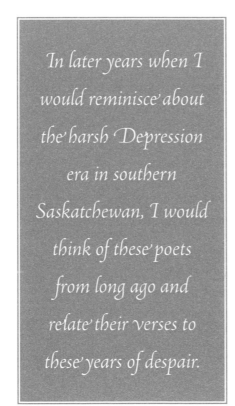

In later years when I would reminisce about the harsh Depression era in southern Saskatchewan, I would think of these poets from long ago and relate their verses to these years of despair.

In the same fashion as an intellectual from the Indian subcontinent or Africa in our day writes in both his or her own language and English, many of the literary figures in the medieval world of Islam wrote not only in their own vernacular tongues but also in Arabic.

Khayyam, like many of his countrymen, knew the language and literature of the Arabs and wrote not only in his native Persian tongue, but also in Arabic, the language of Islam.

Many in the West, unacquainted and unfamiliar with the Arabic language and Arabic literature, think that Khayyam is the father of the *rubaiyat* type of poetry. This is not the case. Abū 'Alā' al-Ma'arrī, a renowned Syrian Arab poet, born in 973 CE, forty-four years before Khayyam, is believed to be the poet who was the pathfinder for the well-known *Rubaiyat* made famous by Fitzgerald.

Abū 'Alā' was a blind poet who, in his verses, expounded unconventionality, pessimism, and cynicism about the revealed religions and questioned life—all of which one finds in the verses of Khayyam. There were other poets who wrote this type of poetry before Khayyam, in both their native tongues and Arabic, but in my opinion no one influenced Khayyam more than this blind Syrian poet.

In my youth I read and enjoyed the *Rubaiyat* of Omar Khayyam, but as time passed and I became proficient in Arabic, the language of my ancestors, I found a larger world of enjoyable *rubaiyat*. In later years when I would reminisce about the harsh Depression years in southern Saskatchewan, I would think of these poets from long ago and relate their verses to these years of despair. Perhaps it was my Arab background that made me think of the *Rubaiyat*'s message as I remembered the harsh years of my youth. There is no doubt that the flowery poetry of the Arabs, especially the *rubaiyat* form, had a great influence on my literary thinking.

Although the Depression left its scars on me, there were glimpses of beauty even in those barren years. Imitating the poets of yore who wrote in the *rubaiyat* form, I wrote stanzas to explain or reminisce about a problem, enjoyable moment, or situation. In the 1980s, while travelling through Mexico during a long winter vacation, the cold Canadian winter with its ice and storms became only a memory as I romped on the beaches and enjoyed the sun. The exhilarating feeling of the cool ocean breezes and warm soft sands inspired me to finish my own *Rubaiyat*.

As I wrote, using both Abū ʿAlāʾ al-Maʿarrī and Omar Khayyam as my inspirations, I finished my *Prairie Rubaiyat*. I was amazed how my verses carried the same messages as those found in the poetry of these famous literary men.

In my *rubaiyat* verses—as well as those of Abū ʿAlāʾ and Khayyam— one finds both pessimism and the inevitability of fate. Discussing how all things fade away, never to return, Abū ʿAlāʾ, through the translation by Henry Baerlein, says:

> The rolling, ever-rolling years of time
> Are as a diwan of Arabian Song;
> The poet, headstrong and supremely strong,
> Refuses to repeat a single rhyme.

In the same vein, Khayyam through Fitzgerald ponders:

> The Moving Finger writes;
> and, having writ,
> Moves on: Nor all thy
> Piety nor Wit
> Shall lure it back to cancel half a Line,
> Nor all thy Tears wash out a Word of it.

In my *Prairie Rubaiyat*, I reminisce about life and write:

> The caravan of our allotted time rolls on and on.
> Halt it awhile and the robe of merriment don.
> Enjoy the moments and from their pleasures sup,
> Pour out the wine, our lives are almost gone.

The Middle East was the cradle of civilization and in this cradle many of humanity's ideas and ways of life had their beginnings. From the onset, when humans began to clothe and feed themselves, they knew there were other forces which affected life. Searching for these forces one found religion and ever since it has been most often the mainstay of human life. Here the religions of today's Western world sprouted and began to flourish.

These religions, nourished in the Arabian Peninsula and its environs, were all built on a belief that an Unknown Hand guided human destiny and thus controlled fate. The vast majority of Arab and Muslim poets who wrote in the *rubaiyat* form came to an identical conclusion. They were of the opinion that this Unknown Hand manages the affairs of man. Abū ʿAlāʾ thought of life as only a passing phenomenon controlled by some Unknown Manipulator. Thus, he muses:

> I think our world is not a place of rest,
> But where a man may take his little ease,
> Until the landlord whom he never sees
> Gives that apartment to another guest.

In the Graves-Shah translation of the *Rubaiyat*, Omar Khayyam also reflects:

> In agitation I was brought to birth
> And learned nothing from life but wonder at it;
> Reluctantly we leave, still uninformed
> Why in the world we came, or went, or were.

In my *Prairie Rubaiyat*, I, too, meditate about life and its mysteries:

How can we mortals our
   allotted lives rearrange
Or another world for this
   world exchange?
When our lives have been
   plotted in that book
Kept by Him who knows
   there can be no change.

There is no doubt that from
the early days when religions were
first established, they have been
the cause of much fanaticism and
dissension. Instead of the love
for humankind expounded by all
religions, hate and wars were more
often than not practiced by their
followers. There are not many
who will dispute the fact that all
religions arouse in people love and
passion, but also envy and hate.
They unify, and at the same time,
divide. Abū ʿAlāʾ, thinking about
the revealed religions, ponders:

   Lo! there are many ways
      and many traps
   And many guides, and
      which of them is lord?
   For verily Mahomet
      has the sword,
   And he may have the truth—
      perhaps! *perhaps*!

In Fitzgerald's translation,
Omar Khayyam reflects:

Oh Thou, who Man of bas-
   er Earth didst make,
And who with Eden didst
   devise the Snake;
For all the Sin wherewith
   the Face of Man
Is blacken'd, Man's Forgiveness
   give-and-take!

I also question the ways of
religion when I muse:

   In a Western church a voice
      of a preacher cries
   And in an Eastern mosque a
      muezzin's voice replies.
   For man struggling on earth
      since the dawn of time
   Is hypnotized, and on that
      unknown world relies.

Poets, perhaps because of their
interest in both the joys and tribulations of life, usually do not seek
to control the fate of others. They
look on power as something not
worth the struggle since it is only a
transitory phenomenon. Writing
of how all power and glory end
in oblivion, Abū ʿAlāʾ meditates:

   There is a palace, and
      the ruined wall
   Divides the sand, a very
      home of tears,
   And where love whispered
      of a thousand years

The silken-footed cat-
   erpillars crawl.

In the same vein, Omar Khayyam
through Fitzgerald ruminates:

   They say the Lion and
      the Lizard keep
   The Courts where Jamshyd
      gloried and drank deep:
   And Bahrám, that great
      Hunter—the Wild Ass
   Stamps o'er his Head, and
      he lies fast asleep.

I do not disagree with them when I
write:

   Where are the Pharaohs and
      their cherished gods?
   Where are the Conquistadors
      and their killer squads?
   The wheels of history turn
      and grind. Today them,
   Tomorrow unknown oth-
      ers will get the nods.

A subject on which most bards
agree, especially the *rubaiyat* poets, is love and beauty. No one will
question the fact that these versifiers
add much to the enjoyment of life
with both their down-to-earth and
metaphoric description of nature's
beauty or the charms of women. In
the *rubaiyat*, since each stanza is
an entity by itself and carries its

own message, each forms a separate image. These images become a series of colourful pictures, easily absorbed and remembered by the reader. Abū ʿAlā metaphorically compares a maid's laughter to a waterfall in a verse uniting nature and beauty. He counsels:

> Run! follow, follow happiness, the maid
> Whose laughter is the laughing waterfall;
> Run! call to her—but if no maiden call,
> 'Tis something to have loved the flying shade.

The image conjured in Fitzgerald's Omar Khayyam does not differ appreciably from that of Abū ʿAlā:

> I sometimes think that never blows so red
> The Rose as where some buried Caesar bled;
> That every Hyacinth the Garden wears
> Dropt in its Lap from some once lovely Head.

In my *Prairie Rubaiyat*, I sketch an illustration encompassing the beauty of both nature and women when I muse:

> Look! As she waters the blooming roses red,
> A fresh tender blossom crossing the flower bed.
> This beauty and the roses with perfumed flowers,
> From the same soil, were they both not bred?

To be enjoyed, poetry, in my opinion, has to be simple, and even if in metaphoric form, easily understood by the reader. Unlike many of the Eastern *rubaiyat* poets, I have written mine in a straightforward fashion. Over the past few years, I have compiled these verses as a summary of my life and how I interpret the laws of nature.

The first chapter of my *Prairie Rubaiyat*, which I call "Where the Breezes Blow," relates mainly to the western Canadian prairies and is really the story of my life and thoughts. In this section, I reminisce about the harshness of the land, the winter winds, and the days of my youth. If in my verses the cold winter storms seem to be all important, it is no accident. With no central heating in those Depression years, it seemed I was cold all through the winter months. Although many years have slipped by, I still vividly remember those cold blustery years as portrayed in the following chapter. ✂

THE PRAIRIE RUBAIYAT

CHAPTER I

Where the Breezes Blow

The wind blowing across Saskatchewan's desert waste
Blew me misery and hardship and a bitter taste,
Made me forget my youthful thrills and joys
After I grew in years and worldly ways embraced.

In past years I hunted on the cold western plain
Wild animals for pleasure or for monetary gain.
Awakening came on the bloody field of battle
When I was the hunted waiting to be slain.

An antelope gliding across the prairie green,
A coyote eating his stolen chicken unseen,
And a farmer ploughing his rock-filled field,
A perfect scene on that upper movie screen.

Biting are the winds which across prairies blow,
Carrying with them the misery of ice and snow.
The chilled traveller asks: Why seek heaven?
Is it not better that place where fires glow?

At my parents' feet I listened to many a tale
About that land from where the prophets hail.
Why they left to dwell in the cold barren west
I know not, but did wealth over history prevail?

In a Western church the voice of a preacher cries,
And in an Eastern mosque a muezzin's voice replies.
For man struggling on earth since the dawn of time
Is hypnotized, and on that unknown world relies.

In stolen native lands I dug a burial mound
Where it was said, rich treasures could be found.
In later years I knew, alike they were,
He who steals the land or takes what's underground.

A bottle of forbidden booze in that field of wheat.
A book of poetry and stolen sandwiches for a treat,
And two lovers cooled by the gentle prairie breeze.
An earthly heaven, if the One above is discreet.

The western trails I trudged in blowing snow,
And the drought-shrivelled grain I used to mow
Are now sad memories of my yesteryears.
Why can I not forget them? Ask Him who knows.

Hark! Hear the wind blowing in the prairie wild.
That sound which haunted me as a growing child.
Unnumbered were the times it aroused my fears.
In those years, the world of terror on me smiled.

The cold winds which chilled my youthful bones,
Blew across a barren land of dust and stones,
Creating a harsh world of sorrows and pains.
I can still hear my parents' sighs and moans.

In western villages when the beer flowed free
Men sang, "Bury me not on the lone prairie."
Were they only words of anxiety and fear, or
Did they feel the afterlife more than you or me?

In bygone years no plough touched the prairie sod,
And in this virgin grassy land very few men trod
Till from across the oceans conquering hordes came
To destroy the handiwork of Him who gave the nod.

They say the palms swaying in the blazing sun,
And the snows of the northern lands are one.
I know it's not true even if some say it's so.
Was it not from under palms human history sprung?

Both the wintery gales which our bodies pierce
And the teaching of Godly men bring us fears.
Why do we loathe the one and the other praise,
All of us Adam's children from peasants to emirs?

Ripening grain swaying in the summer breeze
And gardens overflowing with their tender peas
Are but a little link in the chain of life.
So it has been from the days of Hercules.

In this land, Native and buffalo once did roam,
And men were free to call any place their home,
Then conquerors came to free and civilize, but
Was it not prison to put each one under a dome?

Gophers and rabbits, the joy of prairie life
Are hunted by men with rifle, trap, and knife.
Why is there no pity? Was there no promise made
To them for earth, and the unknown afterlife?

Once, prairie rivers flowed without their dam,
And in their waters men and animals swam,
Then came man with his machines to remake
The landscape, unchanged since the days of Abraham.

Once, in the virgin forests trod the Mohawk,
A proud hunter carrying his stone tomahawk,
Then came traders with gaudy trinkets and booze
To erase his pride and tales of the mighty hawk.

A cowboy roaming the west is a prairie bard
Whose western tunes our tortured ears bombard.
For some it is joy, for others piercing pain.
Remember, that which lifts souls, never discard.

In my adolescent years I rode the western freight
In freezing cold, without food, such was my fate.
Now in luxury I live but it will not fade away
The picture of biting cold and meals I never ate.

Often in the winter cold, I heard Mother weep,
Crying for a better life for us who were asleep.
I ask, "Is it fair, some must starve and suffer
While others, their ripened harvest reap?"

Cruel were my schoolmates, taunting me "infidel"
And "foreigner" who came in their land to dwell.
They must've all feared the strange and unknown,
The bully and even the beautiful mademoiselle.

On the prairie plains a stranger is a friend,
For on each other scattered farmers depend.
'Tis the same. Country folks, no matter whether
They be Bedouins or pioneers, hospitality extend.

Long did I bear dust storms in Canada's west,
And blowing thistles which that land infest.
In those days, paradise was in other lands.
Oh! How green are the fields over yonder crest.

Did Natives live in ignorance and unbelief,
And did they rob and kill from brave to chief?
They are here no more, you have their lands,
Walk with shame when they say you are the thief.

Hiawatha's pride was a code for every tribe.
To his lifestyle, every brave ascribed,
Then invaders came with gods and books and guns
To modernize, but also teach the ways to bribe.

Cold and barren is the northern land I dislike.
To it man came for a little gold to strike.
It was a fleeting mirage which passed away.
Today, are there men or gold in the Klondike?

The hot wind is playing with a sandy dune.
In a hayloft two lovers were beginning to spoon.
Each has been programmed to follow a chosen way
By Him who is manipulating both sun and moon.

Many were the winter nights we would retire
To sleep around a stove made red by fire.
Man loves to feel the heat of a biting flame
Whether it be hearth or a passionate spitfire.

Dreadful are the prairies in a winter storm.
Shivering are its humans, trying to keep warm,

But soothing are their dreams of sunny isles
Where from the cold tourists flock and swarm.

In far Saskatchewan, I heard church bells chime,
A friend in Syria heard words of an imam rhyme.
Each had a message, a message that was clear,
Man to be different is an unforgivable crime.

Birds flying south searching for waters warm.
Geese in formation escaping the winter storm.
Man struggling in the cold, bemoaning his fate.
Was He just? Why was not migration uniform?

See the cows gather, fearing the coming storm,
And see how the chickens in the barnyard swarm.
All are terrorized of the dark unknown, as man
Has from the days when he wrote in cuneiform.

By a dry river bed, there bloomed many a rose
Beautifying the prairie lands, ere winter snows.
Wait! We too mature, blossom, then fade away
When the inevitable wind of our winter blows.

Strange as it may seem, I never tasted the grape,
Nor did I have the chance its influence to escape.
For in the arid western plains only thistle blew,
No vine to arouse our souls or our morals rape.

In the Alberta wheat fields men would toil
To harvest the golden kernels from the soil.
I ask, "Would they have sweated to reap the grain
If they knew that below the land was the oil?"

Still, still I cannot forget the blowing dust
To which in my tender years I could not adjust.
I roamed the wide world searching for its joys,
Yet, that still the piercing sand my soul incrust.

CHAPTER 28

CONCLUSION

My love for Arab cuisine has a winding history. The healthy and tasty foods my mother cooked when we were growing up and of which I was ashamed, in later years, became my world of culinary passion.

When the Second World War began and I left the farm for Regina to work in a war industry factory, I would take my meals at a restaurant. For lunch, I would order either bologna or sardine sandwiches. The proprietor must have thought that I was from another world. The fact that they were not on the menu meant he had to make them especially for me. However, this craving for bologna and sardines and other restaurant foods, like French fries and hamburgers, only lasted a few weeks. Soon, I began to yearn for my mother's food, but I refused to admit this to myself.

In 1943, I joined the Royal Canadian Air Force, and after training in various parts of Canada, I was sent to Great Britain. There, I found that the people did not even have the luxury of bologna and sardines. Sawdust sausages and gamey-tasting mutton were the dishes of the day. Now I began to truly pine away for my mother's meals. I would even dream of *Ilba*—a simple boiled and sweetened wheat dish—which our family often ate for breakfast or for an evening snack. Even a dish which my mother at times made, called *Hareesa*, now seemed palatable. Made by boiling bones with a little meat and crushed wheat—not burghul—and a few spices until the meat and wheat are almost dissolved together, it was the only food from my mother's kitchen that I detested—the dish that, even now, I have no desire to eat.

Yet, this simple food is considered to be a traditional mainstay in many Arab countries. I remember, at the end of the 1980s, I was invited to a wedding banquet in one of the plush restaurants in Dubai, the thriving heart of the United Arab Emirates. One of the main dishes on the menu was *Hareesa*.

In true Arab hospitality, the host urged us on to eat. As soon as our plates began to empty, the waiters would refill them with another delicacy. I can still sense that feeling when I saw before me my plate completely filled with this meat and wheat dish. Of course, in a polite manner, I tried to eat a little, but to no avail. It was no different than my mother's *Hareesa*. There was only one consolation. There was no refilling of my plate that evening.

However, with the exception of *Hareesa*, the foods I have included in this book and numerous others that my mother cooked during my youth are now for me fond culinary memories. It is a part of my life that I cherish. Passionate memories are part of the essence of being human. The foods we thrived on in the lean years of my youth have for many years been the spice of my life.

With our Syrian foods, we survived the Depression years as healthy as any affluent family in our times. Yet, growing up with a different cuisine than that of our peers, we children always thought we were deprived and not equal. We yearned for the neighbours' white bread and their canned foods. Broad beans, burghul, chickpeas, and lentils were staples, we believed, that kept us backward.

How could it be otherwise when we could not disappear into mainstream society and were not accepted as "normal" Canadians. As young children, we spoke the same, played the same, and lived in the same environment as our Canadian neighbours. Why then were we considered different? What we saw as naïve young children was that our food and meals were not the same as those of our schoolmates and neighbours. We felt that this was the main reason why we were called "foreigner" and "black Syrian."

By eating bologna and sardines, we hoped that perhaps we would be like the others. Realizing that our food was more nutritious and tasty than white bread and cold cuts would come later, when most of us had integrated completely into this new Euro-Canadian society in every way, except in looks. As we grew up, we began longing for the food we had rejected and were embarrassed by as children. No different than the vast majority of other immigrants, we spent much of our lives trying to disappear.

However, this was not the true intention of the early immigrants. I am sure that when, in 1882, the first Arab, Abraham Bounadere, stepped on the soil of Canada, he did not think that this northern land would be his everlasting home. Like many others who followed him, he had left a sunny country full of fruit-laden orchards to find his fortune. The stories of cities and towns having streets paved with gold had lured him to this northern part of the Americas. Here he thought that he would find wealth and then return to live in luxury in his tranquil village. But this was not to be. As the years slipped by, he found that an easy fortune was not to be had, and his village became but a memory as he gradually assimilated into Canadian society.

The story of Abraham Bounadere's life is the story of the early Arab immigrants. Most came to Canada from villages in the Syrian region of the Ottoman Empire that later became the French mandated territory of Syria and Lebanon. Most of them were uneducated or, at best, semi-educated, and intended to return after making their fortune. Yet, with the exception of a tiny number, they were eventually to make Canada their permanent home.

The Arab immigrants assimilated into Canadian society at a faster pace than immigrants from other countries. Today, their descendants, almost without exception, I believe, do not even know the village or region whence their ancestors came. A few dishes of Arab food and some mispronounced family names are the only connection these descendants of the first newcomers have with the land of their ancestors.

After the Second World War, new types of Arab immigrants came. Unlike the early pioneers, they arrived from all parts of the Arab world and were, in most cases, educated. Many knew either English or French or both better than their

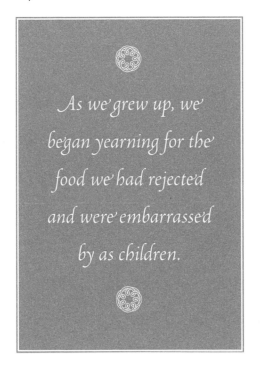

As we grew up, we began yearning for the food we had rejected and were embarrassed by as children.

native tongue. This tended to make them feel more at home in Canada than in the lands from which they originated. Like the first wave of Arab immigrants, most of these second-wave immigrants assimilated quickly. When in the last half of the twentieth century multiculturalism became Canadian government policy, a few of these new arrivals and a small number of the descendants of the first immigrants began to work for the preservation of the Arab heritage in Canada. The majority, however, remained on the sidelines.

The saga of the Arab immigrants is truly the story of Canada. As I update this book, in the 135 years that the Arabs settled in Canada, many prospered and in the process contributed much to their new land. But it is a sad fact that as we look back on these people of Arab heritage, we can identify hardly any as Arab-Canadians. In a few generations, they will have seemed to have disappeared completely into either English or French societies. Only in historical research will they be remembered, and perhaps in the faint memories of the hearty Arab foods that kept us healthy during the Depression years. Perhaps this is as it should be, but I feel that before this becomes a reality, fellow Canadians and others, after

reading our family's saga, will agree that Arab-Canadians have contributed greatly to Canada's history.

Although these contributions span the nation, one of the most important gifts Canada received was in Saskatchewan. Here, Arab pioneers helped to develop, populate, and create the province. Determined to survive and to "make it" in this, their new adopted land, they tenaciously clung to their traditional work ethic, and put to work their ingenuity and their skills in dry-land farming. Despite the harsh forces of nature and the harsh bullying by schoolmates and others, my family stood its ground to make a secure future for their children and for later generations. Through all this, my strongest and most pleasant memories are of Mother's Syrian dishes, which were part of our daily life. This was her connection

to Syria, a connection that she wanted to pass on to her children. Her kitchen was her pride, for it was here that she would create the flavours and aromas of our ancestors in the midst of the prairie dust and drought, through good times and bad, all part of a growing Canadian nation. Foods that at one time we were embarrassed to present to non-Syrian neighbours, friends, and co-workers ironically have now become part of the Canadian culinary scene and part of Canada's future. ❈

REFERENCES

Abraham, Sameer Y., and Nabeel Abraham. *Arabs in the New World: Studies on Arab-American Communities*. Detroit: Wayne State University, 1983.

Abū-Laban, Bahā. *An Olive Branch on the Family Tree: The Arabs in Canada*. Toronto: McClelland and Stewart, 1980.

——."Arabs." *The Canadian Encyclopedia*. Vol. I, Second Edition. Edmonton: Hurtig Publishers, 1988. 90.

Abū-Laban, Bahā, and Faith T. Zeadey. *Arabs in America: Myths and Realities*. Wilmette, Illinois: Medina UP International, 1975.

Arberry, A.J."A Baghdad Cookery Book," a translation of al-Baghdadi's *Kitab al-Tabikh* with notes by C. Perry, in *Medieval Arab Cookery, Essays and Translations* by Maxime Rodinson, A.J. Arberry and Charles Perry. Devon (U.K.): Prospect Books, 2001.

Atalla, Theophile."Lebanese." *Encyclopedia Canadiana*, Vol. 6. Toronto: Grolier of Canada, 1977. 108–9.

Baerlein, Henry. *The Diwan of Abu'l-Ala*. London: John Murray, 1948.

Baker, Peter. *Memoirs of an Arctic Arab: A Free Trader in the Canadian North: The years 1907–1927*. Yellowknife Publishing Co., 1976.

Barclay, Harold B."The Perpetuation of Muslim Tradition in the Canadian North." *Muslim World* 59 (January 1969): 66–83.

Blatty, William Peter. *Which Way to Mecca, Jack?* New York: Curtis Publishing Co., 1958.

Elkholy, Abdo A."The Arab Americans: Nationalism and Traditional Preservation." In *The Arab Americans: Studies in Assimilation*. Wilmette, Illinois: Medina UP International, 1969.

Fodor's Morocco. Fodor's Travel Publications, Inc., 1991.

Fortin, Michel. *Syria, Land of Civilizations*. Montreal: Les Editions de l'Homme, 1999.

Groves, Robert and Omar Ali-Shah. *Rubáiyát of Omar Khayyám*. Translated by Edward Fitzgerald. Middlesex, England: Penguin Books, 1972.

Hamod, Sam. *Dying with the Wrong Name*. New York: Anthé Publications, 1980.

Harris, Lloyd J. *The Book of Garlic*. Berkeley: Aris Books, 1975.

Hendrickson, Robert. *Lewd Food: The Complete Guide to Aphrodisiac Edibles*. Radnor, PA.: Chilton Book Co., 1974.

Jabbra, Nancy Walstrom, and Joseph G. Jabbra. *Voyageurs to a Rocky Shore: The Lebanese and Syrians in Nova Scotia*. Halifax: Institute of Public Affairs, Dalhousie University, 1984.

Johnson, Gilbert. "The Syrians in Western Canada." In *Saskatchewan History* 7 (1959): 31–32.

Mallos, Tess. *The Complete Middle East Cookbook*. Toronto: McGraw-Hill, 1979.

Mardam-Bey, Farouk. *Ziryab: Authentic Arab Cuisine*. Woodbury, Connecticut: Ici La Press, 2002.

Massoud, Muhammad Said. *I Fought As I Believed: An Arab Canadian Speaks Out on the Arab-Israeli Conflict*. Montreal: Ateliers des Sourds, 1976.

Nafzāwī, Umar ibn Muhammad. *The Perfumed Garden*. Translated by Richard Francis Burton. New York: Kegan Paul International, 1999.

Rizk, Salom. *Syrian Yankee*. New York: Doubleday, 1943.

Roden, Claudia. *A Book of Middle Eastern Food*. Middlesex, England: Penguin Books, 1970.

Root, Waverley Lewis. *The Food of Italy*. New York: Atheneum, 1971.

Salloum, Habeeb. *Arabian Nights Cookbook: From Lamb Kebabs to Baba Ghanouj, Delicious Homestyle Middle Eastern Cooking*. North Clarendon, Vermont: Tuttle Publishing, 2010.

———. *Asian Cooking Made Simple: A Culinary Journey Along the Silk Road and Beyond*. Helena, Montana: Sweet Grass Books/Farcountry Press, 2014.

———. *Bison Delights: Middle Eastern Cuisine, Western Style*. Regina: Canadian Plains Research Center, 2010.

———. *Classic Vegetarian Cooking from the Middle East and North Africa*. New York and Northampton: Interlink Books, 2000.

———. "Foods of the Arab Homesteaders." *Backhome Magazine* 7 (Spring 1992): 18–20.

———. "George J. Salloum Family." In *Neville, The Golden Years, 1900-1980*. The Neville Celebrate Saskatchewan Heritage Committee: Neville, Saskatchewan, 1980.

———. "A Gourmet Sunday Dinner on the Homestead." *Countryside & Small Stock Journal* 93, no. 2 (March/April 2009): 68–70.

———. "Homesteading in Southern Saskatchewan." In *Arab-Canadian Writing: Stories, Memoirs, and Reminiscences*, edited by Kamal Rostom, 16–21. Fredericton: York Press, 1989.

———. "Homesteading in Southern Saskatchewan." In *Images: Canada through Literature*, edited by John Borovilos, 34–43. Toronto: Prentice Hall Ginn Canada, 1996.

———. *Journeys Back to Arab Spain*. Toronto: Middle East Studies Centre, 1994.

———. "Reminiscence of an Arab Family Homesteading in Southern Saskatchewan." *Canadian Ethnic Studies* 15, no. 2 (1983): 130–38.

———. "The Syrians." *Encyclopedia of Canada's Peoples*. Toronto: University of Toronto Press, 1999. 1241–46.

———. "Thrifty Homestead Cooking with a Difference." *Recipes Only* 4, no. 4 (September 1986) 248–270.

———. "The Urbanisation of an Arab Homesteading Family." *Saskatchewan History* 42, no. 2 (1989): 79–84.

———. "The Urbanisation of an Arab Homesteading Family." *World Review* 32, no. 2 (1993): 18–30.

———. "Yogurt: Medicinal Food on the Homestead." *Countryside & Small Stock Journal* 97, no. 5 (September/October 2013): 53–55.

Salloum, Habeeb (with Leila Salloum Elias and Muna Salloum). *Scheherazade's Feasts: Foods of the Medieval Arab World*. Philadelphia: University of Pennsylvania Press, 2013.

Salloum, Habeeb (with Leila Salloum Elias and Muna Salloum). *Sweet Delights from a Thousand and One Nights: The Story of Traditional Arab Sweets*. London: I. B. Tauris, 2013.

Salloum, Habeeb, and James Peters. *Arabic Contributions to the English Vocabulary: English Words of Arabic Origin, Etymology and History*. Beirut: Librarie du Liban, 1996.

Salloum, Habeeb, and James Peters. *From the Lands of Figs and Olives: Over 300 Delicious and Unusual Recipes from the Middle East and North Africa*. New York: Interlink Books, 1995.

Service, Robert W. *The Best of Robert Service*. Toronto: McGraw-Hill Ryerson, 1940.

Trager, James. *The Bellybook*. New York: Grossman, 1972.

Waines, David. *In a Caliph's Kitchen*. London: Riad El-Rayyes Books, 1989.

———. "The Culinary Culture of al-Andalus." In *The Legacy of Muslim Spain*, edited by Salma K. Jayyusi, 725–738. Leiden: E.J. Brill, 1992.

Walker, Morton. *Garlic: Nature's Healer*. Old Greenwich, CT: Devin-Adair Publisher, 1984.

Wood, Frances. *Did Marco Polo Go to China?* Colorado: Westview Press, 1996.

Woodsworth, J. S. *Strangers Within Our Gates: or, Coming Canadians*. Toronto: University of Toronto Press, 1972.

Wright, Clifford A. *A Mediterranean Feast: The Story of the Birth of Celebrated Cuisines of the Mediterranean, from the Merchants of Venice to the Barbary Corsairs*. New York: William Morrow and Company, 1999.

INDEX

ABOUT THE AUTHOR

Born in Syria in 1924, Habeeb Salloum arrived in Canada as a baby in 1925. He grew up in Saskatchewan during the "dirty thirties," and went on to join the Royal Canadian Air Force during the Second World War. He then worked for the Canadian Department of National Revenue for thirty-six years. For the past thirty years, Salloum has been a full-time author and freelance writer, specializing in food, history, and travel writing. In addition to his ten previously published books, Salloum has published hundreds of articles about culture, food, travel, and homesteading in western Canada in publications such as *Saveur Magazine*, *Toronto Star*, *The Globe and Mail*, *The Western Producer*, and *Contemporary Review*.

His award-winning cookbooks include: *Bison Delights*; *From the Lands of Figs and Olives*; *Journeys Back to Arab Spain*; *Arabic Contributions to the English Vocabulary*; *Classic Vegetarian Cooking from the Middle East and North Africa*; and *The Arabian Nights Cookbook*. He co-authored, with Leila Salloum Elias and Muna Salloum, two major research studies on medieval Arab cookery: *Scheherazade's Feasts* and *Sweet Delights from A Thousand and One Nights*.

His list of international accolades include the Silver Award winner of the Cuisine Canada and Culinary Culture Taste Canada Book Awards, and two Gourmand World Cookbook Awards. In 2013, Salloum was awarded the Tourism Travel Media Award by the Province of Saskatchewan for his literary work on travel, tourism, and the culinary arts of that province. He currently resides in Toronto, Ontario.

DIGESTIONS

Publishing established and emerging scholars and writers, Digestions is a book series that considers the history of food, the culture of food, and the politics of what we eat from both a Canadian and a global perspective.

SERIES EDITORS

SARAH ELTON
author of *Locavore* and *Consumed*

and

LENORE NEWMAN
author of *Speaking in Cod Tongues: A Canadian Culinary Journey*
and Canada Research Chair in Food Security and Environment
at University of the Fraser Valley

For more information about publishing in the series, please contact:

Karen May Clark, Acquisitions Editor
University of Regina Press
3737 Wascana Parkway
Regina, Saskatchewan s4s 0a2 Canada
karen.clark@uregina.ca
www.uofrpress.ca

COOKING/MIDDLE EASTERN

> "The real deal for people who like Middle Eastern cuisine' and a fine piece of cultural history."

BRIAN FAWCETT, *BOOKS IN CANADA*

"Arab Cooking on a Prairie Homestead *has long been one of my favourite books, not only because of the delectable recipes, but because it is a unique work of prairie history. It weaves recipes into a beautifully written memoir about growing up on a Saskatchewan farm, the son of homesteaders from Syria."*—SARAH CARTER, from the Foreword

In the 1920s, Habeeb Salloum's parents left behind the orchards and vineyards of French-occupied Syria to seek a new life on the windswept, drought-stricken prairies. With recollections that show the grit and improvisation of pioneers, *Arab Cooking on a Prairie Homestead* demonstrates Salloum's love of traditional Arab cuisine. By growing "exotic" crops brought from home—such as lentils and chickpeas—the Salloums survived the dirty thirties and helped change the landscape of Canadian farming.

Over 200 recipes in this updated classic—from dumplings to lentil pies to zucchini mint soup—provide today's foodies and urban farmers with dishes that are not only delicious, but also gentle on the wallet and climate-friendly.

University of Regina Press

ISBN 9780889775183

52995

9 780889 775183

34.95 CDN / 29.95 USD